IØ131139

Political Psychology of Turkish Political Behavior

The primary motivation for this book is to focus on something crucial that is missing in Turkish political science: well-founded theories on the Turkish voter and empiricism in scholarly research. Given the absence of such theories, one could ask what then the best model is for explaining a Turkish citizen's vote choice and political behaviour, and what schools of thought Turkish political science has. Unfortunately, it is not possible to offer a satisfactory response to either question at this point, and among the clear deficiencies in the current literature the primary one is the lack of a robust model explaining how Turkish citizens form their political attitudes, engage in political participation, or cast their votes. With these important questions in mind, this book aims to generate an interest in the theoretical and methodological tools that one can employ to conduct research contributing to the needs of the literature, particularly in political behaviour and political psychology. This book expands our understanding about the processes and the mechanisms of Turkish political behaviour, and contributes to the foundations of theory building in the literature.

This book was published as a special issue of *Turkish Studies*.

Cengiz Erişen (PhD, Stony Brook University, USA) is Associate Professor of Political Science at TOBB University of Economics and Technology, Turkey. His research interests include comparative political behaviour, political psychology, public opinion analysis, and quantitative methods. He has published papers in *Political Psychology*, *Journal of Common Market Studies*, *Political Research Quarterly*, *American Politics Research*, and *Turkish Politics* in addition to a number of book chapters.

Political Psychology of Turkish Political Behavior

Edited by
Cengiz Erişen

Routledge
Taylor & Francis Group

LONDON AND NEW YORK

First published 2015 by Routledge

2 Park Square, Milton Park, Abingdon, Oxfordshire OX14 4RN
711 Third Avenue, New York, NY 10017

Routledge is an imprint of the Taylor & Francis Group, an informa business

First issued in paperback 2018

Copyright © 2015 Taylor & Francis

All rights reserved. No part of this book may be reprinted or reproduced or
utilised in any form or by any electronic, mechanical, or other means, now
known or hereafter invented, including photocopying and recording, or in
any information storage or retrieval system, without permission in writing
from the publishers.

Notice:
Product or corporate names may be trademarks or registered trademarks,
and are used only for identification and explanation without intent to infringe.

British Library Cataloguing in Publication Data
A catalogue record for this book is available from the British Library

ISBN 13: 978-1-138-81985-6 (hbk)
ISBN 13: 978-1-138-37950-3 (pbk)

Typeset in Times New Roman
by RefineCatch Limited, Bungay, Suffolk

Publisher's Note
The publisher accepts responsibility for any inconsistencies that may have
arisen during the conversion of this book from journal articles to book chapters,
namely the possible inclusion of journal terminology.

Disclaimer
Every effort has been made to contact copyright holders for their permission to
reprint material in this book. The publishers would be grateful to hear from any
copyright holder who is not here acknowledged and will undertake to rectify
any errors or omissions in future editions of this book.

Contents

Citation Information

The chapters in this book were originally published in *Turkish Studies*, volume 14, issue 1 (March 2013). When citing this material, please use the original page numbering for each article, as follows:

Chapter 1
The Political Psychology of Turkish Political Behavior: Introduction by the Special Issue Editor
Cengiz Erişen
Turkish Studies, volume 14, issue 1 (March 2013) pp. 1–12

Chapter 2
Research Methods in Political Psychology
Cengiz Erişen, Elif Erişen and Binnur Özkeçeci-Taner
Turkish Studies, volume 14, issue 1 (March 2013) pp. 13–33

Chapter 3
Values, Religiosity and Support for Redistribution and Social Policy in Turkey
Gizem Arikan
Turkish Studies, volume 14, issue 1 (March 2013) pp. 34–52

Chapter 4
The Impact of Party Identification and Socially Supplied Disagreement on Electoral Choices in Turkey
Elif Erişen
Turkish Studies, volume 14, issue 1 (March 2013) pp. 53–73

Chapter 5
Analyzing the Determinants of Group Identity Among Alevis in Turkey: A National Survey Study
Çiğdem V. Şirin
Turkish Studies, volume 14, issue 1 (March 2013) pp. 74–91

Chapter 6

Ethnicity and Trust in National and International Institutions: Kurdish Attitudes
toward Political Institutions in Turkey
Ekrem Karakoç
Turkish Studies, volume 14, issue 1 (March 2013) pp. 92–114

Chapter 7

Emotions as a Determinant in Turkish Political Behavior
Cengiz Erişen
Turkish Studies, volume 14, issue 1 (March 2013) pp. 115–135

Chapter 8

Leadership Traits of Turkey's Islamist and Secular Prime Ministers
Barış Kesgín
Turkish Studies, volume 14, issue 1 (March 2013) pp. 136–157

Chapter 9

Public Opinion toward Immigration and the EU: How are Turkish Immigrants
Different than Others?
Başak Yavçan
Turkish Studies, volume 14, issue 1 (March 2013) pp. 158–178

Please direct any queries you may have about the citations to
clsuk.permissions@cengage.com

Notes on Contributors

Gizem Arikan is Assistant Professor in the Department of International Relations, Yaşar University, Turkey. Her research focuses on the effect of political culture and values on public opinion and policy. She also conducts research on religiosity and attitudes towards democracy. Her publications have appeared in journals such as *British Journal of Political Science, Political Behavior, International Journal of Public Opinion Research and Political Studies*.

Cengiz Erişen (PhD, Stony Brook University, USA) is Associate Professor of Political Science at TOBB University of Economics and Technology, Turkey. His research interests include comparative political behaviour, political psychology, public opinion analysis, and quantitative methods. He has published papers in *Political Psychology, Journal of Common Market Studies, Political Research Quarterly, American Politics Research*, and *Turkish Politics* in addition to a number of book chapters..

Elif Erişen received her BAs in Political Science and International Relations and in Management from Boğaziçi University, Turkey, and her MSc degree from the London School of Economics, UK. She received her PhD in Political Science from Stony Brook University, USA, in 2008 and has been working as Assistant Professor in the Department of Political Science and Public Administration at Hacettepe University, Turkey. Her research focuses on the political psychology of social network influence in the US and from a comparative perspective, and has been featured in *Political Psychology*. Her research on political behavior and public opinion focuses on the EU enlargement and electoral choices in the US and in Turkey.

Ekrem Karakoç received his doctorate in Political Science from the Pennsylvania State University, USA, in 2010. He is Assistant Professor in the Department of Political Science at Binghamton University, SUNY, USA. He is specialized in Comparative Politics with a focus on political institutions, political behavior and democratization. His works have appeared in *World Politics, Comparative Politics, Comparative Political Studies, Electoral Studies, European Political Science Review, Canadian Journal of Political Science* and *International Journal of Comparative Sociology*.

NOTES ON CONTRIBUTORS

Barış Kesgin (PhD, University of Kansas, USA) is Assistant Professor of Political Science at Susquehanna University, USA. He specializes in foreign policy analysis and political leadership—more specially, of Israel and Turkey. His research on the role of parliaments in foreign policy-making appeared in *International Studies Perspectives*; most recently, he published on Tansu Çiller's leadership traits and foreign policy in *Perceptions*.

Bínnur Özeçeci-Taner is Associate Professor of Political Science at Hamline University, USA. Her teaching and research interests include foreign policy analysis, politics of the Middle East, regional and international security, coalition governments and party politics, and Turkish foreign policy. She has written extensively and some of her articles have appeared in *Foreign Policy Analysis*, *International Studies Review*, *Contemporary Security Policy*, *British Journal of Middle Eastern Studies*, and *Turkish Studies*. Her book, *Role of Ideas in Coalition Government Foreign Policymaking: The Case of Turkey between 1991 and 2002*, was published in 2009.

Çíğdem V. Şirin is Assistant Professor in the Department of Political Science at the University of Texas, EL Paso, USA. Her main areas of interest are conflict behavior and political psychology. She has published articles in *Acta Politica*, *Armed Forces & Society*, *Civil Wars*, the *International Journal of Conflict Management*, the *International Journal of Public Opinion Research*, *International Political Science Review*, *Presidential Studies Quarterly*, and *Terrorism and Political Violence*.

Başak Yavçan received her PhD in Political Science from Pittsburg University, USA, in 2011. She is Assistant Professor of Political Science at TOBB University of Economics and Technology. Her research interests include comparative politics, political behavior, public opinion and European politics.

The Political Psychology of Turkish Political Behavior: Introduction by the Special Issue Editor

CENGİZ ERİŞEN
Department of Political Science, TOBB University of Economics and Technology, Sögütözü, Ankara, Turkey

This special issue aims to contribute to Turkish politics literature through a novel, unexplored aspect of Turkish political behavior. Primarily motivated by behavioral theories, political psychology offers a key perspective to explore and disentangle the multifactorial and multidimensional nature of Turkish political behavior. This introduction gives an account of the general motivation behind this special issue by briefly discussing the goals of this special issue, providing a brief history of the political psychology discipline, introducing the articles in this special issue, and outlining political psychology-related work in Turkey. The article concludes by presenting the acknowledgements.

Goals for This Special Issue

The primary motivation for this special issue is to focus on something crucial that is missing in Turkish political science: well-founded theories on the Turkish voter and empiricism in scholarly research. Given the absence of such theories, one could ask what then the best model is for explaining a Turkish citizen's vote choice and political behavior, and what schools of thought Turkish political science has. Unfortunately, it is not possible to give a satisfactory response to either question at this point, and among the clear deficiencies in the current literature the primary one is the lack of a robust model explaining how Turkish citizens cast their votes. This is not to ignore, however, all that productive Turkish scholars have done so far. Among these, one can list (in alphabetical order) Ali Çarkoğlu, Yılmaz Esmer, Metin Heper, Ersin Kalaycıoğlu, Sabri Sayarı, and others. Nevertheless, there is a

1

substantial need for more scholarly work in the discipline to build empirically grounded theories and models of Turkish political behavior, although theory building is not an easy task. It requires not only a team of scholars with a collective mindset to produce robust scholarly work, but also researchers with the methodological tools to generate empirical research. Thus, political scientists first need to come together to form a scholarly understanding to conduct projects that can lead to theories of Turkish political behavior.

With respect to the latter issue, it is necessary to expand the amount of empirical work in the literature to the high levels produced in the international literature in the USA and across Europe. Top political science journals in both these areas already mostly publish studies using empirical models, and the usage of quantitative methods is consistently increasing. Considering the political behavior literature in particular, without a doubt empiricism dominates and future scholarly work will likely continue in that direction. In contrast, when examining the Turkish political science literature, one can see only a limited engagement with empiricism.[1] Therefore, in order to keep up with the standards of the international literature, Turkish scholars need to prioritize empiricism and advance their understanding, while at the same time developing new and better theories.

With these goals in mind, this special issue aims to generate an interest in the theoretical and methodological tools that one can employ to conduct research contributing to the needs of the literature, particularly in political behavior. This special issue does not solely focus on the psychological determinants of political attitudes and behavior in the Turkish context. The goal is to expand our understanding about the processes and the mechanisms of Turkish political behavior, and contribute to the foundations of theory building in the literature.

Political psychology is a sub-discipline of political science that focuses on the mechanism of political behavior. Political behavior studies the underpinnings of voter attitudes, decisions, preferences, and behavior. The topics of interest vary greatly with the aim of exploring the behavioral determinants of politics. At the center of this interest, political psychology focuses on the psychological aspects of political behavior by exploring the mechanism. That is, political psychology employs the tools needed to understand how individuals develop their political attitudes, reach political decisions, form political preferences or engage in political action. From a general standpoint, political psychology researches a wide range of topics: personality, values, ideology, political attitudes, emotions, political behavior, information processing, public opinion, foreign policy, strategic interaction, conflict analysis and resolution, communication and media, decision-making, intergroup relations, group identity, prejudice and racial issues, and gender. In researching these domains, political psychology has become the dominant paradigm for explaining citizen attitudes and behavior. The field includes diverse theories and methodological tools. Since both political scientists and psychologists conduct political psychology research, political psychology is, by definition, truly interdisciplinary.

Four Eras of Political Psychology Research

The goal in this section is to give the reader a sense of the initial discussions in the literature and the current status of political psychology in the discipline of political science.[2] There have been four eras of research in political psychology.[3] The first stems from early political psychology studies focusing on personality and psychoanalysis in the aftermath of the World War II. Political psychology in this era primarily focused on understanding obedience to authority and how the authoritarian personalities of Europe's fascist regimes could have prospered before initiating the conflict that engulfed first the region and eventually the world. This era, from the 1940s to the 1960s, relied strongly on psychoanalysis and behaviorism, with the use of content analysis and interviews as research tools. The theoretical and empirical discussions of the discipline of the time tried to answer some critical questions about war and leader personalities, which became the research priorities of political psychology. In essence, this era provided the introduction to what would later evolve into a key perspective in understanding citizen behavior.

The second era, from the 1960s to the 1980s, focused on political attitudes and electoral behavior, under the influence of the fast developing discipline of economics. The influence of economic rationality on political science theories in this era changed the course of scholarly work in the discipline. Political psychology greatly contributed to the debate about the rationality of political behavior and the dimensions of rational political decision-making.[4] The effort of examining rational preference formation and citizen behavior produced important scientific studies of political behavior that advanced the previous era's aims of making qualitative analyses of individual psychology. Seminal works in this era aimed to understand how individuals cast their votes, list their political preferences and form political attitudes. In this era, seminal works of political behavior began to take into account psychology as a critical factor in voting behavior.[5] Political ideology was also a key topic of interest.[6] In these studies, survey research was the major tool for data collection and hypothesis testing.

In close connection with the end of the previous era, the third era focused on political ideology, belief systems, and information processing from the 1980s to 2000. Most research examined how citizens process political information and reach decisions. Cognitive heuristics, theories on decision-making, and the division between cold and hot decision processes determined the debate, particularly in the first decade. However, by the early 1990s, the cognitive paradigm was being strongly challenged by the old enemy in the discipline, emotions. With the return of emotions, through powerful experimental studies in social psychology[7] and developments in neuroscience,[8] the discipline came to understand the nature of political behavior as a function of both cognition and emotion.[9] As various studies demonstrated the greater and prior influence of affect and emotion over cognition,[10] the discipline began to understand emotion's effects and incorporate affective indicators into new models of political behavior. An additional domain of research in this era concerned social networks. Considering citizens as a single entity making political choices is rather limited, while research on social networks and social influences considers citizens within a net of social relations, and develop the tools that control for these effects on political attitudes, participation, and decisions.[11] During this era, both experimental and survey methodologies were used to find answers to research questions in political psychology.

While the fourth era has continued earlier work on the nature of political attitudes, affect and emotions, social networks, political ambivalence and framing, at the same time a separate strand of research within political psychology has developed since the early 2000s. With strong connections to natural sciences, neuroscience, biology, and genetics in particular, recent political psychology research has expanded its reach further across disciplines. Today, rigorous scientific research, particularly experimental, is being conducted on the influence of affect and emotions, genetics and biology in understanding many facets of political behavior, from voting decisions to policy preferences, to political participation. Other hot research topics include affective priming studies showing affective influences on political judgments and thinking,[12] neuro-politics examining the neural reactions to political stimuli in one's brain,[13] twin studies to determine the genetic underpinnings of political behavior,[14] and evolutionary psychology.[15]

From a wider perspective, political psychology does not simply contribute to research in political behavior. The discipline influences several other domains of political science such as public opinion, media and framing, political communication, race and gender studies, intergroup relations, and conflict resolution. For instance, research in international relations, particularly foreign policy decision-making,[16] leadership traits analysis,[17] foreign policy analysis,[18] perception and misperception,[19] and threat perception[20] have all greatly benefited from political psychology's insights.

Articles in This Special Issue

With the aim of being more theory-oriented, each article in this special issue proposes research hypotheses and tests them using a clear research method. The general goal is to explore the mechanisms beyond individual political decisions, attitudes, and behavior. Therefore, in order to set up a methodological foundation for the articles that follow, the special issue first begins by introducing the major methods used in the discipline.

Research Methods in Political Psychology

Given the interdisciplinary nature of political psychology research, the tools employed to produce scientific knowledge should reflect this multitude of approaches. First, one should note that quantitative and qualitative methods are complementary to each other. As shown in this special issue, all articles employ different research methods (experiments, surveys, and content analysis) to answer their research questions. This multitude of methods used in political psychology provides a variety of options for those interested in conducting research in political science. In this article by Cengiz Erişen, Elif Erişen and Binnur Özkeçeci-Taner, each author discusses one method in detail that they have already employed in published scholarly research. Cengiz Erişen focuses on experiments, Elif Erişen discusses survey research (particularly with respect to novel measurement techniques) and survey experiments, and Binnur Özkeçeci-Taner explains content analysis. Each method is discussed in sufficient detail for understanding what can be achieved by using them. However, the authors were not able to delve into the statistical aspects of these methods, so the reader is advised to refer to relevant statistical texts for further training. The methodological discussion provided in this article can be used to better understand the conceptual articles of this special issue.

Values, Religion, and Redistribution

Political values and religion are among the most important factors affecting political behavior. To that end, Gizem Arıkan provides an analysis of core values and religiosity in political preferences and attitudes toward social redistribution and social policies. Using European Social Surveys (ESS), she shows that self-transcendence (associated with universalism and benevolence) and conservation values (associated with conformity, tradition, and security) enhance support for redistributive governmental policies. Her study also neatly distinguishes two types of religiosity: self-identified religiosity versus social religiosity. The analyses show that self-identified religiosity positively affects one's level of support for governmental responsibility in providing public social services, whereas social religiosity decreases such support. This finding indicates that an understanding of religiosity in Turkey needs to be multidimensional, and that a single indicator of religiosity would be a poor measure, particularly with respect to social policies and redistribution. Another important contribution of this study is that political ideology (on a left-right continuum) is an insignificant indicator of political preferences with respect to governmental spending, suggesting that the Turkish political system is fundamentally different from Western democracies in this respect.

Social Networks and Political Attitudes

Research on social networks is a fast growing research domain in political science, particularly in political psychology. Current studies show that an individual's social network influences their political attitudes and decisions. Most importantly, individuals are subject to social forces and desirability effects that influence their political behavior. Considering the relatively weak levels of party affiliation in Turkey, Elif Erişen's study analyzes the effects of individuals' social network in forming their attitudes toward political candidates, and determining their vote choice. Employing an experimental study, she shows us that young voters are sensitive to both partizan cues and socially supplied disagreements in forming and changing their attitudes toward political candidates. The results also show that, unlike most developing countries with weak parties, the party label in Turkey is an important heuristic for making electoral choices.

Religious and Ethnic Identity

Another critical point of discussion in Turkish political behavior concerns minorities, with Kurds and Alevis being the two minority groups that require the most critical scholarly attention. Two articles in this special issue focus on the ethnic and religious aspects of the Turkish public. Çiğdem V. Şirin assesses the social psychological trade-off that Turkish and Kurdish Alevis make in forming their identity. Relying on social identity theory, she employs a snowball sampling method to collect survey data for her analyses. She finds that Kurdish Alevis report lower levels of attachment to their religious identity compared to Turkish Alevis, and that the more individuals encounter discrimination in social life as Alevis, the more likely they are to prioritize their Alevi identity. Another interesting finding is that there are no differences with respect to group identity between Alevis who live in urban versus rural areas.

From a different perspective, Ekrem Karakoç explores a clear study of differences in the level of trust in national and international institutions, both between Turks and Kurds, and among Kurds themselves. His analysis of the ESS dataset reveals a number of important points. First, Turks and Kurds trust national and international institutions differently. While Turks trust the national institutions more, Kurds are more likely to trust international institutions. Second, among Kurds, those who voted for the Adalet ve Kalkınma Partisi (AKP) in the 2007 elections are not more likely to trust state institutions because they voted for the winning party in the elections. With respect to the level of trust in political parties, his analyses show that higher trust in political parties occur among Kurdish voters, but voting for AKP does not increase trust among Kurdish voters. The critical finding is that regardless of ethnic identity religious voters hold higher trust in state institutions and political parties. His assessment of trust and political attitudes suggests that the attitudinal mechanism can be explored through social identity theories in political psychology.

Emotions and Political Behavior

In order to explore the mechanisms behind Turkish political behavior, Cengiz Erişen focuses on the influence of emotions in Turkish politics, arguing that emotions are critical in Turkish political life. He postulates that if one aims to understand the mechanisms underlying Turkish political behavior it is necessary to take into account emotional reactions to political events, leaders, and issues. The article uses one of the most currently debated topics of contemporary Turkish foreign policy, the Syria crisis, to assess how experimentally manipulated emotions raised by an issue can change individual political attitudes on the issue, intention to seek political information, and evaluations of Turkey's current Prime Minister, Recep Tayyip Erdoğan. This study shows that experimentally induced emotions influence political attitudes and behavior, although the degree of effect differs between negative and positive emotions. In addition, while negative emotions promote support for risk-taking behavior in foreign policy, positive emotions have an insignificant influence. Similarly, negative emotions make individuals more likely to intend to seek further information about the crisis and keep track of the events. Finally, those who were more hopeful about the crisis were more likely to positively evaluate Erdoğan's premiership performance. Overall, these findings suggest that emotions play an important role in determining Turkish political attitudes and thus need to be accounted for in models of political behavior.

Leadership Traits Analysis

At an individual level of analysis, Barış Kesgin's article provides a comprehensive analysis of post-Cold War Turkish prime ministers. With major power changes at the end of Cold War, leadership profiles become a critical notion for understanding a state's foreign policy. Kesgin's contribution is therefore valuable in giving us an overview of the effects of leadership personalities on Turkish foreign policy. Relying on the Leadership Traits Analysis method pioneered by Margaret Hermann, this article examines the role of successive Turkish prime ministers in foreign policymaking. The major finding is that Turkish leaders exhibit different leadership styles beyond a simplistic categorization into secular and religious. Rather, they differ in more complex ways, in which each possesses individual qualities that characterize their unique identity.

Perception of Turkish Immigrants in Europe

Similar to previous experimental approaches, Basak Yavçan examines the perception of Turkish immigrants in Europe, in Germany in particular. This study employs a survey experiment of adults in Germany testing whether an immigrant's descent is important on immigration attitudes of the European public. She finds that the German public's opposition to immigrants from Turkey explains their overall Euroscepticism much better than their attitudes toward immigrants from within EU member states.

As a collection, these articles study a variety of topics with the assistance of distinct research methods. Considered together, the diversity of theories and methodological tools improves our ability to understand possible processes of Turkish political behavior in general. In sum, the articles valuably complement each other, and demonstrate how the interdisciplinary notion of political psychology can contribute to better understanding Turkish politics.

Political Psychology-Related Work in Turkey

Looking back over what have been achieved in political psychology research and related work, there exist a number of psychoanalytical studies on Turkish politics,[21] which rely to a great extent on the earliest political psychology literature from the psycho-politics era of the 1950s. One important difference in the current political psychology literature is that most work now employs experimental design, which was not a research tool used in earlier eras. In more recent psychoanalytical literature, conflict resolution receives great attention, particularly the Kurdish issue, the Turkish–Armenian conflict, the Cyprus issue, and tensions between Turkey and Greece. Vamık Volkan's work is one of the seminal examples taking a psychoanalytical perspective on these conflicts.[22] However, there is also much more to be done with respect to intergroup conflict and conflict resolution through the lens of contemporary political psychology and employing advanced research methods. In terms of identity specifically, the two papers introduced above that focus on ethnic and religious identity provide important findings to motivate further research on conflict resolution using up-to-date theories and methods. Both relations among ethnic and religious groups in Turkey and group processes require more analysis. Because of the critical political and social implications, such future research should aim to explore the multidimensional nature of these attitudes. However, in this quest, neither a rudimentary historical approach nor psychoanalytical examination can significantly contribute to what has been discovered so far.

Background for This Special Issue and Support

It would be relevant to briefly explain how the idea for this special issue originated. The first trigger motivating political psychology research in the Turkish context was the 2011 Annual Meeting of the International Society of Political Psychology (ISPP), held in Istanbul. As members of the Liaison Committee in Turkey, under the leadership of Hale Bolak Boratav at Istanbul Bilgi University, we facilitated and organized one of the most successful ISPP meetings. Before the annual meeting, the aim to introduce political psychology research to interested graduate students and scholars in Turkey was realized through the initiation of the ISPP Summer Academy. More than fifteen Turkish graduate students and scholars participated in this academy through a TÜBİTAK grant. This three-day pre-conference meeting provided participants with the opportunity to learn about specific political psychology topics from a number of world-renowned academics. Along with these two organizations, a core group of young scholars with an interest in political psychology who have either published work in the discipline or done dissertation research is formed.

This latter idea was realized through a special workshop on Turkish political behavior and political psychology, supported by an ISPP grant and TOBB University of Economics and Technology. Several scholars from domestic and foreign academic institutions came to Ankara to present their research and further train those Turkish participants from the previous ISPP Summer Academy. The articles in this special issue were first presented and critiqued in this workshop. I would therefore like to thank all those who participated in this workshop, whether as paper presenters, reviewers or participants, particularly Emre Erdoğan, Kerem Ozan Kalkan, and Zeki Sarıgil.

Finally, I wish to thank a number of people who have made this special issue possible. First, I would like to thank all the authors who have diligently worked on their papers to produce exemplary pieces. Next, I would like to thank all the anonymous reviewers who have given exceptionally valuable comments to the authors and truly improved the quality of the finished articles. Finally, I would like to thank Barry Rubin for giving me the opportunity to be the guest editor of this special issue. With his trust, much has been achieved, culminating in this successful special issue. I can only hope that academics as well as policymakers will benefit from the insights offered here, and advance its content, which aims to provide a humble contribution to the Turkish literature from the perspective of political psychology theories and methodologies.

Notes

1. One can list a number of exemplary studies conducted by two famous Turkish scholars: Kalaycıoğlu and Çarkoğlu. See, for example, Kalaycıoğlu, "Attitudinal Orientation to Party Organizations in Turkey in the 2000s"; Kalaycıoğlu, "Public Choice and Foreign Affairs"; Kalaycıoğlu, "Kulturkampf in Turkey: The Constitutional Referendum of 12 September 2010"; Kalaycıoğlu, "Justice and Development Party at the Helm"; Çarkoğlu, "Political Preferences of the Turkish Electorate"; Çarkoğlu, "The Nature of Left-Right Ideological Self-placement in the Turkish Context"; Çarkoğlu, "Who Wants Full Membership?".
2. Here, I would like to refer the reader to the following sources for more discussion about the discipline: Iyengar and McGuire, *Explorations in Political Psychology*; Lodge and McGraw, *Political Judgment: Structure and Process*; Kuklinski, *Citizens and Politics*; Sears, Huddy, and Jervis, *Oxford Handbook of Political Psychology*; Jost and Sidanius, *Political Psychology*; Houghton, *Political Psychology*; Kuklinski, *Thinking about Political Psychology*; Cottam et al., *Introduction to Political Psychology*.
3. I principally rely on McGuire's well-known chapter discussing the background of political psychology. McGuire, "The Poly-Psy Relationship".
4. Simon, *Models of Bounded Rationality*; Sniderman, Brody, and Tetlock, *Reasoning and Choice*; Lupia, McCubbins, and Popkin, *Elements of Reason*.
5. Campbell et al., *The American Voter*.
6. Converse, "The Nature of Belief Systems in Mass Publics."
7. Zajonc, "Feeling and Thinking: Preferences Need No Inferences"; Lazarus, *Emotion and Adaptation*; Forgas, "Mood and Judgment"; Zajonc, "Feeling and thinking: Closing the debate over the independence of affect."
8. LeDoux, *The Emotional Brain*.
9. Marcus, Neuman, and MacKuen, *Affective Intelligence and Political Judgment*; Redlawsk, *Feeling Politics*; Neuman et al., *The Affect Effect*.
10. E.g. Zajonc, "Feeling and Thinking..."
11. Huckfeldt and Sprague, *Citizens, Politics, and Social Communication*; Mutz, "Cross-cutting Social Networks"; Erisen and Erisen, "The Effect of Social Networks on the Quality of Political Thinking".
12. Erisen, Lodge, and Taber, "Affective Contagion in Effortful Political Thinking."
13. Schreiber and Iacoboni, "Huxtables on the Brain."
14. Alford, Funk, and Hibbing, "Are Political Orientations Genetically Transmitted"; Fowler, Baker, and Dawes, "Genetic Variation in Political Participation"; For more recent discussion on this topic: the flagship journal of the discipline, *Political Psychology*, recently published a special issue on Biology, Genetics and Behavior, Hatemi and McDermott "The Political Psychology of Biology, Genetics, and Behavior."
15. Alford and Hibbing, "The Origin of Politics"; Lopez and McDermott, "Adaptation, Heritability, and the Emergence of Evolutionary Political Science".

16. Snyder, Bruck, and Sapin, *Foreign-Policy Decision Making*; Mintz and DeRouen, *Understanding Foreign Policy Decision-Making*.
17. Hermann, "Explaining Foreign Policy Behavior Using the Personal Characteristics of Political Leaders"; Kaarbo and Hermann, "Leadership Styles of Prime Ministers."
18. Singer and Hudson, *Political Psychology and Foreign Policy*; Breuning, *Foreign Policy Analysis*. For a general overview of the interaction between political psychology and foreign policy analysis, please refer to the special issue recently published in *Perceptions*, particularly Erişen, "An Introduction to Political Psychology for International Relations Scholars."
19. Jervis, *Perception and Misperception in International Politics*.
20. Jervis, Lebow, and Stein, *Psychology and Deterrence*; Stein, "Building Politics into Psychology."
21. For a general overview, see Hasta, "Siyaset Psikolojisi Kapsamında Türkçe Yayımlanmış Araştırma ve Yazılar."
22. Volkan, "The Need to Have Enemies and Allies"; Volkan, *Politik Psikoloji*; Volkan, *Bloodlines*.

References

Alford, John R., Carolyn L. Funk, and John R. Hibbing. "Are Political Orientations Genetically Transmitted." *American Political Science Review* 99, no. 2 (2005): 153–167.

Alford, John R., and John R. Hibbing. "The Origin of Politics: An Evolutionary Theory of Political Behavior." *Perspectives on Politics* 2, no. 4 (2004): 707–723.

Breuning, Marijke. *Foreign Policy Analysis: A Comparative Introduction*. New York: Palgrave, 2007.

Campbell, Angus, Philip Converse, Warren Miller, and Donald Stokes. *The American Voter*. New York: Wiley, 1960.

Çarkoğlu, Ali. "Who Wants Full Membership? Characteristics of Turkish Public Support for EU Membership." *Turkish Studies* 4, no. 1 (2003): 171–194.

Çarkoğlu, Ali. "Political Preferences of the Turkish Electorate: Reflections of an Alevi-Sunni Cleavage." *Turkish Studies* 6, no. 2 (2005): 273–292.

Çarkoğlu, Ali. "The Nature of Left-Right Ideological Self-placement in the Turkish Context." *Turkish Studies* 8, no. 2 (2007): 253–271.

Converse, Philip. "The Nature of Belief Systems in Mass Publics." In *Ideology and Discontent*, edited by David Apter, 206–261. New York: Free Press, 1964.

Cottam, Martha L., Beth Dietz-Uhler, Elena Mastors, and Thomas Preston. *Introduction to Political Psychology*. New York: Psychology Press, 2009.

Erişen, Elif. "An Introduction to Political Psychology for International Relations Scholars." *Perceptions* XVII, no. 3 (Autumn 2012): 9–28.

Erisen, Elif, and Cengiz Erisen. "The Effect of Social Networks on the Quality of Political Thinking." *Political Psychology* 33, no. 6 (2012): 839–865.

Erisen, Cengiz, Milton Lodge, and Charles S. Taber. "Affective Contagion in Effortful Political Thinking." *Political Psychology* (forthcoming).

Forgas, Joe P. "Mood and Judgment: The Affect Infusion Model (AIM)." *Psychological Bulletin* 11, no. 1 (1995): 39–66.

Fowler, James H., Laure A. Baker, and Christopher T. Dawes. "Genetic Variation in Political Participation." *American Political Science Review* 102, no. 2 (2008): 684–687.

Hasta, Derya. "Siyaset Psikolojisi Kapsamında Türkçe Yayımlanmış Araştırma ve Yazılar." *Türk Psikoloji Bülteni* 11, no. 37 (2005): 97–105.

Hatemi, Peter K., and Rose McDermott "The Political Psychology of Biology, Genetics, and Behavior: An Introduction by Special Issue Editors." *Political Psychology* 33, no. 3 (2012): 307–312.

Hermann, Margaret. "Explaining Foreign Policy Behavior Using the Personal Characteristics of Political Leaders." *International Studies Quarterly* 24, no. 1 (March 1980): 7–46.

Houghton, David P. *Political Psychology: Situations, Individuals, and Cases.* New York: Routledge, 2008.

Huckfeldt, Robert, and John Sprague. *Citizens, Politics, and Social Communication: Information and Influence in an Election Campaign.* New York: Cambridge University Press, 1995.

Iyengar, Shanto, and William J. McGuire, eds. *Explorations in Political Psychology.* Durham, NC: Duke University Press, 1993.

Jervis, Robert. *Perception and Misperception in International Politics.* Princeton: Princeton University Press, 1976.

Jervis, Robert, Richard Ned Lebow, and Janice G. Stein. *Psychology and Deterrence.* Baltimore, MD: Johns Hopkins University Press, 1985.

Jost, John T., and Jim Sidanius, eds. *Political Psychology: Key Readings.* New York: Psychology Press, 2004.

Kaarbo, Juliet, and Margaret G. Hermann. "Leadership Styles of Prime Ministers: How Individual Differences Affect the Foreign Policymaking Process." *Leadership Quarterly* 9, no. 3 (1998): 243–263.

Kalaycıoğlu, Ersin. "Attitudinal Orientation to Party Organizations in Turkey in the 2000s." *Turkish Studies* 9, no. 2 (2008): 297–316.

Kalaycıoğlu, Ersin. "Public Choice and Foreign Affairs: Democracy and International Relations in Turkey." *New Perspectives on Turkey* 40 (2009): 59–83.

Kalaycıoğlu, Ersin. "Justice and Development Party at the Helm: Resurgence of Islam or Restitution of the Right-of-Center Predominany Party?" *Turkish Studies* 11, no. 1 (2010): 29–44.

Kalaycıoğlu, Ersin. "Kulturkampf in Turkey: The Constitutional Referendum of 12 September 2010." *South European Society and Politics* 17, no. 1 (2012): 1–22.

Kuklinski, James H, ed. *Citizens and Politics: Perspectives from Political Psychology.* New York: Cambridge University Press, 2001.

Kuklinski, James H, ed. *Thinking about Political Psychology.* New York: Cambridge University Press, 2009.

Lazarus, Richard S. *Emotion and Adaptation.* New York: Oxford University Press, 1991.

LeDoux, Joseph E. *The Emotional Brain: The Mysterious Underpinnings of Emotional Life.* New York: Simon and Schuster, 1995.

Lodge, Milton, and Kathleen M. McGraw, eds. *Political Judgment: Structure and Process.* Ann Arbor, MI: University of Michigan Press, 1995.

Lopez, Anthony C., and Rose McDermott. "Adaptation, Heritability, and the Emergence of Evolutionary Political Science." *Political Psychology* 33, no. 3 (2012): 343–362.

Lupia, Arthur, Mathew D. McCubbins, and Samuel L. Popkin, eds. *Elements of Reason: Cognition, Choice, and the Bounds of Rationality.* New York: Cambridge University Press, 2000.

Marcus, George E., W. Russell Neuman, and Michael MacKuen. *Affective Intelligence and Political Judgment.* Chicago: The University of Chicago Press, 2000.

McGuire, William J. "The Poly-Psy Relationship: Three Phases of a Long Affair." In *Explorations in Political Psychology,* edited by Shanto Iyengar and William J. McGuire, 9–35. Durham, NC: Duke University Press, 1993.

Mintz, Alex, and Karl DeRouen. *Understanding Foreign Policy Decision-Making.* New York: Cambridge University Press, 2010.

Mutz, Diana C. "Cross-cutting Social Networks: Testing Democratic Theory in Practice." *American Political Science Review* 96, no. 1 (2002): 111–126.

Neuman, W. Russell, George E. Marcus, Ann Crigler, and Michael MacKuen, eds. *The Affect Effect: Dynamics of Emotion in Political Thinking and Behavior.* Chicago: University of Chicago Press, 2007.

Redlawsk, David. *Feeling Politics: Emotion in Political Information Processing*. New York: Palgrave, 2006.

Schreiber, Darren, and Marco Iacoboni. "Huxtables on the Brain: An fMRI Study of Race and Norm Violation." *Political Psychology* 33, no. 3 (2012): 313–330.

Sears, David O., Leonie Huddy, and Robert Jervis, eds. *Oxford Handbook of Political Psychology*. New York: Oxford University Press, 2004.

Simon, Herbert. *Models of Bounded Rationality*. Cambridge, MA: MIT Press, 1982.

Singer, Eric, and Valerie Hudson, eds. *Political Psychology and Foreign Policy*. Boulder, CO: Westview Press, 1992.

Sniderman, Paul M., Richard A. Brody, and Phillip E. Tetlock. *Reasoning and Choice: Explorations in Political Psychology*. New York: Cambridge University Press, 1993.

Snyder, Richard C., H. W. Bruck, and Burton Sapin, eds. *Foreign-Policy Decision Making*. Glencoe, IL: The Free Press, 1962.

Stein, Janice G. "Building Politics into Psychology: The Misperception of Threat." *Political Psychology* 9, no. 2 (1988): 245–271.

Volkan, Vamık D. "The Need to Have Enemies and Allies: A Developmental Approach to Political Psychology." *Political Psychology* 6, no. 2 (1985): 219–247.

Volkan, Vamık D. *Politik Psikoloji*. Ankara: Ankara Üniversitesi Rektörlüğü Yayınları, 1993.

Volkan, Vamık D. *Bloodlines: From Ethnic Prode to Ethnic Terrorism*. Boulder, CO: Westview Press, 1998.

Zajonc, Robert. "Feeling and Thinking: Preferences Need No Inferences." *American Psychologist* 35, no. 2 (1980): 151–175.

Zajonc, Robert. "Feeling and Thinking: Closing the Debate Over the Independence of Affect." In *Feeling and Thinking: The Role of Affect in Social Cognition*, edited by Joe P. Forgas, 31–58. Cambridge, MA: Cambridge University Press, 2000.

Research Methods in Political Psychology

CENGİZ ERİŞEN*, ELİF ERİŞEN** & BİNNUR ÖZKEÇECİ-TANER†

*Department of Political Science, TOBB University of Economics and Technology, Söğütözü, Ankara, Turkey; **Department of Political Science, California Polytechnic State University, San Luis Obispo, CA, USA; †Department of Political Science, Hamline University, St Paul, MN, USA

ABSTRACT *Given the interdisciplinary nature of political psychology research, the methods employed to produce scientific knowledge should be able to answer the questions raised in the discipline. The multitude of methods used in political psychology offers a variety of options for those interested in conducting research in political science. This article explains the basic structure of experimental design, survey research, and content analysis and briefly discusses the recent developments and interest growing on certain methods in the discipline. Each method is discussed in detail to the extent that would be sufficient to understand what one could achieve by using it.*

Introduction

This article aims to provide the methodological background to better understand and interpret the articles included in this special issue that employ diverse methods commonly found in political psychology research from experimental design to survey research and to the content coding of speeches. These methods are not solely used in political psychology or political behavior research. Since a method can be used for any type of research question, no single discipline can claim a particular method. The important point here is that political science as well as other social science disciplines could implement any methodology that would make the hypothesis testing possible and provide the necessary answers to a research question.

This special issue's focus on research methodology in political psychology stems from the following reasoning: training on research methodology is essential for scholarly work. Today's political science harbors several sub-disciplines such as political psychology, political behavior, comparative politics, and international relations all of which strongly rely on the proper use of methodology. It is critically important that scholarly work is designed in a way that employs a specific type of research tool to test its hypotheses or investigate its propositions. A set of hypotheses or propositions cannot be explored without a proper research design. This is critical not only for the improvement of the models depicting citizen behavior (in the case of political psychology and behavior) but also for the development of the discipline in general. Without proper methods of inquiry we cannot learn from our findings and cannot accumulate scientific knowledge.

This article develops in three sections: first, experimental design as the most important method of inquiry in political psychology is discussed. Next, survey research with its main assumptions and the recent improvements to understand individual attitudes and behavior is explained. Finally, content analysis is examined.

Experimental Method

Experimental method is the thriving research methodology within political science since the early 1990s. The number of articles implementing experimentation is exponentially increasing. There is also a growing debate about the methodology and its capabilities for research questions in political science. Recently, major books and handbooks are being published to explain and delineate certain aspects of the methodology.[1] The development of political psychology within political science has initiated the interest on experimental studies. There is also a similar interest in social sciences in general: today, experiments are being used in economics and marketing. A growing number of studies are published on behavioral and experimental economics.[2] In business administration, experiments are being increasingly used to delineate decision-making on day-to-day individual decisions as well as investment choices in the business market.[3] Relatedly, decision-making literature primarily relies on experimental findings on decisions under uncertainty and time-constraints.[4]

The consistently growing interest in experiments particularly stems from the social sciences' desire to be more scientific and to get closer to the scientific standing of the life sciences (e.g. neuroscience and biology).[5] By its nature, experimental design is the best method to define causal effects between variables. Building theories, testing hypotheses, and ultimately reaching scientifically valid knowledge are essential for social scientists. In that respect, experimentation gives the researcher the opportunity to clearly tease out the causal associations between the dependent variable and various independent effects. In simple terms, an experiment is the only tool that would directly tell one the degree of causal impact of the independent effect on a dependent variable.

Attributes of an Experimental Design

Experimental design has two major attributes:

(1) Administration of the experimental treatment: Experimental design is simply distinguished from other research designs by its comparison of two conditions of the

world. In one condition, an experimental treatment or a stimulus is used whereas in the other condition no treatment or stimulus is used. The comparison of these two conditions would reveal the effect of the experimentally administered treatment or stimulus on the dependent variable of interest. In other words, the only difference between the two states of the world is the experimental treatment and nothing else. Given this, one knows that the difference between the two conditions occurs only due to the experimental treatment. In turn, one can tell the causal effect of the experimental treatment on the interested political phenomenon.

The researcher should administer the experimental treatment with outmost control. To that end, several environment related external factors such as time, light, sound, weather conditions, and others should be controlled. The higher the control over the external factors, the higher the control over the administration of the experimental treatment on the participant would be. This control would strengthen the internal validity of the findings by making sure that participants are exposed to the experimental manipulation under similar conditions.

(2) Random assignment: In an experimental design, participants should be randomly assigned to experimental treatment and control groups. The treatment groups (could be one or more) refer to the conditions in which participants are exposed to a certain causal intervention. For instance, one experimental treatment group would read a pro article on a foreign policy decision, while a second experimental treatment group would read a con article on the same topic. Preferably, there should also be a control group in which participants are exposed to a completely neutral situation (e.g. read a non-political article on running shoes) or kept as they are (e.g. skip the treatment section in the experiment). The control group would function as the neutral condition of the world in which no experimental treatment would exist. Given these conditions, it is critical that participants are randomly assigned with equal probability to these groups without any particular reason.

Random assignment enables the researcher to estimate the average treatment effect across the experimental conditions. By this assumption, the experimental treatment group would have behaved in the same way as the control group had it not received the treatment. So, by comparing the average outcome of the treatment group to the control group one can determine the average treatment effect. If a researcher randomly distributes individuals to different states of the world, he can later define what exactly makes those individuals behave or decide differently from each other. Statistically, if the averages between the groups are significantly different from each other this is a result of the experimental intervention.

Random Assignment and Convenience Samples

Random assignment is the most important feature of experiments. It is the critical factor that actually determines causality. The major assumption in random assignment is that it does not require that the participants be randomly drawn from the population. Simple random sampling is not a statistical concern for experiments. Rather, it is critical that the participants are assigned to experimental groups randomly.

A convenience sample or a university student sample can be used for experimental tests as well as a randomly drawn sample. For an experimental study, under certain conditions there would be no theoretical or methodological differences across different types of samples. The scholarly accepted agreement in the literature is that so long as one can argue that the experimental treatment effect is homogeneous in the population, any type of sample would generate the results that would be theoretically and methodologically valid.[6] In other words, if the experimental treatment effect differs between a convenience sample and a randomly drawn sample, then one needs to find solutions to the generalizability problem. But it is also important not to forget that external validity does not necessarily mean that the sample should be representative. External validity requires that the findings are generalizable across different contexts and time as well.

Types of Experiments

There are three types of experiments mostly used in political science: laboratory, field, and survey experiments. The only factor differentiating these types of experiments from each other is the context or place where the participant receives the experimental treatment. In lab experiments, participants receive the stimulus in a controlled environment. The external conditions like location of the study, temperature, light, sound, decoration, and others are controlled in a lab setting. The lab experiments are probably the most used ones in political science due to their ability to provide high internal validity. The lab experiments can be given on computers or on paper-and-pencil. The usage of computers makes data collection and analysis procedure extremely easier. If one needs to collect experimental data fast and cheap, paper-and-pencil studies can be conducted in locations like classrooms and libraries. Because most of the external conditions are controlled in these contexts, external factors would not pose any problems. There are two exemplary experimental studies in this special issue. Strongly relying on a theoretical set-up, Elif Erişen and Cengiz Erişen conduct two paper-and-pencil experiments with a convenience student sample that test the distinct effects of social networks and emotions on political attitudes, evaluations, and behavior.

In field experiments, participants receive the stimulus in an environment that is closer to their everyday life setting where the events naturally occur in the course of daily events. So, instead of having the individual to travel from one place to another, the researcher can take the study to the individual's daily environment. The individual can also participate in the study over the Internet or TV at his home. Alternatively, to conduct a face-to-face study the researcher would need to reach the individual at his home. With face-to-face studies, researchers can ask a number of questions whereas there are always limits when it is done on the Internet and TV.

Another way of conducting the field experiments is to reach the individual closer to his daily life. So, if one conducts a study in which the difference between rural and urban would be important, then the study can use convenience samples drawn in rural and urban locations. These studies can be conducted in a controlled environment as much as possible. As long as every participant taking the study has a similar environment then the basic conditions would be met for an experiment.

Finally, a survey experiment can be conducted on paper, on Internet, on TV, and over the phone (Computer Assisted Telephone Interviewing, CATI surveys). A survey experiment would generate a randomly drawn sample in which participants were randomly assigned to experimental groups. Today, there is great interest in survey experiments considering the contributions they can provide to the researchers (the section on survey research discusses survey experiments in greater detail).

A Note on Theory Building Through Experiments

Finally, it is important to note that experiments are critical for theory building and testing. The key benefits of using experiments are the ability to disentangle the hypothetical associations and the causal effects among the indicators. These benefits allow the researcher to make a clear definition and inference of how independent (or explanatory) variables would influence dependent variables in a research hypothesis. In that respect, one can define the hypothetical associations in a theory, which is probably the most important goal in empirical research.

The current urge in Turkish political science is producing more methodologically valid research and develops theories that explore and infer citizen behavior. In turn, scientific advancement in the discipline would greatly benefit from experimental studies in different ways that it would also form other research methods.[7] As used in the discipline internationally, future research in Turkish political science regardless of the sub-discipline (whether it is political psychology/behavior or international relations or comparative politics) could truly benefit from experimental design in making progress.

Survey Research

Political science owes much of what is known about mass political behavior and public opinion to survey methodology. Survey methodology ranks at the top in a survey of all the methods used in leading political science journals from 1940 to 2000.[8] Among all the methods used in understanding the political world, survey methodology presents social scientist with an optimal balance between the richness of the information the method provides and its level of scientific rigor. Surveys with representative samples make it possible to draw reliable and unbiased conclusions about millions of people with 1000 or 2000 participants. Moreover, researchers can look into the nature of and the linkages among a plethora of variables at once. Moreover, experiments embedded in surveys allow researchers to make causal inferences about political phenomena. They can do so at a given point in time, or indicate trends over time using data generated by surveys. Hence, survey methodology has been particularly useful for measuring public opinion nationally and across several nations. Examples in Turkey include international survey programs' studies in Turkey such as the Eurobarometer,[9] International Social Survey Program, World

Value Surveys, and the European Social Survey studies with Turkish samples as well as several studies of public opinion and electoral behavior conducted by scholars such as Ersin Kalaycıoğlu and Ali Çarkoğlu.[10] In addition to shedding light on Turkish citizens' attitudes on domestic political issues and their electoral behavior, the international survey programs' studies in Turkey made it possible to study topics such as the determinants of public opinion in Turkey vis-à-vis the European Union (EU) and Turkey's membership to the EU using survey methodology.[11] You will find in this special issue two contributions to the study of citizen attitudes and behavior in Turkey by Gizem Arıkan and Ekrem Karakoç who use data from the large representative Turkish samples of European Social Surveys.

Because survey methodology is intimately linked to public opinion research, its contributions are not only to the academic study of citizen attitudes and behavior but also to democratic societies by facilitating the links between democratic deliberation in the public and democratic institutions. This is perhaps best evidenced by research funds made available by governments to survey studies that monitor the public's political and social attitudes and electoral behavior over decades. Prominent examples are American National Elections Study, the General Social Survey, the British Election Study, Canadian Election Study, European Election Studies, Mexico Panel Study of Elections, and New Zealand Election Study. In fact, one can cite thousands of SSCI articles in political science using the American National Election Study databases alone. This core data source sustains a lively and rigorous academic study of domestic politics from the American public's perspective. Such initiatives would be no less promising in Turkey, and could constitute the backbone of the scientific study of Turkish political behavior. By generating publicly available data collected in line with cutting-edge theoretical and methodological developments in the field, it would help fill the theoretical vacuum in several studies of Turkish public opinion, and present consistent measurements on the Turkish public for generations. The current data on electoral politics do not include consistent measurements on the Turkish public using similar/same scales across studies, neither these studies have time-series cross-sectional or panel designs that extend to several decades. Hence, our ability to make scientific inferences about trends in the Turkish citizens' political attitudes and behavior remains fairly limited.

Measurement in Survey Research

Having discussed the prominence of survey research for understanding political attitudes and behavior, one might rightly ask the following: How do surveys achieve the task of being the fundamental data collection method for political science by simply asking questions to people? The fact that surveys rely on asking questions does not mean that surveys are simple collections of questions, or items using the methodological terminology. Significant scholarly effort has been devoted to the development of both psychological and measurement theories that explain how a response is obtained and what it means.[12] The early models of the survey response process were the one developed by psychometricians such as Guttman, Guildford, Likert,

Thurstone, and their colleagues. They explained for the first time how attitudes can be systematically measured and their strengths quantified. For instance, Thurstone's seminal formal model of attitudes relies on his psychological theory of judgment.[13] According to this theory, people represent stimuli as points or regions in an internal dimension. They first identify which dimension to use (the psychological dimension), then assign scale values based on their reaction to the stimulus (the discriminal process), and compare pairs of stimuli (the calculation of discriminal difference). Earlier psychometric models, however, could not account for the anomalies in survey response that the later literature using surveys demonstrated.

First, people tend to give a different answer to a question when phrased differently or when different options are provided, or when the same is presented at a different point in time. Hence, widespread evidence on response instability that does not resemble meaningful attitudinal change motivated the formulation of new models on attitudes and survey response, which emphasize how people draw the relevant information from memory and how a response is formulated. For instance, while Fazio and his colleagues argue for the existence of real attitudes and explain variation in responses as a function of motivation and opportunity, Zaller and his colleagues consider survey response as the summary of a number of fleeting considerations that people usually carry in their minds at any point in time.[14] Zaller's theory explaining how people can so readily change their responses from one measurement to the other while being perfectly sincere has become the most impactful explanation of survey response in the literature. He argues that when people are responding to a survey item, they are not looking for an attitude already stored away in memory. Instead they sample from positive and negative considerations on the issue that happen to be salient at the time of the administration of the survey and produce a response averaging those considerations. Hence, as the considerations triggered by the item and the context change so does the response.

Second, social scientists now have a better understanding of different sources of random and non-random error that may make the findings based on survey data unreliable and biased. Unlike experiments, surveys rely on sampling of people from the larger population; hence, sampling error is unavoidable and minimizing it is often the first concern in designing a survey study.[15] Although different research questions may require different kinds of samples, if the aim of the survey researcher is to make inferences about the population, then a probability sample becomes a must. The error generated by such a sample would not bias the results unlike sampling error found in non-probability samples such as convenience samples. One should be aware of the fact that the results generated by convenience samples, which also include quota samples commonly used by opinion polling firms, are biased before drawing any conclusion from data for the population. Moreover, bias remains in the results regardless of the size of the convenience sample. Another issue related to sampling is the proper use of sampling weights.

Despite a probability sample, if the sample is stratified or a cluster, researchers may end up with biased estimates if they ignore the sampling weights in their analysis of survey data. Just to give an example, Eurobarometer surveys sample about 1000 individuals from each EU country regardless of the country's population. Running analyses on a combined EU-wide dataset ignoring the sampling weights would bias the results toward the small country citizens' opinions as these respondents would have a higher probability of entering the sample. Another error related with the representativeness of the sample is the unit non-response error. Despite probability sampling from a representative sampling frame, if a significant portion of those who are contacted for a survey decline the offer or their refusal is a product either of the survey topic, or a specific contextual variable, or certain personal characteristics, once again the sample becomes not representative of the larger population, and the results become biased.

Another group of errors, called measurement error, refers to a variety of ways in which the composition of the survey, the wording of the survey items, the qualities of the interviewer, and their interaction with the respondent's characteristics get in the way of correctly measuring the construct that the researcher is interested in. Several psychological factors such as social desirability or an unwillingness to respond to sensitive items with moral or legal implications can lead to mistakes in measurement. Simplicity in wording, use of intensity items instead of scale midpoint, avoiding agree–disagree items with response sets all can reduce measurement error.[16] Also, using items that have been tried before or, if available, using existing scales with known strengths and weaknesses can also make measurement error more predictable and easier to account for in the analysis stage. Also, although some researchers recommend the use of a no-opinion response to reduce measurement error,[17] others[18] caution against it because many real attitudes are missed by offering such an option and those who feel uncomfortable with the items choose the no-opinion option leading to measurement error.

As the discussion on possible errors above indicates, it is fairly easy to make claims about the population using survey data, which are in fact biased or simply wrong. Consumers of public opinion data should pay attention to the details of survey studies, particularly the sample and the response rate in gauging the reliability of the findings. Moreover, analysis of survey data requires at a minimum a basic knowledge of psychometrics and econometric modeling, and even those with statistical training make theoretical mistakes in modeling,[19] and it is possible to arrive at substantively different conclusions due to choices one can make in analyzing the data as with other types of data.

New Techniques in Survey Research

Despite all these potential problems, researchers continue relying on survey research because no other method presents the ability to investigate a multitude of substantively interesting variables together. Surveys fare far better in terms of what they can tell about the real world, their external validity, compared to experiments. Moreover, new techniques in survey research also increase the method's internal validity, improving the researchers' ability to isolate the impact of the independent variables in their hypothesis. For instance, survey experiments are surveys with embedded experimental manipulations. They combine the strengths of representative surveys with the ability to make causal inference even with cross-sectional data.[20] In interpreting the results form survey experiments, however, one should exercise caution, as they are different from laboratory experiments. Real life events are outside the researcher's control and are likely to contaminate the experimental results when they matter politically. In addition, political scientists should find ways of measuring the duration of the experimental treatment's effect. Several treatment effects important from a psychologist's perspective may not be as important for political scientists interested in voting or public opinion if they do not last.[21]

New methods for dealing with measurement error due to sensitive questions such as those on support for militant groups, illegal practices, corruption, or racial prejudice also benefit from the logic of experiments. List experiments have attracted much scholarly attention as they present the researcher with the ability to recover truthful responses from aggregated answers in response to indirect questioning.[22] In a list experiment, the sample is split into control and treatment groups and those in the control group are presented with a set number of non-sensitive control items and asked how many they would respond in the affirmative. The respondents in the treatment group receive all the control items and the additional sensitive item and are also asked how many they would respond in the affirmative. Significant differences between the two numbers would indicate support for the sensitive item.[23] Endorsement experiments are also used for measuring the levels of political support for socially sensitive actors such as ethnic minorities, militant groups, and authoritarian regimes.[24] In endorsement experiments, the treatment group receives a set of policies said to have the endorsement of the sensitive political actor and those in the control group are given the policies without any endorsement information. The difference between the control and the treatment groups' support for the policies indicates the level of support for the sensitive political actor. Both list and endorsement experiments improve response rates and uncover more truthful responses, but they nonetheless are indirect measures for support for sensitive actors and issues.

Another set of techniques embedded in surveys aimed at uncovering the true response in sensitive issues such as racial prejudice involve the use of indirect, or implicit, measurement of attitudes such as the Implicit Association Test (IAT)[25] and its variants or the Affect Misattribution Procedure (AMP).[26] What makes these sets of measures implicit is the fact that the respondent is completely unaware of what is being measured. In IAT, the respondent pairs words with visual stimuli such as human faces. A statistically significant difference in association strength between negative versus positive word–visual stimulus pairs indicates like or dislike for certain stimulus group. In AMP, the respondent receives subliminal stimuli on the sensitive issue that runs through the screen in milliseconds without entering conscious processing. Next, respondents report whether they find a Chinese ideograph, an unrelated and not meaningful stimuli for most of the research population, pleasant or unpleasant. Here, a significant difference between pleasant and unpleasant ideograph counts among subliminal stimuli categories indicate like or dislike for the stimuli.

In addition to new techniques that primarily improve the internal validity of surveys, how surveys are administered has also changed since the early face-to-face studies of the 1940s through to the 1970s primarily due to changes in telecommunications. As telephone networks in many countries increased their coverage of the population, phone-survey sampling frames increasingly resembled face-to-face sampling frames in developed countries. The introduction of CATI whereby random digit dialing from a representative phone number sampling frame is done using software reduced costs of interviewing greatly.[27] The response rates, however, are lower compared to face-to-face surveys. Moreover, because household phone numbers are used in sampling, those who are often at home such as the elderly are over-represented and working-age adults are under-represented in phone surveys. Online surveys further reduce survey costs, but unlike current telephone interviewing their representativeness of the population is fairly poor. The young and the educated are over-represented in online surveys, particularly in places where there is a socio-economic and generational gap in Internet use. Researchers, however, found innovative ways of overcoming this sampling problem. Recent ANES studies, for example, are conducted online though simple computers with Internet access distributed to a representative sample of the American population who would be surveyed repeatedly.

These technological changes are making the use of surveys increasingly common at a global scale. Cross-country survey research in the 1960s up until 1990s was rare and confined mostly to American institutions. Notable examples include the Five Nation Civic Culture Study,[28] Political Participation and Equality in Seven Nations,[29] and Eight Nation Political Action Study.[30] Cross-national surveys such as the World Values Survey, the International Social Survey Program, the European Social Survey, and the various Global Barometers including the Eurobarometers have globalized public opinion research,[31] raising several new methodological and sub-stantive issues in survey research. First, population coverage, response rates, and non-response bias all change from country to country causing variation in the quality of the same survey across nations. It also necessitates altering the mode of survey administration. While phone surveys are desirable in one country, face-to-face surveys may increase the response rates and help avoid excessive sampling error in another country. Moreover, international survey research programs led to questions on whether diverse country contexts allow for meaningful comparisons of public opinion. Lack of common concepts or inconsistencies in their interpretation, as well as poor translation may hinder the standardization of surveys necessary for cross-country comparisons. Using back translation, vignettes,[32] a set of items called scales instead of a single item to measure a given concept all can help reduce comparability concerns but not eradicate them. Hence, acquiring information on specific country contexts is necessary to correctly design surveys and interpret the results in cross-national studies.

Having discussed the various ways in which new developments in survey research is strengthening its internal validity, and given its already strong ability to inform us of the real political world, it is safe to argue that the social survey will continue to be the fundamental data collection method for political science. The study of Turkish politics, particularly Turkish public opinion, could benefit greatly from the new tech-niques in survey research that incorporate features improving the ability to make causal inferences. Panel studies or cross-sectional time-series studies in Turkey similar to the American National Elections Study could greatly enhance our ability to understand the ebb and flow of Turkish public opinion and electoral behavior. The absence of this public data source has hindered and will slow down the develop-ment of empirical studies on the Turkish mass public. However, creation of this survey facility could not be sufficient to improve the academic study of public opinion in Turkey. Improvements both on the methodological and theoretical fronts are necessary. First, a higher number of graduate study programs in political science should offer courses in survey methodology and in quantitative data analysis. Second, the study of public opinion should be better informed of the current theories in political psychology, which has increasingly become the dominant paradigm in explanations of citizen attitudes and behavior. Without a sound and up-to-date theor-etical basis in the hypotheses tested using Turkish survey data, researchers will find it hard to tie their research programs to ongoing scholarly debates on citizen attitudes and behavior. Consequently, how Turkish citizens are portrayed politically using survey data will lack coherence and consistency so valuable in understanding change over-time. Given that the number of young scholars informed of political psy-chology and keen in proper methods use is on the rise, there is reason to be optimistic about the possibility of these methodological and theoretical improvements in the study of Turkish citizens' political attitudes and behavior.

Content Analysis

As scholars who often focus on the effect of communication with meaning in social and political life, political psychologists use content analysis as an important method in examining various topics. Content analysis is the systematic, replicable method used in many social science disciplines for inferring meaning from data sources into fewer content categories based on explicit rules of coding. Political scientist Ole Holsti defines content analysis as "any technique for making inferences by objec-tively and systematically identifying specified characteristics of messages."[33] It is a method "capable of throwing light on the ways [people] ... use or manipulate symbols and invest communication with meaning."[34] This method presents any type of communicative message in a reliable and replicable way in summary and representative form,[35] as it enables researchers to sift through large volumes of data with relative ease in a systematic fashion. In general, then, content analysis helps researchers to uncover what Harold Lasswell, a leading American political scientist and communications theorist, suggested as the core question in communi-cation [and political life]: *who (says) what (to) whom (in) what channel (with) what effect.*

Political psychologists have used content analysis to examine a variety of issues and topics. Some of these include among others the followings:

(1) To analyze traits and/or styles of individuals (e.g. presidents and terrorists).[36]
(2) To analyze techniques of persuasion (e.g. mediation and negotiations).[37]
(3) To describe and differentiate political parties and other ideological groups (e.g. party documents and manifestoes).[38]
(4) To infer cultural aspects and change (e.g. characteristics of a culture and public opinion).[39]
(5) To relate known characteristics of audiences to messages produced for them (e.g. advocacy groups and social movements).[40]

There is a wide range of materials that are available for content analysis: books, films, pamphlets, party programs, speeches, interviews, commercials, diaries, letters, and even cartoons, as the material does not need to involve words. The type(s) of relevant material in general depends on the research question.[41] Such materials for world leaders and other important figures located in governments outside of the United States are collected in the *Foreign Broadcast Information Services Daily Report* and are reported by other governments' information agencies on their websites. For scholars and students, such databases as *Lexis-Nexis*, *ProQuest Newstand*, and *New York Times Index* provide such materials and others from a diverse number of new sources. Given these, content analysis has been a useful method used in political psychology for allowing researchers to discover, describe, and examine the focus, mode, and character of individual, group, institution, or social attention.[42] A significant strength of content analysis is that it allows inferences to be made in an unobtrusive way, which can be then corroborated using other methods of data collection.[43]

Researchers usually consider a series of at least six sets of questions before beginning the content analysis:[44]

(1) Does the research question require extracting meaning from communication?
(2) What kinds of data materials (e.g. documents, speeches, or poems) are available? What is the population from which these materials are drawn? Are they accessible?
(3) Are these materials to be used representational or instrumental in understanding the subjects you are studying?
(4) What will be the coding rules and procedures?
(5) Can one contextualize to take into account situation, culture, and history?
(6) Can others replicate the analysis?

Content analysis is an appropriate method for certain types of research topics, and the kinds of data required for analysis depend on the nature of questions being asked. An important consideration is that however important a question might be, in order to prevent incomplete or invalid analysis, researchers should be careful about the missing documents for the study, or inappropriate or un-codable (e.g. unreadable or ambiguous content) records that may be gathered during the data gathering process.[45]

Content analysis can be done quantitatively or qualitatively, though the most common notion in qualitative research is that a content analysis simply means doing a word-frequency count. According to this view, the words and phrases that are mentioned most often are the words that reflect the salient concerns in one's speech or in a document. In quantitative content analysis, the most crucial step is to identify words and then to use, preferably, computer software to test for the consistency of their usage. Indeed, computer-assisted software such as Atlas.ti, Nudist, and Profiler+ and the increase in Internet sources that record material from news services, television, and archives have facilitated the use of and reduced the time necessary for conducting content analysis.[46] After a careful data cleaning process, sources such as interviews, press conferences, speeches of leaders, party documents, opinion polls, and survey results can easily be entered into these software programs, which can then complete the word-frequency count and provide statistical data for analysis.

There are certain issues with word-frequency count that a researcher needs to consider though. First, some words can have ambiguous meaning or can lead to misunderstanding. Similarly, some words have synonymous and researchers who use content analysis as a research method should be careful about synonymous words used throughout a document. Missing synonymous words in an analysis may lead the researchers to underestimate the importance of a particular concept.[47] There is also the problem that certain word having multiple meanings. Researchers should spend some time to ensure that a particular word has the same meaning throughout the document. There are certain software programs such as Key Word in Context that helps researchers to examine if a particular word is used in a consistent manner. In short, by using quantitative content analysis a researcher sets up a list of categories derived from the frequency list of words while controlling the distribution of words and their respective categories over the texts in an attempt to transform observations of found categories into quantitative statistical data. For example, by using quantitative content analysis, political scientists have found out that "the rhetoric of advocacy groups suggests that on emotionally charged issues such as slavery, [and] abortion ... integrative complexity is lower for both extremes than for groups taking the middle position."[48] In other words, simple quantitative content analysis provides important information but does not necessarily go into any detail or depth for why certain things happen or provide a very clear picture about the possible significance of the salient concerns.

Contextualization of data and findings has become an essential component of qualitative content analysis. As Hermann suggests, it is important to account for the nuances and complexities that are part of any political phenomenon.[49] For example, Hermann has first developed a method for constructing integrated, multivariate personality profiles of political leaders from their scores on several different motivational, cognitive, and trait-style component variables by content analyzing leaders' speeches and interviews.[50] She then suggested a series of other factors, including situational variables that "filter" the effects of personality on political behavior to contextualize their (foreign policy) actions. Similarly, others have considered the cultural and social factors in their examination of political parties by way of focusing on certain themes rather than simple words to ascertain their ideo-logical roots and possible courses of action in domestic and foreign politics.[51]

In this sense, in qualitative content analysis, the researcher examines more than just plain word counts; he will have to carefully examine the documents to clean out the data and create objective guidelines for data entry, analysis, and discussion of the findings. An important decision in qualitative content analysis is how to code and classify or categorize the data. The process of coding in qualitative content analysis is a creative approach to variables that exert an influence over textual or non-verbal content and involves defining the coding units

(1) in terms of their exact meanings and natural borders,
(2) by separating the data into words, sentences, or paragraphs, depending on the nature of the content analysis, and finally
(3) through the use of referential units (e.g. M.K. Ataturk, the first President of Turkey, the founding father of Turkey, Mustafa Kemal refer to the same political leader).[52]

In general, a researcher can choose from two approaches to coding data. In the first approach—emergent coding—categories are established following some pre-liminary examination of the data. A researcher first reviews the material and comes up with a set of features that form a checklist and then applies coding. In the second approach—a priori coding—the categories are established prior to the analysis based upon some theory. Accordingly, researcher agrees on the categories, and the coding is applied to the data. Revisions are made as necessary, and the cat-egories are tightened up to the point that maximizes mutual exclusivity and exhaus-tiveness.[53] Once the decisions are made regarding the coding, researchers are faced with designing the rules and procedures they are going to follow in drawing infer-ences from the materials.[54] In this sense, the qualitative content analysis focuses more on what certain words, groups of words or symbols mean (e.g. intentionality) and their implications.

In order for inferences to be valid, it is important that the coding and classification procedure be reliable—in the sense of being consistent and objective. First, a researcher must be able to make the same inferences from the same data (stability or intra-coder reliability) and second, "different people should code the same text in the same way [reproducibility or inter-coder reliability]."[55] Developing rules that allow researchers to categorize and code the same data in the same way over a period of time is essential to the success of a content analysis. Coding is important to both organize the data and provide a means to make inferences following the content analysis. The researchers read the data carefully, demarcating segments that labeled with a "code"—usually a word or a word group. When coding is com-plete, the researcher prepares a codebook.

It is suggested that the coding and categorization is done by more than one researcher alone for reasons related to reliability of the analysis. When there is inter-coder reliability, which means that there is an agreement between two or more than two researchers about how to code and categorize certain words or groups of words, the coding can be applied on a large-scale basis, though, a periodic quality control check is always desirable. Inter-coder reliability is needed in content analysis because that is how researchers can assess the internal validity of their conclusions.[56] Similarly, one can suggest, "high levels of disagreement among [coders] suggest weaknesses in research methods, including the possibility of poor operational definitions, categories, and judge training."[57] In order to achieve intra- and inter-coder reliability,[58] the most critical step in content analysis is to develop clear and precise instructions as to how to code and record variables. When possible it also helps to share these instructions in order to allow other researchers to replicate the study.[59]

In this special issue, Barış Kesgin uses the leadership trait analysis in assessing the traits of Turkey's post-Cold War prime ministers. A computerized program, the ProfilerPlus, is used to content analyze and then quantify leaders' speeches, interviews, and the like into seven traits following a carefully developed coding scheme. The scores are then compared to a norming group in order to contextualize and make valid and reliable inferences. His article also shows the particular strengths of the content analysis as a research method—reducing a large amount of data into a manageable size and making inferences in an unobtrusive way—while exemplifying the six steps discussed above that researchers must take when conducting such a study at the same time.

Conclusion

We offer two brief concluding notes for this article: First, as one can tell from the discussion, every method has strengths and drawbacks. The question one should ask is not "which one is the best method out there?" it is rather "which method would provide the best test for the research question?" It is critical to understand that every method would provide a distinct aspect of the unknown phenomenon. The researcher should then seek and answer the following question: which method best fits in with the research question?

Second comes the interval versus external validity tradeoff. Interval validity refers to the degree of control in a study over all possible factors that the participants are exposed to. External validity in contrast refers to the degree of generalization across different people, places, and times. So, while one asks whether there is control over the causal inferences between the conditions the other one asks whether one can generalize from the findings to different populations. In this setting, the tradeoff between external and internal validity is not easy to solve. The possible solution would be to accept the realities of the research method and acknowledge the benefits and downsides of the method. Through this acknowledgement one can reach reliable inferences. The other option would be to follow the debate in the methodology and statistics literature within political science and advance the methods accordingly. Today, there is either a methodological or a statistical solution developed for the potential problems encountered in quantitative research methods.

Proper usage of a research methodology is the backbone of reaching empirically and theoretically valid inferences. Without these analytical methods, answers to research questions will be rather limited and debatable. In turn, future research in any domain of Turkish political science should pay more attention to research methodology with the aim of advancing scientific knowledge in the discipline.

Notes

1. Kinder and Palfrey, *Experimental Foundations of Political Science*; Druckman et al., "The Growth and Development of Experimental Research Political Science"; Druckman et al., *Cambridge Handbook of Experimental Political Science*; and Morton and Williams, *Experimental Political Science and the Study of Causality*.
2. Camerer, *Behavioral Game Theory* and Henrich et al., *Foundations of Human Sociality*.
3. Gladwell, *Blink*; Gigerenzer, *Gut Feelings*; Ariely, *Predictably Irrational*; and Taleb, *Fooled by Randomness*.
4. Kahneman et al., *Judgment under Uncertainty*.
5. Since early 2000s, the interest towards neuroscience and genetics in political science is on significant rise. We see that neuro-politics and geno-politics are the two sub-disciplines within political psychology that promote scientific studies in understanding and modeling citizen behavior on vote choice, party identification and emotional reactions (for a general discussion on this topic, please refer to the special issue of Hatemi and McDermott, "The Political Psychology of Biology, Genetics, and Behavior").
6. Druckman and Kam, "Students as Experimental Participants."
7. For a broader discussion as to how experiments can contribute to theory-building in Turkish political science, refer to Erişen, "Deneysel Yöntem."
8. Brady, "Contributions of Survey Research to Political Science."
9. Esmer, *Measuring and Mapping Cultures*.
10. See for example: Carkoglu and Kalaycioglu, *Turkish Democracy Today*.
11. Erişen and Erişen, "The Effect of Social Networks on the Quality of Political Thinking"; Erişen and Erişen, "Attitudinal Ambivalence in the EU Towards Turkey's EU Membership"; Erişen and Erişen, "Cognitive Versus Emotional Evaluations as the Foundations of Public Perceptions of the EU in Turkey"; and Kentmen, "Determinants of Support for EU Membership in Turkey."
12. Tourangeau et al., *The Psychology of Survey Response* and Krosnick, "Survey Research."
13. Thurstone, "A Law of Comparative Judgment."
14. Fazio, "Multiple Processes by Which Attitudes Guide Behavior"; Zaller, *The Nature and Origins of Mass Opinion*; and Zaller and Feldman, "A Simple Theory of the Survey Response."
15. Weisberg, *The Total Survey Error Approach*.
16. Converse and Presser, *Survey Questions*,
17. Ibid.
18. Berinsky, *Silent Voices* and Krosnick, "The Causes of No-Opinion Responses to Attitude Measures in Surveys."
19. King, "How Not to Lie With Statistics."
20. Cassino and Erişen, "Priming Bush and Iraq in 2008."
21. Gaines et al., "Rethinking the Survey Experiment."
22. Holbrook and Krosnick, "Social Desirability Bias in Voter Turnout Reports"; Janus, "The Influence of Social Desirability Pressures on Expressed Immigration Attitudes"; Redlawsk et al., "Voters Emotions, and Race in 2008"; and Imai, "Multivariate Regression Analysis for the Item Count Technique."
23. Blair and Imai, "Statistical Analysis of List Experiments."
24. Bullock et al., "Statistical Analysis of Endorsement Experiments."
25. Greenwald et al., "Measuring Individual Differences in Implicit Cognition."
26. Payne et al., "An Inkblot for Attitudes."

27. Lavrakas, *Telephone Survey Methods.*
28. Almond and Verba, *The Civic Culture.*
29. Verba et al., *Participation and Political Equality.*
30. Jennings and Van Deth, *Continuities in Political Action.*
31. Heath et al., "The Globalization of Public Opinion Research."
32. King et al., "Enhancing the Validity and Cross-Cultural Comparability of Measurement in Survey Research."
33. Holsti, *Content Analysis for the Social Sciences and Humanities*, 14.
34. Moyser and Wagstaffe, *Research Methods for Elite Studies*, 20.
35. Neuendorf. *The Content Analysis Codebook*, 10.
36. For example, George, "The 'Operational Code' "; Hermann and Hermann, "Who Makes Foreign Policy Decisions and How"; Hermann et al., "Who Leads Matters"; Kaarbo, "Linking Leadership Style to Policy"; and Post, "Saddam Hussein of Iraq."
37. For example, Winter et al., "The Personalities of Bush and Gorbachev Measured at a Distance"; Keltner et al., "Power, Approach, and Inhibition"; and Suedfeld et al., "Changes in Integrative Complexity among Middle East Leaders During the Persian Gulf Crisis."
38. For example, Ozkececi-Taner, "The Impact of Institutionalized Ideas in Coalition Foreign Policy Making" and Benoit and Laver, "Estimating Party Policy Positions."
39. Iyengar and Simon, "News Coverage of the Gulf Crisis and Public-Opinion"; Gelpi, "Public Opinion Toward War"; and Goldsmith et al., "American Foreign Policy and Global Opinion?"
40. Dillon, "Argumentative Complexity of Abortion Discourse" and Tetlock et al., "The Slavery Debate in Antebellum America."
41. Hermann, "Content Analysis."
42. Weber, *Basic Content Analysis.*
43. Krippendorff, *Content Analysis.*
44. Krippendorff, *Content Analysis* and Hermann, "Content Analysis." In addition to these, Hermann (2010) considers two more questions: (1) What is the unit of analysis? and (2) Does the analysis capture what you are interested in learning about?
45. US General Accounting Office, *Content Analysis.*
46. Hermann, "Content Analysis."
47. Weber, *Basic Content Analysis.*
48. Winter, "Personality and Political Behavior."
49. Hermann, "Content Analysis."
50. Hermann, "Foreign Policy Role Orientations and the Quality of Foreign Policy Decisions."
51. Ozkececi-Taner, "The Impact of Institutionalized Ideas in Coalition Foreign Policy Making"; Benoit and Laver, "Estimating Party Policy Positions" and Ozkececi-Taner, *Role of Institutionalized Ideas in Coalition Government Foreign Policymaking.*
52. Krippendorff, *Content Analysis*; Stemler gives the example of the concept of "state," an oft-used word in political science, which could "mean a political body, a situation, or a verb meaning 'to speak'."
53. Stemler, "An Overview of Content Analysis" and Weber, *Basic Content Analysis.*
54. Hermann, "Content Analysis."
55. Weber, *Basic Content Analysis*, 12 and Krippendorff (2003) suggests that sometimes researchers establish "shared and hidden meaning of the coding" because they have been working with each other for a long time. This may result in an artificially high inter-coder reliability that can create problems.
56. Tinsley and Weiss, "Interrater Reliability and Agreement."
57. Kolbe and Burnett, "Content-Analysis Research."
58. There are different ways to measure the appropriate level of inter-coder reliability. An extensive review of the "agreement indices" can be seen in Lombard et al., *Content Analysis in Mass Communication.*
59. It is important to note that the data be durable in nature so that the content analysis could be replicable.

Bibliography

Almond, Gabriel, and Sidney Verba. *The Civic Culture: Political Attitudes and Democracy in Five Nations.* Boston, MA: Little, Brown, 1963.

Ariely, Dan. *Predictably Irrational: The Hidden Forces That Shape Our Decisions.* London: Harper Collins, 2008.

Benoit, Kenneth, and Michael Laver. "Estimating Party Policy Positions: Comparing Expert Surveys and Hand-Coded Content Analysis." *Electoral Studies* 26, no. 1 (2007): 90–107.

Berinsky, Adam J. *Silent Voices: Opinion Polls and Political Representation in America.* Princeton: Princeton University Press, 2004.

Blair, Graeme, and Kosuke Imai. "Statistical Analysis of List Experiments." *Political Analysis* 20, no. 1 (2012): 47–77.

Brady, Henry. "Contributions of Survey Research to Political Science." *PS: Political Science & Politics* 33, no. 1 (2000): 47–57.

Bullock, Will, Kosuke Imai, and Jacob N. Shapiro. "Statistical Analysis of Endorsement Experiments: Measuring Support for Militant Groups in Pakistan." *Political Analysis* 19, no. 4 (2011): 363–384.

Camerer, Colin. *Behavioral Game Theory: Experiments on Strategic Interaction.* Princeton: Princeton University Press, 2003.

Carkoglu, Ali, and Ersin Kalaycioglu. *Turkish Democracy Today.* London: I. B. Tauris, 2007.

Cassino, Dan, and Cengiz Erişen. "Priming Bush and Iraq in 2008: A Survey Experiment." *American Politics Research* 28, no. 2 (2010): 372–394.

Converse, Jean M., and Stanley Presser. *Survey Questions: Handcrafting the Standardized Questionnaire.* Thousand Oaks, CA: Sage Publications, 1986.

Dillon, Michelle. "Argumentative Complexity of Abortion Discourse." *Public Opinion Quarterly* 57, no. 3 (1993): 305–314.

Druckman, James N., Donald P. Green, James H. Kuklinski, and Arthur Lupia. "The Growth and Development of Experimental Research Political Science." *American Political Science Review* 100, no. 4 (2006): 627–636.

Druckman, James N., Donald P. Green, James H. Kuklinski, and Arthur Lupia. *Cambridge Handbook of Experimental Political Science.* New York: Cambridge University Press, 2011.

Druckman, James N., and Cindy Kam. "Students as Experimental Participants: A Defense of the 'Narrow Data Base'." In *Cambridge Handbook of Experimental Political Science*, edited by James N. Druckman, Donald P. Green, JamesH. Kuklinski, and Arthur Lupia, 70–101. New York: Cambridge University Press, 2011.

Erişen, Elif, and Cengiz Erişen. "The Effect of Social Networks on the Quality of Political Thinking." *Political Psychology* 33, no. 6 (2012): 839–865.

Erişen, Cengiz, and Elif Erişen. "Cognitive Versus Emotional Evaluations as the Foundations of Public Perceptions of the EU in Turkey." In *The Great Catalyst: European Union Project and Lessons from Greece and Turkey*, edited by Bülent Temel. New York: Lexington Books, forthcoming.

Erişen, Cengiz, and Elif Erişen., "Attitudinal Ambivalence in the EU Towards Turkey's EU Membership," Presented at the annual meeting of the American Political Science Association, Seattle, WA, 2011.

Erişen, Cengiz,. "Deneysel Yöntem." In *Farklı Pencereler, Farklı Manzaralar: Sosyal Bilimlerde Yöntem Tartışmaları*, edited by Pınar Uyan Semerci and Emre Erdoğan, 121–146. İstanbul: Hiperlink, 2013.

Esmer, Yilmaz. *Measuring and Mapping Cultures: 25 Years of Comparative Value Surveys.* Leiden, The Netherlands: Brill Academic Publishers, 2007.

Fazio, Russell H. "Multiple Processes by Which Attitudes Guide Behavior: The MODE Model as an Integrative Framework." In *Advances in Experimental Social Psychology*, Vol. 23, edited by M.P. Zanna, 75–109. New York: Academic Press, 1990.

Gaines, Brian J., James H. Kuklinski, and Paul J. Quirk. "The Logic of the Survey Experiment Reexamined." *Political Analysis* 15, no. 1 (2007): 1–20.

Gelpi, Christopher. "Performing on Cue? The Formation of Public Opinion Toward War." *Journal of Conflict Resolution* 54, no .1 (2010): 88–116.

George, Alexandre L. "The 'Operational Code': A Neglected Approach to the Study of Political Leaders and Decision-Making." *International Studies Quarterly* 13, no. 2 (1969): 190–222.

Gigerenzer, Gerd. *Gut Feelings: The Intelligence of the Unconscious.* New York: Viking, 2007.

Gladwell, Malcolm. *Blink: The Power of Thinking Without Thinking.* New York: Back Bay Books, 2007.

Goldsmith, Benjamin E., Yasaku Horiuchi, and Takashi Inoguchi. "American Foreign Policy and Global Opinion: Who Supported the War in Afghanistan?" *Journal of Conflict Resolution* 49, no. 3 (2005): 408–429.

Greenwald, Anthony G., Debbie E. McGhee, and Jordan L. K. Schwartz. "Measuring Individual Differences in Implicit Cognition: The Implicit Association Test." *Journal of Personality and Social Psychology* 74, no. 6 (1998): 1464–1480.

Hatemi, Peter K., and Rose McDermott. "The Political Psychology of Biology, Genetics, and Behavior: An Introduction by Special Issue Editors." *Political Psychology* 33, no. 3 (2012): 307–312.

Heath, Anthony, Stephen Fisher, and Shawna Smith. "The Globalization of Public Opinion Research." *Annual Review of Political Science* 8 (2005): 297–333.

Henrich, Joseph, Robert Boyd, Samuel Bowles, Colin Camerer, Ernst Fehr, and Herbert Gintis. *Foundations of Human Sociality: Economic Experiments and Ethnographic Evidence from Fifteen Small-Scale Societies.* Oxford: Oxford University Press, 2004.

Hermann, Margaret G. "Foreign Policy Role Orientations and the Quality of Foreign Policy Decisions." In *Role Theory and Foreign Policy Analysis*, edited by Scott Walker, 123–140. Durham, NC: Duke University Press, 1987.

Hermann, Margaret G. "Content Analysis." In *Qualitative Methods in International Relations*, edited by Audie Klotz and Deepa Prakash, 151–167. New York: Palgrave MacMillan, 2010.

Hermann, Margaret G., and Charles Hermann. "Who Makes Foreign Policy Decisions and How: An Empirical Inquiry." *International Studies Quarterly* 33, no. 4 (1989): 361–388.

Hermann, Margaret G., Thomas Preston, Baghat Korany, and Timothy M. Shaw. "Who Leads Matters: The Effects of Powerful Individuals." *International Studies Review* 3, no. 2 (2001): 83–131.

Holbrook, Allyson L., and Jon A. Krosnick. "Social Desirability Bias in Voter Turnout Reports: Tests Using the Item Count Technique." *Public Opinion Quarterly* 74, no. 1 (2010): 37–67.

Holsti, Ole. *Content Analysis for the Social Sciences and Humanities.* Reading, MA: Addison-Wiley, 1969.

Imai, Kosuke. "Multivariate Regression Analysis for the Item Count Technique." *Journal of the American Statistical Association* 106, no. 494 (2011): 407–416.

Iyengar, Shanto, and Adam Simon. "News Coverage of the Gulf Crisis and Public-Opinion: A Study of Agenda Setting, Priming, and Framing." *Communication Research* 20, no. 3 (1993): 365–383.

Janus, A. L. "The Influence of Social Desirability Pressures on Expressed Immigration Attitudes." *Social Science Quarterly* 91, no. 4 (2010): 928–946.

Jennings, Kent M., and Van Deth, J., eds. *Continuities in Political Action: A Longitudinal Study of Political Orientations in Three Western Democracies.* Berlin: Walter de Gruyter, 1990.

Kaarbo, Julliet. "Linking Leadership Style to Policy: How Prime Ministers Influence the Decision-Making Process." In *Profiling Political Leaders: Cross-Cultural Studies of Personality and Political Behavior*, edited by Ofer Feldman and Linda O. Valenty, 81–96. Westport, CT: Praeger, 2001.

Kahneman, Daniel, Paul Slovic, and Amos Tversky. *Judgment under Uncertainty: Heuristics and Biases.* New York: Cambridge University Press, 1982.

Keltner, Dacher, Deborah H. Gruenfeld, and Cameron Anderson. "Power, Approach, and Inhibition." *Psychological Review* 110, no. 2 (2003): 265–284.

Kentmen, Çigdem. "Determinants of Support for EU Membership in Turkey: Islamic Attachments, Utilitarian Considerations, and National Identity." *European Union Politics* 9, no. 4 (2008): 487–510.

Kinder, Donald R., and Thomas R. Palfrey. *Experimental Foundations of Political Science.* Michigan: University of Michigan Press, 1993.

King, Gary. "How Not to Lie with Statistics: Avoiding Common Mistakes in Quantitative Political Science." *American Journal of Political Science* 30, no. 3 (1986): 666–687.

King, Gary, Murray, Christopher J. L., Salomon, Jashua A., and Ajay Tandon. "Enhancing the Validity and Cross-Cultural Comparability of Measurement in Survey Research." *American Political Science Review* 98, no. 1 (2004): 191–207.

Kolbe, Richar H., and Melissa S. Burnett. "Content-Analysis Research: An Examination of Applications with Directives for Improving Research Reliability and Objectivity." *Journal of Consumer Research* 18, no. 2 (1991): 248.

Krippendorff, Klaus. *Content Analysis: An Introduction to Its Methodology*. Newbury Park, CA: Sage, 2003.

Krosnick, Jon A. "Survey Research." *Annual Review of Psychology* 50, no. 1 (1999): 537–567.

Krosnick, Jon A. "The Causes of No-Opinion Responses to Attitude Measures in Surveys: They Are Rarely What They Appear to Be." In *Survey Non Response*, edited by R. M. Groves, D. A. Dillman, J. L. Eltinge, and R. J. A. Little, 87–100. New York: Wiley, 2002.

Lavrakas, Paul J. *Telephone Survey Methods: Sampling, Selection, and Supervision*. Thousand Oaks, CA: Sage Publications, 1993.

Lombard, Matthew, Jennifer Snyder-Duch, and Cheryl Companella Bracken. "Content Analysis in Mass Communication: Assessment and Reporting of Intercoder Reliability." *Human Communication Research* 28, no. 4 (2002): 587–604.

Morton, Rebecca B., and Kenneth C. Williams. *Experimental Political Science and the Study of Causality*. New York: Cambridge University Press, 2010.

Moyser, George, and Margaret Wagstaffe, eds. *Research Methods for Elite Studies*. London: Allen & Unwin, 1987.

Neuendorf, Kimberly A. *The Content Analysis Codebook*. Thousand Oaks, CA: Sage Publications, 2002.

Ozkececi-Taner, Binnur. "The Impact of Institutionalized Ideas in Coalition Foreign Policy Making: Turkey as an Example, 1991–2002." *Foreign Policy Analysis* 1, no. 3 (2005): 249–278.

Ozkececi-Taner, Binnur. *Role of Institutionalized Ideas in Coalition Government Foreign Policymaking: Turkey as a Case Study, 1991–2002*. Leiden, The Netherlands: Brill & RoL Publishers, 2009.

Payne, B. Keith, Clara Michelle Cheng, Olesya Govorun, and Brandon D. Stewart. "An Inkblot for Attitudes: Affect Misattribution as Implicit Measurement." *Journal of Personality and Social Psychology* 89, no. 3 (2005): 277–293.

Post, Jerrold. "Saddam Hussein of Iraq: A Political Personality Profile." *Political Psychology* 12, no. 2 (1991): 279–289.

Redlawsk, David P., Caroline J. Tolbert, and William Franko. "Voters, Emotions, and Race in 2008: Obama as the First Black President." *Political Research Quarterly* 63, no. 4 (2010): 875–889.

Stemler, Steve. "An Overview of Content Analysis." *Practical Assessment, Research, and Evaluation* 7 (2001). Accessed May 15, 2012. http://PAREonline.net/getvn.aspv=7&n=17

Suedfeld, Peter, Michael D. Wallace, and Kimberly L. Thachuk. "Changes in Integrative Complexity among Middle East Leaders During the Persian Gulf Crisis." *Journal of Social Issues* 49, no. 4 (1993): 183–199.

Taleb, Nassim Nicholas. *Fooled by Randomness: The Hidden Role of Chance in Life and in the Markets*. New York: Rando House, 2008.

Tetlock, Phillip E., David Armor, and Randall S. Peterson. "The Slavery Debate in Antebellum America: Cognitive Style, Value Conflict, and the Limits of Compromise." *Journal of Personality and Social Psychology* 66, no. 1 (1994): 115–126.

Thurstone, Louis Leon. "A Law of Comparative Judgment." *Psychological Review* 34, no. 4 (1927): 273–286.

Tinsley, Howard E. A., and Weiss, David J. "Interrater Reliability and Agreement." In *Handbook of Multivariate Statistics and Mathematical Modeling*, edited by Howard E. A. Tinsley and Steven D. Brown, 95–124. New York: Academic Press, 2000.

Tourangeau, Roger, Lance J. Rips, and Kenneth Rasinski. *The Psychology of Survey Response*. New York: Cambridge University Press, 2000.

US General Accounting Office. *Content Analysis: A Methodology for Structuring and Analyzing Written Material*. Washington, DC: US General Accounting Office, 1996 (GAO/PEMD-10.3.1).

Verba, Sidney, Joseph Nie, and Jae-On Kim. *Participation and Political Equality: A Seven Nation Comparison*. Cambridge: Cambridge University Press, 1978.

Weber, Robert P. *Basic Content Analysis*. 2nd ed. Newbury Park, CA: Sage, 1990.

Weisberg, Herbert F. *The Total Survey Error Approach*. Chicago: University of Chicago Press, 2005.

Winter, David. "Personality and Political Behavior." In *Oxford Handbook of Political Pscyhology*, edited by David O. Sears, Leonie Huddy, and Robert Jervis, 124. New York: Oxford University Press, 2003.

Winter, David G., Margaret G. Hermann, Walter Weintraub, and Scott G. Walker. "The Personalities of Bush and Gorbachev Measured at a Distance: Procedures, Portraits, and Policy." *Political Psychology* 12, no. 2 (1991): 215–245.

Zaller, John. *The Nature and Origins of Mass Opinion*. Cambridge: Cambridge University Press, 1992.

Zaller, John, and Stanley Feldman. "A Simple Theory of the Survey Response: Answering Questions Versus Revealing Preferences." *American Journal of Political Science* 36, no. 3 (1992): 579–616.

Values, Religiosity and Support for Redistribution and Social Policy in Turkey

GIZEM ARIKAN

Department of International Relations, Yaşar University, İzmir, Turkey

ABSTRACT   *This paper investigates the individual level factors that influence support for social redistribution and social policy in Turkey by focusing on the role of core values and religiosity. The analysis of data from Round 4 of European Social Surveys shows that self-transcendence and conservation values enhance support for government provision of social safety nets. Different aspects of religiosity have different effects on attitudes toward redistribution and social policy, with self-identified religiosity having a positive and social religious behavior having a negative effect on support for government responsibility in providing social insurance.*

The welfare state continues to be an important topic for scholarly inquiry, yet few studies address the personal motives that drive support for redistribution and welfare policies.[1] Existing research mostly focuses on the role of self-interest, ideology and subjective beliefs, while the effects of other psychological predispositions remain relatively unexplored. This paper investigates the effect of core values and religiosity on attitudes toward redistribution and social policy in Turkey. Although both values and religiosity are seen as important psychological motivations that drive a variety of political attitudes, research on their impact on attitudes toward redistribution and welfare policy remains limited. Using data from the European Social Surveys (ESS) collected in 2008, this paper finds that self-transcendence and conservation values, as well as religiosity, are important factors driving support for government responsibility in social welfare policy, while the social behavioral aspect of religiosity diminishes support for such policies.

Apart from establishing the effects of values and personal religious experience, the results also suggest that differences in institutional and political contexts are reflected in the way attitudes and opinions are structured. While comparative studies on advanced industrialized nations find self-interest, class cleavages and ideology to be important factors, in the present study, in line with some previous studies,[2] there is little empirical evidence for the effect of these variables on attitudes toward redistribution and social policy in the Turkish case. The relative unimportance of these factors suggests that a limited, invisible welfare state, together with a low information environment in which neither political elites nor the media provide enough content on social policy, seem to make it hard for individuals to make the cognitive connection between these factors and policy outcomes. Thus, besides providing an insight into the sources of attitudes toward redistribution in Turkey, these results also compliment some of the crucial findings in the political psychology literature on the importance of elite and media framing of issues,[3] as well as the importance of context in influencing individual attitudes and behavior.

Explaining Attitudes toward Redistribution and Social Policy

Research on attitudes toward redistribution and social welfare policies focuses on advanced industrialized countries with fairly developed welfare states. This literature extensively discusses the effect of material self-interest, arguing that those who are economically more vulnerable, and who are thus more likely to receive welfare state benefits, tend to be more supportive of redistribution and welfare policy.[4] Conversely, more affluent individuals, who are less likely to benefit from government provision of social safety nets, are usually less supportive of such policies compared to those who face greater economic risks, such as people with low income or low education, as well as women, the retired and the unemployed.[5] In fact, although the political psychology literature often fails to find consistent effects of self-interest on public opinion[6], comparative studies have established robust effects of income, education and social status indicators on attitudes toward redistribution and welfare in the West.

Ideological orientations are also among the important factors explaining attitudes toward redistribution and welfare spending.[7] Social equality and redistribution are the core issues in the left–right distinction in many contexts[8], and ideological identifications emerge as consistent and strong predictors of support for social policies.[9] Some recent studies have also uncovered the effect of subjective beliefs and perceptions on attitudes toward redistribution. For example, those who attribute poverty to individual laziness or lack of individual effort are less supportive of redistribution and increased welfare spending compared to those who believe that poverty is caused by circumstances beyond individual control, such as luck or lack of opportunity.[10] Similarly, those who believe that hard work is the key to success tend to be less supportive of government actions to reduce income inequalities.[11] Finally, individuals who believe that their society creates few impediments to upward mobility tend to oppose governmental redistribution.[12]

Thus, while the role of symbolic factors such as subjective beliefs and perceptions has been addressed, values and religiosity still remain less understood psychological motivations in the study of public opinion toward redistribution and welfare policy.

Although economic individualism or egalitarianism has been widely discussed in the case of welfare attitudes in the USA,[13] there is not much interest in values in the comparative literature on attitudes toward redistribution.[14] This paper aims to fill this gap. By studying the effects of core values and religiosity on welfare attitudes in the case of Turkey, it strives to provide a better understanding of the psychological factors that influence attitudes toward government responsibility in social welfare policy. The next two sections define both concepts, discuss their relevance to welfare attitudes, and present the hypotheses that are tested in this study.

Value Dimensions and Support for Redistribution and Social Welfare

Scholars from different disciplines offer different conceptualizations of individual values, some of which correspond both theoretically and empirically with each other.[15] Here, social psychologist Shalom Schwartz's value framework is adopted. Schwartz's theory of universal human values offers a comprehensive, theory-based approach, has been validated using data from over 80 countries, and can be considered to be one of the most appropriate instruments for cross-cultural research on individual and societal values.

Values are psychological constructs defined as desirable and trans-situational goals that serve as guiding principles in the selection and the justification of actions and the evaluation of people (including the self) and events.[16] Values are highly relevant in explaining a wide array of political attitudes.[17] Whereas attitudes are beliefs concerning specific objects or situations, and tendencies to evaluate particular objects positively or negatively, values are abstract, general and evaluative, transcend specific situations, and are more enduring[18]. This property makes them essential for understanding attitudes, preferences and actions.

Schwartz's value theory identifies ten types of values, which form two higher-order bipolar value dimensions.[19] The first dimension contrasts *openness to change* with *conservation*. Openness to change is associated with values of self-direction, stimulation and (partly) hedonism; in contrast, conservation values emphasize conformity, tradition and security. The second higher-order value dimension is *self-transcendence* versus *self-enhancement*. While the former set of values is associated with universalism and benevolence, which concern transcendence of selfish interests, self-enhancement emphasizes motivational goals that reflect personal success, such as achievement and power.

Self-transcendence values embrace motivational goals that include concern for the well-being of others, helping those in need and protecting the welfare of all people. Intuitively, this value dimension seems highly relevant to attitudes toward redistribution. Since they emphasize transcendence of selfish interests in favor of social equality, concern with the interests of others and social justice,[20] self-transcendence values are expected to be associated with greater support for redistribution and government responsibility (Hypothesis 1).

The link between conservation values and redistribution is less obvious, however, and may even appear contradictory. Conventional wisdom usually equates social policy and redistribution with altruism, concern for others or support for equality—values that are not relevant to the motivational goals of conservatism.[21] Conservatism is also frequently associated with limited government and a desire for lower government spending.[22] Therefore, if conservatism were related to welfare attitudes at all, many would think the effect would be in the negative direction. However, while most studies refer to conservatism as identification with the political right,[23] conservatism is defined here as a fundamental psychological predisposition, a core value orientation that emphasizes the goals of social order, tradition and conformity. This makes it different from political philosophies and contemporary ideologies and should not be confused with them.[24] That is, the fact that many right-wing or centrist political ideologies and political parties combine the goals of political order, stability, security and preservation of status quo with free market economics does not necessarily mean that conservatism as a value orientation is automatically associated with rejection of government responsibility. In addition, the political right usually combines these value orientations with the ideal of limited government; this does not necessarily have to be the case in all contexts. On the contrary, conservatism may actually have a positive impact on support for equal outcomes. For example, the conservative's concern for social order and security might call for government intervention to alleviate poverty to prevent social unrest.[25] In fact, political scientist Karen Stenner's analysis of data from 80 independent samples from 59 nations shows that conservatism is negatively, although modestly, correlated with support for laissez-faire policies.

While conservation values could be theorized to increase support for government intervention in general, it is also possible that their effects depend on the political context. Types of welfare regimes and outcomes of welfare policies may matter in determining conservatism's influence on support for social welfare. For example, some welfare states provide benefits only to a limited privileged group in the society[26] and help uphold traditional status distinctions, which may draw support from more conservative, traditional groups. Turkey is considered to be a type of "protective" welfare state with conservative tendencies, such as the preservation of authority, in which the leaders prefer social rights that promote loyalty to the state.[27] These types of welfare states typically regulate most spheres of social life and dominate social interests in the society.[28] As a result, conservative individuals, who tend to be more accepting of state authority and traditional social structures, may support its welfare policies. On the other hand, there is nothing in these debates that suggests that conservatism is associated with a vision of an egalitarian society. Therefore, while conservation values are not necessarily expected to increase support for redistribution, they are expected to have a positive impact on support for government responsibility to provide basic social security benefits to disadvantaged groups (Hypothesis 2).

Dimensions of Religiosity and Attitudes toward Redistribution and Welfare

Similarly to core values, the effect of religiosity on attitudes toward redistribution is also less understood. The fact that different conceptualizations and measures of individual religiosity abound further complicates this. In this paper, religious experience is described as a multifaceted phenomenon comprising belief, behavior and belonging dimensions.[29] While the different dimensions of religiosity seem to be highly related, research shows they may often produce different and even conflicting outcomes on volunteering,[30] voting behavior,[31] party support[32] and support for democracy.[33]

The belief dimension of religiosity embraces an understanding of the divine and humanity's relationship to it, connects the individual to the world, and refers to belief in God, heaven, hell, life after death and tendencies of people to characterize themselves as religious.[34] Religious belief has many aspects that may influence attitudes toward redistribution and welfare policy. Since almost all religions embrace compassion and the responsibility to help those who are in need,[35] piety is generally expected to increase support for redistributive policies.[36] It has also been argued that the religiously orthodox are both culturally and economically communitarian, in the sense that they believe the community must enforce divinely mandated moral standards on individuals and should also watch over or take care of those who are in need.[37] On the other hand, evidence in favor of religiosity's influence on attitudes toward redistribution in Muslim countries is mixed. For example, survey data from 25 countries with Muslim majorities show that while pious Muslims are more likely to favor state ownership of economic enterprises, they are generally opposed to government efforts to eliminate income inequalities.[38] Another study finds that religious orthodoxy, measured as support for Shari'a, is associated both with support for government intervention to ensure that everyone in the society is provided for and also support for government ownership of business, although this does not necessarily extend to support for more equal outcomes.[39] Thus, while religious teachings preach compassion and caring, it does not seem that this is translated into concern for more equal incomes. Therefore, more religious individuals may not necessarily hold positive attitudes toward redistribution, but they are expected to be more supportive of government provision for those who are in need (Hypothesis 3).

The behavioral component of religiosity consists of the private and social practice of a religion, including private devotion (prayer or reading of holy texts) and social religious behavior, which involves participation in organized religious communities and attendance at places of worship.[40] According to political scientists Kenneth Scheve and David Stasavage, the social practice of religiosity serves as a type of insurance for individuals against the effects of adverse life events, such as unemployment, illness or retirement.[41] They argue that participation in religious networks allows individuals to draw upon communal material support in times of difficulty, making individuals more confident in individual effort and less supportive of government intervention in the economic sphere. In addition, it is also possible that those who are engaged in religious social networks desire more private action and charity to correct for social inequalities. In many Muslim countries, including Turkey,[42] Islamic charities and non-governmental organizations are highly effective in redistributing income and helping those who are in need[43]. Thus, those who tend to be more involved in religious social networks are expected to be less supportive of government responsibility in redistribution of income and the provision of social benefits (Hypothesis 4).

Data, Variables and Methods

Data from the Round 4 of the ESS collected in 2008 is used to test the hypotheses. The fieldwork was carried between November 2, 2008 and May 17, 2009. The dataset contains 2415 observations from respondents, all of whom are above the age of 15.[44]

The first dependent variable is *support for redistribution*, which consists of one item, using a five-point Likert scale ranging from "strongly agree" to "strongly disagree," that asks respondents whether the government should take measures to reduce differences in income levels. The second dependent variable is *support for government responsibility in providing social services*. This is an aggregate index of four items that ask the respondents to rate, on a scale of zero to ten how much responsibility they think governments should have in four areas:

(1) To ensure a job for everyone who wants one;
(2) To ensure adequate health care for the sick;
(3) To ensure a reasonable standard of living for the old and
(4) To ensure a reasonable standard of living for the unemployed (alpha $= 0.87$).

For both dependent variables higher values represent greater support for redistribution and government responsibility.

Regarding the key independent variables, Schwartz values of conservation, openness, self-transcendence and self-enhancement were coded according to the instructions provided by the ESS.[45] To measure the relative weight individuals place on a value on one dimension as opposed to the value on the other dimension, conservation is subtracted from openness, and self-transcendence from self-enhancement. The resulting measures, thus, show the degree to which respondents valued conservation as opposed to openness, and self-transcendence as opposed to self-enhancement.

Due to the lack of religious belief questions in the survey, religious belief was measured by the self-assessed level of religiosity on a zero-to-ten scale. Frequency of prayer and attendance at religious services (both seven-point scales) was used to tap the devotional aspect of religiosity. Although no specific hypothesis concerning the effect of prayer has been put forward, it was still included as a control variable. The sample includes 31 respondents who are non-Muslims (1.33 percent of the sample), but since their number is too small to have any statistical effect, Muslim and non-Muslim respondents were not coded separately in the data analysis. Note, however, that the results shown below remained robust when non-Muslims were excluded from the analysis.[46]

A number of control variables found to affect attitudes toward redistribution and social welfare were also included. The *self-interest* variables used in the analyses

include age (age of respondent), gender (one if the respondent is male), having children (one if the respondent has any children living at home), household income
(measured on an interval scale of zero to ten) and level of education (a ten-category
ordinal variable), and three dummy variables that tap *labor force participation*:
unemployed, retired and others (those who are not in labor force, including the disabled, students, housewives, etc.). The baseline category consists of those who are in
the work force.

Ideology was measured with a zero-to-ten scale left–right identification. Two
measures of *subjective economic perceptions* were included: satisfaction with the
present state of economy in Turkey (zero-to-ten scale), and the respondent's expectation that there will be some periods in the next 12 months when he/she will not have
enough money to cover household necessities. (One-to-four ordinal scale) The other
control variables were union membership (dummy), and whether the most frequently
spoken language at home is Kurdish (dummy).

With the exception of age, all variables were recoded to vary between zero and one.
Since the first dependent variable is measured on an ordinal scale, ordinal logit was
used in the first two models. For the third model, in which the dependent variable is
continuous, linear ordinary least squares (OLS) regression was used. The homosce-
dasticity test for the OLS regression rejected the null hypothesis of constant variance
($\chi^2 = 62.92$, $p > \chi^2 = 0.0000$), so the model was run with robust standard errors.

Some of the independent variables were found to have high pair-wise correlations.[47] However, the variance inflation factor (VIF), which measures how much
the variance of the estimated regression coefficient is inflated due to collinearity,
and the tolerance measure, which represents the proportion of variance in the independent variable that is not related to the other independent variables in the model,
both indicate that multicollinearity was not a significant problem in this case.[48]
Nevertheless, the results of alternative model specifications are also reported.

Results

Table 1 presents the results of the ordered logit model for support for redistribution.
Since the coefficients in the ordered logit or probit models are not directly interpretable, the odds ratios and standard errors, together with changes in predicted probabilities, are presented.[49] The probabilities show the change in predicted probability
when each independent variable moves from its minimum to maximum value,
while the other variables are held constant at their means.[50]

Core values and attendance at religious services all have the expected effects on
support for redistribution. Prioritizing conservation values over openness to change
is associated with lower support for redistribution, while emphasis on self-transcendence values over self-enhancement has a statistically significantly positive effect on
support for government involvement to reduce income differences. Moving from the
least conservative (thus, most open to change) to the most conservative individual
reduces the predicted probability of strongly agreeing with government reducing
income differences by 48 percent. On the other hand, a shift from emphasis on

Table 1. Support for Redistribution: Ordered Logit Regression Results

	Odds ratio (Std. error)	Change in predicted probabilities (Min → Max)				
		0	0.25	0.50	0.75	1
Self-interest/demographic variables						
Age	0.994 (0.004)	0.002	0.015	0.019	0.067	−0.104
Gender (male =1)	1.349 (0.193)***	−0.002	−0.009	−0.012	−0.051	0.074
Has children	1.054 (0.106)	−0.000	−0.001	−0.002	−0.010	0.014
Education	1.231 (0.302)	−0.001	−0.006	−0.008	−0.035	0.049
Income	0.821 (0.186)	0.001	0.006	0.008	0.030	−0.046
Labor force participation						
Unemployed	1.192 (0.204)	−0.000	−0.005	−0.007	−0.032	0.044
Retired	1.342 (0.259)	−0.001	−0.008	−0.011	−0.054	0.074
Not in labor force	1.445 (0.212)***	−0.002	−0.011	−0.015	−0.062	0.089
Subjective economic perceptions						
Satisfied with country's economy	0.288 (0.055)***	0.008	0.051	0.061	0.162	−0.283
Personal risk perception	1.369 (0.036)***	−0.002	−0.010	−0.013	−0.052	0.076
Ideology						
Political right	0.932 (0.191)	0.000	0.002	0.003	0.013	−0.018
Other controls						
Union member	1.030 (0.209)	−0.000	−0.000	−0.000	−0.006	0.006
Kurdish spoken at home	0.991 (0.171)	0.000	0.000	0.000	0.000	−0.002
Core values						
Conservation–openness	0.132 (0.060)***	0.018	0.100	0.110	0.252	−0.480
Self-transcendence–self-enhancement	4.060 (2.198)***	−0.006	−0.036	−0.046	−0.213	0.300
Religiosity dimensions						
Identification as religious	0.923 (0.240)	0.003	0.001	0.002	0.012	−0.015
Attendance at religious services	0.530 (0.104)***	0.003	0.021	0.027	0.104	−0.156
Frequency of prayer	0.968 (0.194)	0.000	0.001	0.001	0.008	−0.009
N	1642					
LR χ^2 (18)	123.51					
Prob $> \chi^2$	0.000					
Pseudo R^2	0.0369					

***$p < 0.01$ level.
**$p < 0.05$ level.
*$p < 0.10$ level.

self-enhancement values to self-transcendence values increases the predicted probability of strongly agreeing with the same statement by 30 percent.

Among the religiosity variables, only attendance at religious services has a statistically significant effect on support for redistribution. Frequent attendance, compared to not attending at all, is associated with a decrease in the probability of strongly supporting redistribution by 15 percent. Only a few of the control variables had statistically meaningful effects on support for redistribution. Contrary to the comparative literature, men were found to be more supportive of redistribution. It is possible that in a country where men are traditionally seen as the primary breadwinners, the pressure on them to take care of the family is higher, and thus they want more equal income distribution to protect themselves and their families against possible risks. In addition, those who are not in the labor force, including housewives, students, disabled, etc., tended to support redistribution more than those participating in the labor force. However, this effect was not replicated for support for social policy (Table 2).

Personal economic experiences are among the most robust predictors of support for redistribution. Satisfaction with the nation's economy is positively associated with opposition to redistribution, in line with theoretical expectations. Good economic conditions and low levels of economic strain are both believed to increase confidence in individual responsibility, making individuals less supportive of redistribution.[51] In this analysis, personal satisfaction with economic conditions at an individual level also seems to have this effect. On the other hand, those who feel that their personal economic security might be at risk in the near future tend to be more supportive of redistribution. As will be seen below, these two variables also have consistent effects on support for social insurance policies.

One interesting finding, discussed in greater detail in the next section, is the null result for the effect of left–right self-placements. Contrary to theoretical expectations and previous findings, in this study, an individual's standing on the left–right political continuum did not have a statistically significant effect on support for income redistribution. In addition, there was no empirical evidence for the effect of this variable on support for government responsibility in providing social safety nets either (Table 2).

Table 2 presents the OLS regression results when the dependent variable is a support for government responsibility in providing social services. While many of the results of the previous models are replicated here as well, in this second analysis, adding or dropping the highly correlated core values items made a substantial difference to the results for the effect of self-transcendence. Therefore, three models are presented below; two with each value item entered into the regression separately, and one in which both are included (Model 3).

As hypothesized, self-transcendence increases support for social insurance. All else being equal, emphasizing self-transcendence over self-enhancement is expected to increase support for government responsibility by about 0.1 points, which is about one-tenth of the range of the dependent variable. While conservation values are associated with opposition to redistribution, they were found to have a positive

Table 2. Support for Government Responsibility in Providing Social Benefits: OLS Regression Results

	Model 1 Coeff. (Robust std. errors)	Model 2 Coeff. (Robust std. errors)	Model 3 Coeff. (Robust std. errors)
Constant	0.688 (0.037)***	0.690 (0.037)***	0.687 (0.037)***
Self-interest/demographic variables			
Age	0.000 (0.000)	0.000 (0.000)	0.000 (0.000)
Gender (male =1)	0.035 (0.013)***	0.035 (0.013)***	0.035 (0.013)***
Has children	0.016 (0.009)	0.014 (0.009)	0.014 (0.010)
Education	0.071 (0.022)***	0.078 (0.022)***	0.078 (0.022)***
Income	−0.028 (0.020)	−0.027 (0.020)	−0.027 (0.020)
Labor force participation			
Unemployed	−0.002 (0.017)	−0.000 (0.017)	−0.000 (0.017)
Retired	−0.000 (0.016)	−0.000 (0.016)	−0.000 (0.016)
Not in labor force	0.012 (0.013)	0.012 (0.013)	0.012 (0.013)
Subjective economic perceptions			
Satisfied with country's economy	−0.158 (0.019)***	−0.158 (0.019)***	−0.158 (0.019)***
Personal risk perception	0.042 (0.014)***	0.040 (0.014)***	0.040 (0.014)***
Ideology			
Political right	0.031 (0.019)	0.028 (0.019)	0.028 (0.019)
Other controls			
Union member	−0.003 (0.018)	−0.001 (0.018)	−0.000 (0.018)
Kurdish spoken at home	−0.019 (0.019)	−0.014 (0.019)	−0.014 (0.019)
Core values			
Conservation−openness	–	0.147 (0.031)***	0.155 (0.039)***
Self-transcendence−self-enhancement.	0.097 (0.038)***	–	−0.016 (0.048)
Religiosity dimensions			
Identification as religious	0.081 (0.025)***	0.077 (0.025)***	0.077 (0.025)***
Attendance at religious services	−0.081 (0.020)***	−0.079 (0.020)***	−0.079 (0.020)***
Frequency of prayer	0.052 (0.013)***	0.043 (0.20)***	0.043 (0.20)***
N	1648	1648	1648
F	10.00	10.93	10.31
Prob. > *F*	0.0000	0.0000	0.0000
R^2	0.0998	0.1074	0.1075

***$p < 0.01$ level.
**$p < 0.05$ level.
*$p < 0.10$ level.

effect on support for government provision of social safety nets. The effect of this variable is also quite large: the difference in support for government responsibility between the least and most conservative individual is 0.15 points. Similarly, while people who characterize themselves as more religious are not necessarily supportive of redistribution (Table 1). They tend to support government responsibility in taking care of disadvantaged groups. Thus, it seems that even if they do not envision a more equal society, conservative and religious individuals still want the government to take action to provide a minimum standard of living for disadvantaged groups in the society.

The effect of social religious behavior is also consistent with the first two models. Participation in social religious networks, measured as a frequency of mosque attendance, decreases support for government responsibility. While there was no specific hypothesis concerning the effect of frequency of prayer, this variable was also associated with greater support for government responsibility.

As in the previous model, men were more likely to support government provision of social benefits. In addition, personal economic experiences also emerged as robust and significant predictors of support for government responsibility. Thus, those who were satisfied with the national economy expressed less support for government provision of social services, whereas those who expected economic difficulties in their household in the near future were more likely to support these policies. Table 2 also shows that those with greater levels of education were more likely to support social policies. Again, while the more highly educated were not necessarily in favor of greater social equality (Table 1), they did want the government to play a greater role to provide a minimum standard of living for the disadvantaged.

Robust Analysis

The results found in the OLS regression model also held when running the items that constituted the measure of support for government responsibility as separate dependent variables. A number of additional models also tested the robustness of the findings in both models. While the correlations between the religiosity dimensions were not too high (the highest Pearson's correlation was 0.3), each item was also entered into the regressions separately, omitting the rest of the dimensions for both dependent variables but including all the other control variables. In addition, all religiosity items were run separately while also excluding the measures for values and ideology. These analyses did not lead to any statistically significant change in the regression coefficients or their standard errors.

As will be discussed below, the failure to provide empirical evidence for the effect of the ideology variable on attitudes toward the welfare state may indicate that Turkey's political and the institutional context does not necessarily provide enough information for individuals to make a connection between their ideological stance and social welfare policies. If this is the case, more informed or more sophisticated individuals are still expected to make a connection between left–right orientations and redistribution. That is, information, affluence, or political interest may moderate the relationship between ideological orientation and attitudes toward redistribution and social welfare. To control for this, models in which the interaction terms between ideology and level of education, political interest and following news on TV were specified. This analysis revealed that only when the interaction term with political interest was entered into the equation did being politically right-wing have any statistically significant effect on support for government responsibility—although not on redistribution). Surprisingly, this effect was positive, meaning that the more individuals identified with the right ideologically, the more they tended to be more supportive of the social welfare policy. Again, as will be discussed below, this may mean that the Western left–right categorizations do not seem to fit the case of Turkey.

Discussion

The findings of these analyses provide support for Hypotheses 1 and 2. Self-transcendence values were associated with both support for reducing income differences and providing social assistance to the disadvantaged, while conservation values were associated only with support for the latter. However, focusing on the single case of Turkey makes it impossible to test whether this positive effect applies cross-nationally or whether conservatism has an effect on welfare attitudes only under certain political and institutional contexts, such as the type of welfare regime. Conservatism is also concerned with tradition and preserving the status quo. Thus, in cultural contexts where the government is naturally seen as having a duty to provide for those in need, conservation values may be associated with greater support for welfare policy, in contrast to contexts such as the USA, where the dominant cultural values idealize limited government, so conservation values may lead to the rejection of greater government involvement in the economy.

There is also partial support in this study for the effect of religiosity on redistribution and social policy (Hypothesis 3). While the religiously devout were not necessarily in favor of redistribution, they were supportive of government policies that provide social insurance. Thus, it seems that even if religiosity may be associated with compassion or caring for others, this does not necessarily translate into support for economic equality. This implies that religious individuals may not want government action because of egalitarian orientations, but rather that they prefer government intervention in the economy out of social order or security concerns. The results here also replicate previous findings on the negative effect of social religious behavior on both redistribution and support for government responsibility, thus providing empirical confirmation of Hypothesis 4.

The fact that the two dimensions of religiosity considered here have contrasting effects on attitudes toward redistribution may sound counterintuitive at first since the religiously devout are expected to engage more in the social practice of religion and be more active in religious social networks. Indeed, correlations between the two dimensions of religiosity usually tend to be high.[52] However, while belief or religiosity is a more cognitive aspect of religious experience, associated with authoritarianism, tradition and security values, social religious behavior is an experience in which the individual participates in a community of like-minded individuals. Involvement in religious social networks, therefore, tends to enhance social capital, increase political interest and participation, and help groups solve collective action problems.[53] Thus, it has different effects than religiosity on individual attitudes and behavior. As a result, individuals who are well integrated into their religious social communities can be expected to have different attitudes to individuals who, while equally religious, are not involved in such networks.

Contrary to the literature on public opinion toward welfare, which has established the effects of some of the crucial self-interest variables, in the Turkish case there is not much empirical evidence for the effect of self-interest variables. This could be attributable to the low information environment concerning welfare and redistribution issues in the Turkish context. Self-interest arguments make the implicit assumption that citizens are informed enough to make the connection between self-interest and related policies.[54] However, material self-interest has an effect on individual attitudes when the benefits or harms of proposed policies are substantial, imminent and well publicized.[55] The welfare state and redistributive institutions themselves play an important role in structuring the information environment for citizens.[56] In contrast to increased social spending, certain mechanisms of social policy, such as social support via indirect tax credits, or education or healthcare subsidies, make governance less visible to voters, thus making them less likely to punish or reward officials based on such "submerged state" programs.[57] This is also the case for Turkey, which has a small welfare state with limited social benefits, and in which social policy is based on informal strategies and implicit social pacts.[58] The neoliberal reform pressures after the 2001 financial crisis, the retreat of the state from welfare provision and increasing privatization have all combined to make an already very limited social policy even less visible to citizens. In a context where the welfare state does not provide visible benefits, or where citizens are not even aware of the potential benefits that they may receive from social policy, it is unlikely that individuals will connect policy outcomes with their own material gains. As a result, subjective assessments of the economy and personal economic risks, which are more readily available to individuals, emerge as more consistent predictors of attitudes toward redistribution and social policy in Turkey.

The failure to find a statistically meaningful effect of ideology also deserves further discussion. Ideology can be thought of as a cognitive heuristic that enables people to organize and analyze information about the ideological content of policy issues.[59] Although left–right self-identifications generally help explain a wide array of political attitudes,[60] people adopt these cues via the messages they receive from political elites and the media.[61] For example, in the case of the USA, issues concerning government spending are recurrent and familiar, enabling American citizens to easily connect ideological labels to redistributive policies.[62] In the Turkish case, various issues, including conflicts over government spending, do not involve such clear ideological divisions as, for instance, in the case of the USA. [63] Since Turkish political parties do not communicate economic or political issues in typical left–right packages as political parties often do in, for example, Western Europe, a different identity-based cleavage emerges in the Turkish political landscape.[64] In Turkey, the meaning of left–right ideological labels themselves also seem to be different than most advanced democracies in that they do not necessarily embrace a social class or social equality dimension.[65] Accordingly, studies of Turkey have also failed to find robust effects of ideological self-placements on economic policy, social welfare and human rights policies,[66] and attitudes toward the European Union.[67] It seems then that a low information environment, in which political parties fail to provide clear cues to citizens, makes it hard for them to connect ideological labels to various policies, including redistributive policies. More research is, therefore, necessary in order to reveal the meaning of left–right orientations in Turkey, and how citizens utilize these labels to construct attitudes toward different issues.

Conclusion

This paper aimed at understanding the factors that contribute to support for redistribution and social policy in Turkey by focusing on the role of core values and religiosity. The results provide further evidence for the effects of self-transcendence values and religious social behavior on attitudes toward redistribution and social policy recently found in the literature. The results concerning the effects of conservation values and personal religiosity, on the other hand, deserve more attention. Whether these predispositions are universal elements broadly applicable to all contexts, or whether they are dependent on specific circumstances, such as the type of welfare state, could be tested using cross-national survey data. Even more important, however, is the need to explore further the processes and mechanisms beyond these effects—a line of inquiry consistently advocated by political psychology scholars.[68] Various methods, including mediation tests or experiments, could be used to uncover the specific sources of support for redistribution, social equality and the provision of social benefits to poor and needy groups in society.

This study also supports current findings on the role that the institutional and political context plays in shaping the effects of psychological factors on individual attitudes, highlighting the need for integrating context into both theorizing and empirical analysis. Certain assumptions that are taken for granted should be tested using data from diverse contexts, and the increasing availability of high-quality cross-national survey data makes this possible. Finally, apart from the institutional context, further research could also explore the role of other contextual factors, such as social and cultural orientations in the formation and stability of attitudes toward redistribution and welfare.

Acknowledgements

I thank Emre Erdoğan, Cengiz Erişen, Elif Erişen, Kerem Ozan Kalkan, Ekrem Karakoç, Eser Şekercioglu and Çiğdem V. Şirin for their helpful comments on an earlier version of the manuscript. All remaining errors are my responsibility.

Notes

1. Kulin and Svallfors, "Class, Values, and Attitudes," 2.
2. See, for example, Ersin Kalaycıoğlu, "Does Ideology Matter?" 2009.
3. Erişen, "An Introduction to Political".
4. Hasenfeld, and A. Rafferty, "The Determinants of Public Attitudes," 1027–48; Svallfors, "Worlds of Welfare and Attitudes," 283–304.
5. Hasenfeld and Rafferty, "The Determinants of Public Attitudes"; Iversen and Soskice, "An Asset Theory," 875–95; Jaeger, "Welfare Regimes and Attitudes," 157–70; Jaeger, "What Makes People Support," 321–38; Linos and West, "Self-Interest, Social Beliefs," 393–409.
6. Kinder, "Opinion and Action," 778–867; Sears and Funk, "The Role of Self-Interest," 1–91.
7. Feldman and Zaller, "The Political Culture of Ambivalence," 268–307; Hasenfeld and Rafferty, "The Determinants of Public Attitudes"; Jaeger, "What Makes People Support"; Jacoby, "Public Attitudes Toward Government," 336–61.
8. Bobbio, *Left and Right*, 60.
9. Arıkan, *Economic Individualism and Cross-National*; Arıkan and Ben-Nun Bloom, "Social Values and Attitudes Towards," 2012; Jaeger, "What Makes People Support."
10. Fong, "Social Preferences, Self-Interest," 225–46.
11. Corneo and Grüner, "Individual Preferences for Political," 83–107.
12. Alesina and Ferrera, "Preferences for Redistribution in the Land," 897–931.
13. Economic individualism is argued to be an important value orientation that discourages support for extensive social welfare programs in the USA. See Feldman, "Economic Self-interest and Political," 446–66; Lipset, *American Exceptionalism*; McCloskey and Zaller, *The American Ethos*. Economic individualism also predicts individual attitudes towards welfare policy and redistribution from a comparative perspective (Arikan, *Economic Individualism and Cross-National*). In addition, humanitarian values are associated with higher support for increased spending on social welfare services, while egalitarian values predict support for greater government involvement in providing a decent standard of living for the unemployed and reducing income differences. See Feldman and Steenbergen, "The Humanitarian Foundation of Public Support," 658–77.
14. But see Arıkan, *Economic Individualism and Cross-National*; Kulin and Svallfors, "Class, Values, and Attitudes towards Redistribution."
15. Geert Hofstede's individualism/collectivism values dimension has been used as a point of reference for many studies in cross-cultural psychology. Harry Triandis also adopted the individualism/collectivism dimension. Ronald Inglehart has proposed a two-dimensional values construct consisting of survival/self-expression and traditional/rational-secular values that could be applied to both individual and societal levels. See Hofstede, *Culture's Consequences*; Inglehart, *Modernization and Post-Modernization*; Triandis, *Individualism and Collectivism*.
16. Schwartz, "Universals in the Content and Structure," 1–65; Schwartz, "Are There Universal Aspects," 547–59. Also see Rokeach, *The Nature of Human Values*.
17. For a review, see Feldman, "Values, Ideology, and the Structure," 477–508.
18. Rokeach, *Beliefs, Attitudes, and Values*; Rokeach, *The Nature of Human Values*.
19. Schwartz, "Universals in the Content and Structure of Values"; Schwartz, "Are There Universal Aspects"; Schwartz and Ros, "Values in the West," 91–122.
20. Kulin and Svallfors, "Class, Values, and Attitudes."
21. Titmuss, *Social Policy*, 27.
22. See, for example, Jacoby, "Public Attitudes Toward Government."
23. See, for example, Feldman and Zaller, "The Political Culture of Ambivalence", as well as Conover and Feldman, "The Origins and Meaning of Liberal/Conservative," 617–45; Jacoby, "Public Attitudes Toward Government."
24. Karen, *The Authoritarian Dynamic*, especially 86. See also Stenner, "Three Kinds of 'Conservatism,'" 142–59.
25. Freeden, "The Coming of the Welfare State," 7–44.

26. Rudra, "Welfare States in Developing Countries," 378–96.
27. Huber, "Administering Targeted Social Programs," 141–91; Rudra, "Welfare States in Developing Countries."
28. In fact, despite the latest reforms that aim at shrinking the welfare state, there is evidence of an expansion of state power and control over social interests. Eder, "Retreating State? Political Economy," 152–84.
29. Kellstedt, Green, and Smidt, "Is There a Culture War?" 1997; Wald and Smidt, "Measurement Strategies in the Study," 26–52. While the third dimension of religiosity, belonging, consists of denominational affiliation, that is, identification as a member of a particular organized denomination, and/ or religious movement identification, due to the unavailability of data on denominational or sectarian affiliation, I will not be able to elaborate on the belonging dimension.
30. Dekker and Halman, *The Values of Volunteering*.
31. Kotler-Berkowitz, "Religion and Voting Behaviour," 523–54.
32. Çarkoğlu and Kalaycıoğlu, *Turkish Democracy Today*.
33. Ben-Nun Bloom and Arıkan, "The Differential Effect of Religious Belief," 249–76; Ben-Nun Bloom and Arıkan, "Religion and Support for Democracy."
34. Kellstedt Green, and Smidt, "Is There a Culture War?" 1997.
35. Wilson, *Economics, Ethics and Religion*.
36. Malka et al., "Religiosity and Social Welfare," 763–92.
37. Davis and Robinson, "The Egalitarian Face of Islamic Orthodoxy," 167–90.
38. Pepinsky and Welborne, "Piety and Redistributive Preferences," 491–505.
39. Davis and Robinson, "The Egalitarian Face of Islamic Orthodoxy."
40. Kellstedt Green, and Smidt, "Is There a Culture War?" 1997.
41. Scheve and Stasavage, "Religion and Preferences for Social Insurance," 255–86.
42. Buğra and Keyder, *New Poverty and the Changing*, 2003.
43. See Pepinsky and Welborne, "Piety and Redistributive Preferences", for a good review.
44. For more detailed information about sampling and fieldwork, see http://ess.nsd.uib.no/ess/round4/surveydoc.html.
45. For details, see http://ess.nsd.uib.no/ess/doc/ess1_human_values_scale.pdf.
46. Results are available upon request from the author.
47. These are conservation and self-transcendence values ($r = 0.062$), age and being retired ($r = 0.48$), being male and attendance to religious services ($r = 0.52$), and the others category in labor force participation ($r = -0.62$), and income and education ($r = 0.5$).
48. The highest VIF is 2.31, which is well below the suggested threshold of 5; and the lowest tolerance measure is 0.43, which is well above the threshold of 0.
49. Long, *Regression Models for Categorical*.
50. CLARIFY! software was used to calculate the predicted probabilities. King, Tomz, and Wittenberg, "Making the Most of Statistical Analyses," 347–61.
51. Blekesaune, "Economic Conditions and Public," 393–403.
52. Ben-Nun Bloom and Arıkan, "The Differential Effect of Religious"; Ben-Nun Bloom and Arıkan, "Religion and Support for Democracy."
53. Norris, *Democratic Phoenix*; Putnam, *Bowling Alone*.
54. Donald Kinder, "Opinion and Action in the Realm."
55. Ibid., p. 802.
56. Gingrich, "Visibility, Values and Voters," 2012.
57. Mettler, *The Submerged State*.
58. Eder, "Retreating State?"
59. Huckfeldt et al., "Accessibility and the Political Utility," 888–911.
60. Feldman, "Values, Ideology, and the Structure."
61. Zaller, *The Nature and Origins*.
62. Jacoby, "Public Attitudes Toward Government."
63. Jacoby, "Issue Framing and Public Opinion," 750–67.
64. Secor, "Ideologies in Crisis," 539–60.

65. Çarkoğlu, "The Nature of Left-Right," 253–71.
66. Kalaycıoğlu, "Does Ideology Matter?" 2009.
67. Arıkan, "Attitudes Towards the European Union"; Çarkoğlu, "Who Wants Full Membership?" 171–94.
68. Erişen, "An Introduction to Political."

References

Alesina, Alberto, and Eliano La Ferrera. "Preferences for Redistribution in the Land of Opportunities." *Journal of Public Economics* 89, no. 5–6 (2005): 897–931.

Arıkan, Gizem. "Attitudes Towards the European Union in Turkey: The Role of Perceived Threats and Benefits." *Perceptions: Journal of International Affairs* 17, no. 3 (2012): 81–103.

Arıkan, Gizem. *Economic Individualism and Cross-National Differences in Redistribution*. New York, NY: Stony Brook University, 2010.

Arıkan, Gizem, and Pazit Ben-Nun Bloom. "Social Values and Attitudes Towards Redistribution and Welfare." 70th Annual Midwest Political Science Association Conference, Chicago, IL, April 12–15, 2012.

Blekesaune, Morten. "Economic Conditions and Public Attitudes to Welfare Policies." *European Sociological Review* 23, no. 3 (2007): 393–403.

Ben-Nun Bloom, Pazit, and Gizem Arıkan. "The Differential Effect of Religious Belief and Religious Social Behavior on Opinion and Ambivalence in Democratic Attitudes." *Political Behavior* 34, no. 2 (2012): 249–276.

Ben-Nun Bloom, Pazit, and Gizem Arıkan. "Religion and Support for Democracy: A Cross-National Test of the Mediating Mechanisms." *British Journal of Political Science* (Forthcoming).

Bobbio, Norberto. *Left and Right: The Significance of a Political Distinction*. Cambridge: Polity, 1996.

Buğra, Ayşe, and Çağlar Keyder. *New Poverty and the Changing Welfare Regime of Turkey*, Report prepared for the United Nations Development Programme, Ankara, 2003.

Çarkoğlu, Ali. "The Nature of Left-Right Ideological Self-placement in the Turkish Context." *Turkish Studies* 8, no. 2 (2007): 253–271.

Çarkoğlu, Ali. "Who Wants Full Membership? Characteristics of Turkish Public Support for EU Membership." *Turkish Studies* 4, no. 1 (Spring 2003): 171–194.

Çarkoğlu, Ali, and Ersin Kalaycıoğlu. *Turkish Democracy Today: Elections, Protest and Stability in an Islamic Society*. London: I.B. Tauris, 2007.

Conover, Pamela J., and Stanley Feldman. "The Origins and Meaning of Liberal/Conservative Self-identification." *American Journal of Political Science* 25, no. 4 (1981): 617–645.

Corneo, Giacomo, and Hans Peter Grüner. "Individual Preferences for Political Redistribution." *Journal of Public Economics* 83, no. 1 (2002): 83–107.

Davis, Nancy J., and Robert V. Robinson. "The Egalitarian Face of Islamic Orthodoxy: Support for Islamic Law and Economic Justice in Seven Muslim-Majority Nations." *American Sociological Review* 71, no. 1 (2006): 167–190.

Dekker, Paul, and Loek Halman. *The Values of Volunteering: Cross-Cultural Perspectives*. New York: Kluwer Academic Plenum Publishers, 2003.

Eder, Mine. "Retreating State? Political Economy of Welfare Regime Change in Turkey." *Middle East Law and Governance* 2, no. 2 (2010): 152–184.

Erişen, Elif. "An Introduction to Political Psychology for International Relations Scholars." *Perceptions: Journal of International Affairs* 27, no. 3 (2012): 9–28.

Feldman, Stanley. "Economic Self-interest and Political Behavior." *American Journal of Political Science* 26, no. 3 (1982): 446–466.

Feldman, Stanley. "Values, Ideology, and the Structure of Political Attitudes." In *Oxford Handbook of Political Psychology*, edited by David O. Sears, Leonie Huddy, and Robert Jervis, 477–508. New York: Oxford University Press, 2003.

Feldman, Stanley, and John Zaller. "The Political Culture of Ambivalence: Ideological Responses to the Welfare State." *American Journal of Political Science* 36, no. 1 (1992): 268–307.

Feldman, Stanley, and Marco Steenbergen. "The Humanitarian Foundation of Public Support for Social Welfare." *American Journal of Political Science* 45, no. 3 (2001): 658–677.

Fong, and Christina. "Social Preferences, Self-Interest, and the Demand for Redistribution." *Journal of Public Economics* 82, no. 2 (2001): 225–46.

Freeden, Michael. "The Coming of the Welfare State." In *The Cambridge History of Twentieth Century Political Thought*, edited by Terence Ball and Richard Bellamy, 7–44. Cambridge: Cambridge University Press, 2003.

Gingrich, Jane. "Visibility, Values and Voters: Welfare States and Vote Choice." 70th Annual Midwest Political Science Association Conference, Chicago, IL, April 12–15, 2012.

Hasenfeld, Yeheskel, and Jane A. Rafferty. "The Determinants of Public Attitudes Toward the Welfare State." *Social Forces* 67, no. 4 (1989): 1027–1048.

Hofstede, Geert. *Culture's Consequences: International Differences in Work-Related Values.* London: Sage Publications, 1980.

Huber, Evelyne. "Administering Targeted Social Programs in Latin America: Neoliberal vs. Social Democratic Models." In *Welfare States in Transition*, edited by Gosta Esping-Andersen, 141–191. London: Sage Publications, 1996.

Huckfeldt, Robert, Levine Jeffrey, Morgan William, and Sprague John. "Accessibility and the Political Utility of Partisan and Ideological Orientations." *American Journal of Political Science* 43, no. 3 (1999): 888–911.

Inglehart, Ronald. *Modernization and Post-Modernization: Cultural, Economic and Political Change in 43 Societies.* Princeton, NJ: Princeton University Press, 1997.

Iversen, Torben, and David Soskice. "An Asset Theory of Social Policy Preferences." *American Political Science Review* 95, no. 4 (2001): 875–895.

Jacoby, William G. "Issue Framing and Public Opinion on Government Spending." *American Journal of Political Science* 44, no. 4 (2000): 750–767.

Jacoby, William G. "Public Attitudes Toward Government Spending." *American Journal of Political Science* 38, no. 2 (1994): 336–361.

Jaeger, Mads Meier. "Welfare Regimes and Attitudes Towards Redistribution: The Regime Hypothesis Revisited." *European Sociological Review* 22, no. 2 (2006): 157–170.

Mads Meier Jaeger. "What Makes People Support Public Responsibility for Welfare Provision: Self-Interest or Political Ideology? A Longitudinal Approach." *Acta Sociologica* 49, no. 3 (2006): 321–338.

Kalaycıoğlu, Ersin. "Does Ideology Matter? Turkish Public Opinion and Government in Action." Presented at the Middle East Studies Association's Annual Meeting, Boston, MA, November 21–24, 2009.

Kellstedt, Lyman A., John C. Green, and Corwin E. Smidt. "Is There a Culture War? Religion and the 1996 Election." Paper presented at the Annual Meeting of the American Political Science Association, Washington, DC, August 28–31, 1997.

King, Gary, Michael Tomz, and Jason Wittenberg. "Making the Most of Statistical Analyses: Improving Interpretation and Presentation." *American Journal of Political Science* 44, no. 2 (2000): 347–361.

Kinder, Donald. "Opinion and Action in the Realm of Politics." In *Handbook of Social Psychology*, edited by Daniel T. Gilbert, Susan T. Fiske, and Gardner Lindzey, 778–867. New York: McGraw-Hill, 1998.

Kotler-Berkowitz, Laurence A. "Religion and Voting Behaviour in Great Britain: A Reassessment." *British Journal of Political Science* 31, no. 3 (2001): 523–554.

Kulin, Joakim, and Stefan Svallfors. "Class, Values, and Attitudes towards Redistribution: A European Comparison." European Sociological Review, (Forthcoming).

Linos, Katerina, and Martin West. "Self-Interest, Social Beliefs, and Attitudes to Redistribution: Re-Addressing the Issue of Cross-national Variation." European Sociological Review 19, no. 4 (2003): 393–409.

Lipset, Seymour Martin. American Exceptionalism: A Double Edged Sword. New York: W.W. Norton & Company, 1996.

Long, Scott J. Regression Models for Categorical and Limited Dependent Variables. Thousand Oaks, CA: Sage Publications, 1997.

Malka, Ariel, Christopher J. Soto, Adam B. Cohen, and Dale T. Miller. "Religiosity and Social Welfare: Competing Influences of Cultural Conservatism and Prosocial Value Orientation." Journal of Personality 79, no. 4 (2011): 763–792.

McCloskey, Herbert and John R. Zaller. The American Ethos: Public Attitudes Toward Capitalism and Democracy. Cambridge: Harvard University Press, 1984.

Mettler, Susan. The Submerged State: How Invisible Government Policies Undermine American Democracy. Chicago, IL: University of Chicago Press, 2011.

Norris, Pippa. Democratic Phoenix: Reinventing Political Activism. Cambridge, UK: Cambridge University Press, 2002.

Putnam, Robert D. Bowling Alone: The Collapse and Revival of American Community. New York: Simon and Schuster, 2000.

Pepinsky, Thomas B., and Bozena C. Welborne. "Piety and Redistributive Preferences in the Muslim World." Political Research Quarterly 64, no. 3 (2011): 491–505.

Rokeach, Milton. Beliefs, Attitudes, and Values: A Theory of Organization and Change. San Francisco, CA: Jossey-Bass, 1968.

Rokeach, Milton. The Nature of Human Values. New York: The Free Press, 1973.

Rudra, Nita. "Welfare States in Developing Countries: Unique or Universal?" The Journal of Politics 69, no. 2 (2007): 378–396.

Scheve, Kenneth, and David Stasavage. "Religion and Preferences for Social Insurance." Quarterly Journal of Political Science 1, no. 3 (2006): 255–286.

Shalom S Schwartz. "Universals in the Content and Structure of Values: Theoretical Advances and Empirical Tests in 20 Countries." Advances in Experimental Social Psychology 25, no. 1 (1992): 1–65.

Schwartz, Shalom S. "Are There Universal Aspects in the Structure and Contents of Human Values?" Journal of Social Issues 50, no. 4 (Winter 1994): 547–559.

Sears, David O., and Carolyn L. Funk. "The Role of Self-Interest in Social and Political Attitudes." In Advances in Experimental Social Psychology, edited by Mark Zanna, 1–91. Orlando, FL: Academic Press, 1991.

Secor, Anna J. "Ideologies in Crisis: Political Cleavages and Electoral Politics in Turkey in the 1990s." Political Geography 20, no. 5 (2001): 539–560.

Stenner, Karen. The Authoritarian Dynamic. New York: Cambridge University Press, 2005.

Stenner, Karen. "Three Kinds of 'Conservatism'." Psychological Inquiry 20, no. 2–3 (2009): 142–159.

Svallfors, Stefan. "Worlds of Welfare and Attitudes to Redistribution: A Comparison of Eight Western Nations." European Sociological Review 13, no. 3 (1997): 283–304.

Schwartz, Shalom S., and Maria Ros. "Values in the West: A Theoretical and Empirical Challenge to the Individualism-Collectivism Cultural Dimension." World Psychology 32, no. 3 (1995): 91–122.

Titmuss, Richard. Social Policy. New York: Pantheon Books, 1965.

Triandis, Harry C. Individualism and Collectivism. Boulder, CO: Westview Press, 1995.

Wald, Kenneth D., and Corwin E. Smid. "Measurement Strategies in the Study of Religion and Politics." In Rediscovering the Religious Factor in American Politics, edited by David C. Leege and Lyman A. Kellstedt, 26–52. New York: M.E. Sharpe, 1993.

Wilson, Rodney. Economics, Ethics and Religion: Jewish, Christian and Muslim Economic Thought. New York: New York University Press, 1997.

Zaller, John. The Nature and Origins of Mass Opinion. Cambridge: Cambridge University Press, 1992.

The Impact of Party Identification and Socially Supplied Disagreement on Electoral Choices in Turkey

ELİF ERİŞEN

Department of Political Science, California Polytechnic State University, San Luis Obispo, CA, USA

ABSTRACT   *The relative impacts of social influence and political party affiliation on electoral choices depend on the maturity of the political party system. In established democracies political party affiliation has a decisive impact on electoral choices whereas in democratizing countries political discussion influences over-time volatility in electoral outcomes. This paper investigates the significance of both factors on individual attitudes toward political candidates in Turkey. Findings from an experiment where social disagreement and candidate political party affiliation are manipulated indicate that young voters are sensitive to both partisan cues and socially supplied disagreement in forming and changing their attitudes toward political candidates. The results also show that, unlike most developing countries with weak parties, party label in Turkey is an important heuristic for making electoral choices. However, social disagreement can make political attitudes unstable. The findings suggest that Turkey presents us with a case in between the developed country voters' iron clad partisan attachment and the developing country voters' high susceptibility to socially communicated persuasive messages.*

Introduction

In established democracies with old party systems, the single most important cue in making electoral choices is party identification.[1] The impact of social context on vote choice pales in comparison to that of party identification. For instance, informal political discussion affects political participation, attitudes, and electoral choices in the USA; however, party affiliation remains the strongest predictor of vote choice. On the other hand, party identification in the electorate tends to be weak in relatively new democracies. Because political parties are in the process of defining themselves, the electorate may not face as coherent a set of partisan cues in the political environment as the electorate in countries with old party systems. As a result, social

53

environment may play a significantly more important role in determining electoral choices compared to the impact of party identification. Previous research points to the importance of social networks as a specific social context of political information flow in determining election outcomes in Brazil; however, the social networks literature did not address the issue for other developing countries.[2]

Social networks defined as networks of informal political discussion with friends, family, neighbors, and colleagues have been shown to affect political attitudes, attitude strength, and political participation in the USA and Western Europe. This particular web of relationships creates a specific social context, a social network, for political information flow. Despite widespread agreement and similarity, political discussion in such networks involves substantial amounts of disagreement.[3] Disagreement and political heterogeneity, in turn, have attitudinal and behavioral consequences significant for deliberative and participatory perspectives on democracy. Exposure to disagreement has been shown to increase awareness of others' views and more tolerance, but it also lowers attitude strength, and creates more ambivalence. Moreover, the literature presents us with mixed evidence on social network effects on political participation in the US context.[4]

The impact of social network disagreement on attitude change and political behavior may play a significant role in explaining the volatility in attitudes toward political candidates in developing countries. Because parties are typically weak, electoral stability introduced by partisan attachment is mostly lacking in such countries. Individuals operate without a strong partisan information filter and are affected more by political information coming from their social networks. Hence, social network disagreement's impact on attitude change, hence electoral instability, might be magnified in developing countries with weak parties.

This paper investigates the relative significance of party identification and the socially supplied disagreement for electoral attitudes in the context of Turkey. Although Turkey has a history of coup d'états and judicial interventions in her political party system, emerging political parties trace their lineage to earlier ones. Moreover, the ruling Justice and Development Party (AKP, *Adalet ve Kalkınma Partisi*) has been successful in cultivating a body of loyal supporters that repeatedly carry the party to electoral success. In addition, the current challenger, Republican People's Party (CHP, *Cumhuriyet Halk Partisi*), has a core supporter group whose vote for the party remained stable over recent election cycles. Hence, as a developing country with a relatively new party system, partisan attachment in the masses might not be as weak as it is in other developing countries, but still not as strong as it is in most developed countries.

As a result, partisan attachment's power to predict electoral choices might not be as decisive as it is in developed country contexts. Other determinants such as socially supplied disagreement on electoral choices might play a larger role in determining electoral choices. Because the level of political disagreement that surrounds a citizen changes more frequently compared to changes in her partisan attachment, social disagreement may create attitudinal instability toward electoral choices. Also, the new generation of voters has been politically socialized in a relatively stable political system compared to the experience of the past generations in Turkey, which might make party identification an important factor in determining electoral attitudes together with social disagreement among the new generation of voters.

This paper tests these claims using data from a survey experiment where the partisan label of the attitude object, an MP candidate, and disagreement reported by potential social contacts are manipulated. In this experimental setting, this paper investigates socially supplied disagreement in the context of informal political discussion networks, and it addresses the latter literature.[5] The findings show that attitudes toward the candidate are determined by the similarity of the candidate's party label; however, socially supplied disagreement seems to make these attitudes less stable when party cues are absent.

Below, the partisan attachments' electoral significance in developing and developed country contexts is first discussed, explain why social networks in general and network disagreement in particular matter for electoral choices in developing countries, introduce the relevant social networks literature, and discuss what would be a reasonable expectation regarding partisan attachments in Turkey. Next, the research hypotheses and the study design are introduced, followed by a discussion of the data and measures used in the analyses. Last, the findings and their implications are discussed.

Political Party Affiliation and Attitude Stability with Strong and Weak Parties

Most models and theories explaining electoral behavior are based on the premise that the party system is old and strong. Hence, partisan attachment is portrayed as stable and symbolic in the political psychology literature.[6] Partisan attachment is the product of political socialization in an environment where party labels and what they mean, despite slight realignments, remain stable over the course of one's life. In the short-run, it serves as a filter for processing political information, labeling incongruent information, and helping voters absorb partisan information.[7] Hence, political party affiliation serves as the most important cognitive heuristic, a decisional shortcut, in making electoral choices.[8] Voters do not need to understand and evaluate all the details of political life in making electoral choices; they refer to the party label to figure out the match between their own preferences and those of a political candidate, or their issue stances and policy proposals introduced by a specific political party.

Although research shows that using such cognitive heuristics leaves less politically sophisticated individuals at a disadvantage in making good electoral choices,[9] the use of partisan affiliation as a short-cut makes such choices more stable.[10] Previous research on electoral volatility lends credit to this claim: in the USA less than ten percent and in Western Europe slightly more than ten percent of the voters change sides from one election to the other.[11] In both cases, parties have a history of more or less uninterrupted development and deep roots in the electorate. Hence, voters who are socialized into their partisan identification generate electoral stability. At the individual level of analysis, partisan filter on political information processing reduces the attitudinally destabilizing impact of incongruent information coming from other sources such as one's political discussion network.

In new democracies where party systems are young or in transition, these forces of electoral stability at the individual level might be very weak. First, parties' life span might be shorter than that of the average voter, and they typically have a limited presence in the electorate.[12] Hence, voters do not go through the same socialization process in developing their party identification as their counterparts in strong party systems. Second, in relatively young party systems, partisan cues in political messages are weak due to low partisan identification in the masses, thereby making voters more volatile.[13] Because the standing choices that parties provide and many citizens rely upon at the start of every campaign are not clear-cut,[14] one observes high degrees of short-term preference change among voters during the campaign period unlike the limited campaign effects in stable party systems.[15]

For instance, in Mexico, a developing country with a relatively stable party system, almost a quarter of Mexicans change their minds in the final months of presidential election campaigns.[16] In Brazil, winners in the 1989 and 1994 elections entered the campaign with less than ten percent of the initial vote intentions. Fujimori won the 1990 election in Peru with a new party and with just two percent of the pre-campaign vote intentions. Chavez won the 1998 presidential election with the support of small parties, and put an end to the old two party system of Venezuela. Similarly, Yeltsin won the 1996 elections despite an initial eight percent support of the electorate.

This volatility needs a political communication explanation. Because the partisan filter on political information is weak, the destabilizing impact of varying political information coming from other sources becomes strong. The literature has so far focused on the media as a source of destabilizing political information in developing countries. Research shows that news programs in developing countries maintain their pre-transitional authoritarian bias and manage to shape electoral choices. Also, media coverage of the candidate's personality and image influences voters' choices.[17] Media research, however, considers the voter in an informational vacuum lacking any social interaction that might bring about different pieces of political information.

Social networks constitute another important information source that can explain short-term instability in electoral choices. The electoral relevance of political discussion and disagreement in social networks has been well addressed in the literature, but mostly in developed country contexts. Although the impact of political discussion on electoral choices might be relatively stronger due to weak partisan attachments in developing countries, it has been largely unaddressed in the literature. An exception is the study of campaign period volatility in electoral choices in Brazil.[18] In this study, political scientists Baker, Ames, and Renno argue that information gathered through social networks plays a primary role in short-term attitude change and vote choice. It causes rapid preference change and makes electoral outcomes less predictable. The authors show that candidate momentum runs are driven by waves of political discussion, particularly discussion that involves disagreement, in social networks.[19]

The Impact of Political Discussion Networks on Political Attitudes and Behavior

Social networks in the political psychology, political behavior and political communication literatures are defined as webs of mostly informal relationships that involve discussion of personally important matters including those that are political in nature. Research shows that whom one talks about personally important matters such as his satisfaction with his job and important political matters such as the favorite political figure overlap.[20] These people are typically spouses, partners, relatives, friends, neighbors, colleagues, or acquaintances from school, place of worship or some other social context that one frequents. How one feels toward these contacts and how often one converses with them affect the type of political information one is exposed to. Famous sociologist Granovetter, in his seminal work on the strength of weak ties, argues that seemingly weak relationships according to the former two standards are in fact advantageous.[21] Weak relationships are typically found outside the family and close friends circles, and bring about varied information that are often different in subject matter and political views. Consequently, informational variety introduced at the network level affects the quality of decisions and attitudes. Moreover, networks serve as specific social contexts for political information flow to citizens.

These insights have been well taken in the literature. Studies of political discussion networks either in the tradition of social context effects[22] or with the normative concerns of deliberative democracy[23] have reached a level of maturity in showing certain network effects. For instance, people with large networks are more likely to participate in politics[24]; people talk more with political experts despite disagreement, and they correctly identify them[25]; citizens maintain politically diverse networks[26]; and politically diverse networks tend to make people less polarized, more tolerant and aware of others' views,[27] at the same time reducing political participation,[28] an effect that also changes based on how disagreement is measured.[29]

Among the qualities of political discussion networks, disagreement among network members has drawn the most attention because it makes attitudes less stable and it has been shown to reduce political participation. Political scientist Huckfeldt and his colleagues[30] acknowledged the potentially depressing effect of contradictory information causing a type of psychological distress called cognitive dissonance[31] and the inclination to conform to the socially accepted norms, which in turn reduces disagreement in networks. Moreover, partisan diversity and disagreement in networks have been shown to increase one's likelihood of holding contradictory attitudes on the same person or issue,[32] which reduces the likelihood of political participation. Disagreement affects the dynamics of discussion as well. In investigating whether disagreement is an initial filter on discussion, Huckfeldt and Mendez show that discussion likely precedes disagreement, which points to a process of persuasion and attitudinal adjustment.[33]

More recent work on attitudes and social networks combined the insights from research showing how network diversity influences attitude strength with how people process counter-attitudinal information. Network diversity serves as a cue that one's attitudes need to be carefully reexamined in light of new information.[34] Moreover, high quality arguments from diverse discussants make attitude change more likely. The point on network effects on the initiation of thoughtful mechanisms is well in a study of network impacts on political thinking, which shows that cohesive social networks reduce the quality of political thinking, both in the sheer volume of policy relevant thoughts, and in the causality and the complexity of the thoughts.[35]

In brief, the political discussion networks literature reviewed here points to the destabilizing impact of network disagreement on political attitudes. Disagreement may have other effects as well. When people are faced with disagreement in their networks, defensive processing of contrary evidence presented by network members might ensue. People may uncritically bolster their prior evaluation by counter-arguing, discounting, or ignoring the incongruent evidence, which is a phenomenon called motivated reasoning.[36] Motivated reasoning might help people avoid the uncomfortable experience of being exposed to contradictory information caused by network disagreement. The same process might lead individuals to discount the salience of politics in their life and reduce political interest. This may in fact be the mechanism behind the negative impact of network disagreement on political participation in some works where disagreement on a multitude of political issues is measured.[37] Hence, this paper not only addresses the impact of network disagreement on attitudes toward candidates and the stability of such attitudes, but also investigates its impact on political interest.

In the Turkish context, either because of coups or judicial interventions, new parties have emerged and the old ones have redefined themselves. The political socialization process that gives symbolic value to a party label[38] has simply suffered from these developments. The party system in Turkey followed a path of interrupted growth, which is very similar to the experience of other developing countries where one observes high electoral volatility. This has been particularly the case until the 2002 parliamentary election and including the 2002 election where AKP won an outright majority of the seats in the parliament doubling its vote during the campaign. This once again exemplified the electoral volatility generated by weak partisan identification in the masses.

Turkish political parties and the political system have certain distinct qualities that set it apart from other countries with weak parties such as those in Latin America. First of all, Turkey is a political party oriented parliamentary democracy. Voters put their stamp on the party label in the voting booth in the general elections, and the electoral choice is the choice of the ruling political party, and practically its leader as the prime minister. The institutional setting and the shallow roots of the political parties in local districts allow party leaders create their own candidate lists. Hence, the institutional setting in Turkey compensates for the weakness of the political parties.

Moreover, the last coup took place in 1980, and after the 2002 general election both the ruling AKP and the challengers CHP, Nationalist Action Party (MHP, *Milliyetci Hareket Partisi*, and the group of independent MPs under the umbrella of Peace and Democracy Party (BDP, *Baris ve Demokrasi Partisi*) managed to cultivate their respective body of supporters who are more or less stable in how they cast their votes. The new generation of voters, particularly those who for the first time experienced casting a vote in an election in 2002, are experiencing a far more stable political environment compared to the voters from past generations. Although the literature points to the ineffectiveness of political party affiliation and the greater impact of social network disagreement on electoral choices in weak party systems, the impact of party affiliations should be stronger in Turkey. However, such impact might not be as strong as it is in strong party systems of developed countries, allowing network disagreement to create some instability in electoral decisions.

Hypotheses and the Study Design

In light of the discussion above, political party label of a candidate is expected to be a significant predictor of attitudes toward that candidate, and social disagreement to be a significant predictor of the stability of these attitudes, as well as of political interest. Political party affiliation is strong enough in the current Turkish political scene to function as a decisive cue in electoral choices. Hence, when the candidate is from a different party than one's own, lower evaluations toward and a lower willingness to see a candidate as a member of the parliament are to be expected. Moreover, as the social networks literature suggests, social disagreement might make the candidate evaluations less stable in the absence of partisan cues. Also, partisan cues might inter-act with social disagreement in affecting attitudes toward political candidates. Social disagreement may trigger a defensive attitude discounting the value of contradictory information in an effort to protect initial evaluations already formed based on partisan cues, which makes attitude change less likely. Moreover, disagreement might reduce the level of political interest due to the uncomfortable experience of cognitive disso-nance. The research hypotheses that summarize the main expectations are stated below:

H1: Similarity of party affiliation improves attitudes toward a political candi-date.
H2: Social disagreement on a candidate makes attitudes toward that candidate less stable when there is no information on the candidate's party affiliation.
H2a: Candidate party label reverses the negative impact of social disagreement on attitude stability.
H3: Social disagreement reduces political interest.

Before outlining the study design, a discussion on the experimental measurement of disagreement, one of the two independent variables in the hypotheses, is in order. Network disagreement is typically measured by the average disagreement on elec-toral choices among a political discussion network's members.[39] Because the litera-ture relies heavily on survey data, this particular measure has proven to be very useful in showing the relationships between network disagreement and political attitudes and behavior. The literature, however, has not been successful in establishing causal relationships due to the simple fact that social network qualities are hard to generate and manipulate in experiments.[40] Instead proxy measures of network disagreement have been used.[41] To obtain the measure, experimenters typically introduce to the subject a new person who is said to come from a social context that can be found in an informal political discussion network. The deceptive scenario tells the respondent that further contact with the person is very likely after the study and immediate upon consent. Then subjects receive information on the fictitious potential contact's views that are either in line or contrary to those of the subject.

The above-mentioned experimental strategy is adopted here due to its strength in establishing causality. Because what is critical is the social supply of disagreement and what makes it network disagreement is the specific social context of informal political discussion, the experimental manipulation in the literature can tap similar mental processes that are triggered by real-life network disagreement. But because the subjects have their own real life networks and in order to underline the fact that social network disagreement is manipulated in an experimental setting, the paper adopts the term socially supplied disagreement from potential political discussants rather than network disagreement.

The experimental study has a between subjects 3×2 factorial design. The treatments are party affiliation information in the short biography of a political candidate (no party label, same party label, or other party label) and the level of disagreement on the candidate among potential social contacts introduced in the survey. Upon agreeing to participate in the study, subjects read a short text detailing which labeled survey they should pick based on their political party affiliation. Subjects are randomly assigned to one of the three party label conditions: while some pick surveys where there is no party affiliation information on the candidate, almost a third picks surveys where the candidate is from their own party, and the other third picks surveys where the candidate is from a different party than theirs. Subjects first read the biography of a fictitious political candidate. The candidate biography includes family, professional, and political career information. The candidate is said to have a very high likelihood of being an MP candidate in the next general elections. Subjects in the same or other party label conditions read the name of the political party on whose list the name of the candidate will be included. Next, subjects report their feeling thermometer ratings, i.e. whether they feel warm or cool toward the candidate on a 0–100 scale where scores below 50 stand for increasingly cooler and scores above 50 stand for increasingly warmer evaluations, and 50 stands for neither cool nor warm feelings toward the candidate. Afterwards, subjects report whether they would like to vote for her if given a chance. Due to the absence of candidate voting in the Turkish context, this item stands for the subject's willingness to see the candidate as an MP.

Then, subjects are told that there are other volunteers who already participated in the study and whom they will be able to get in touch with, if they so desire, in future iterations of the study to discuss social and political issues and also the candidate. They read three consecutive potential social contact biographies each followed by items on their attitudes toward the potential contacts. The biographies belong to undergraduate students and include information on their families, studies, and social life, and future plans. The three biographies differ in gender and other attributes. The contact biographies also include the second treatment: a sentence on whether the potential social contact would like to cast a vote for her if given a chance, i.e. see the candidate get elected as an MP. Half the subjects are assigned to a condition where all three potential contacts want to see her get elected as an MP (social agreement condition); and the other half read bios where the first candidate approves of the candidate as an MP, the second is undecided, and the third does not want to see her get elected (social disagreement condition). They are then told to report once again their feeling thermometer ratings on the candidate, and whether they would like to see her get elected as an MP. They are once again given the same candidate biography and told to read it if they want to evaluate the candidate, and asked whether they read it, skimmed through it, or not read it again. Last, they answer items on their political interest, political party affiliation, ideological leaning, and other personal characteristics including demographics.[42]

Data, Measures, and Findings

The survey experiment was administered to undergraduate students in Bilkent University, Bilgi University, TOBB University of Economics and Technology (TOBB ETU), and Middle East Technical University (ODTU) in classrooms and within the same time period between November 2011 and February 2012. Hence, controlling for the subject's institution in the analysis below also means controlling for the time of the survey experiment. The study produced 359 valid surveys. Some characteristics of the sample are reported in Table 1. CHP identifiers are over-represented in the sample. Because the study has an experimental design, and because the experimental manipulation of party affiliation involves the same or other party label anchored on the subject's party identification, this should not cause bias in the results from hypotheses testing.[43]

Table 1. Sample Characteristics.

	Frequency	Percent
Female	202	56.27
With private car	80	22.28
Birth-year before 1992	331	92
Bilgi University student	47	13.09
Bilkent University student	138	38.44
ODTU student	104	28.97
TOBB ETU student	70	19.50
Total sample size	359	100

Affective evaluations toward the candidate and the approval of the candidate as a member of the parliament stand for the construct of candidate attitudes in the hypotheses. respondents' affective evaluations are measured using the feeling thermometer rating on the candidate (0–100 scale) taken after the experimental manipulations. Approval of the candidate as an MP is measured by an item that asks the subject whether she would like to vote for the candidate if given the chance so that she can get elected as an MP in the next parliamentary elections (1–3 scale). These measures constitute the first two dependent variables in the analyses below. The third dependent variable is attitude instability. It is measured by the absolute value of the change between the pre-treatment and post-treatment feeling thermometer ratings on the candidate, and ranges between 0 and 80. The last dependent variable, political interest, is measured by a survey item asking the subject the extent to which she is interested in social and political issues, measured on a five-point scale.

Experimental treatments are the main independent variables in the analyses below. The treatment of party affiliation has three groups: no party label, same party label, and other party label. The first two treatment variables included in the regression analyses reported below, same and other party label, are measured on a 0–1 scale. No party label group serves as the base category. Social disagreement stands for the second experimental treatment explained above. It takes on the value of 0 when all three potential social contacts approve of the candidate as an MP, and takes on the value of 1 when all three have different reports of their willingness to see the candidate as an MP. Three dummy variables stand for the party affiliation of the subject, with CHP as the base category. University affiliation dummy variables have Bilkent University as the base category. Owning a personal car stands for socio-economic status, which was directly asked using an ordinal scale. The latter, however, did differentiate the subjects and instead, the car variable is used in the regression analyses. Religiosity is measured by an item asking the frequency of religious practice, measured on a five-point scale running from no religious practice to religious practice every day in the past month.

In order to assess the impact of the experimental manipulations on the dependent variables, this paper first reports the results of the analyses of variance (ANOVA). When the feeling thermometer rating on the candidate is the dependent variable, the experimental treatment of party affiliation of the fictitious candidate becomes highly significant, $F(2, 339) = 11.64$; p-value < 0.001.[44] However, neither social disagreement, which is the other treatment, nor the interaction of the two treatments is significant. Figure 1 illustrates the impact that party affiliation of the candidate has on the thermometer ratings. Because the interaction of the treatments is insignificant, there is no significant change in the pattern of this relationship between social agreement and social disagreement groups. On the other hand, the mean candidate thermometer rating in the no party label and the same party label conditions are significantly different compared to the condition where the candidate biography included a different political party label than the subject's party affiliation $(t(220) = 3.99$, p-value < 0.01; and $t(229) = 4.237$, p-value < 0.01, respectively).

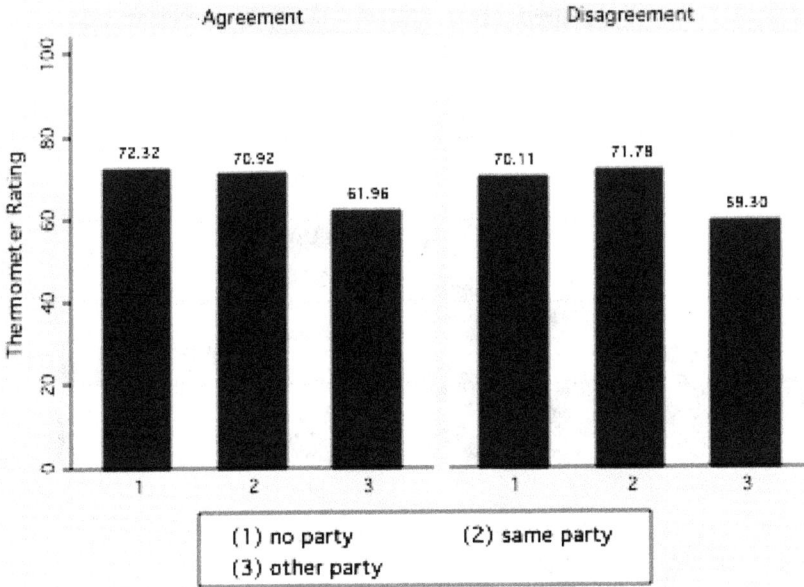

Figure 1. Party Affiliation's Impact on Candidate Ratings.

Moreover, party affiliation of the candidate and social disagreement together significantly affect the size of the changes in the thermometer ratings after the respondent receives the treatments, $F(2, 326) = 2.80$; p-value $= 0.06$. Figure 2 clearly shows that the pattern of the relationship between the dependent variable and party affiliation conditions differs between social agreement and disagreement groups. Within the social agreement group, the gap between the no party label and other party label is significantly large ($t(104) = -2.46$, p-value < 0.05), and people seem to significantly change their ratings for the candidate when they learn that she is affiliated with a different political party than theirs. Although the pattern is reversed in the social disagreement group, the differences in the dependent variable values for the no party label and the other party label conditions are not statistically significant, $t(106)=0.75$, p-value $= 0.45$. In addition, Figure 3 shows that social disagreement matters for changed evaluations particularly within the no-label group. This is to be expected as subjects make their evaluations in this condition without any reference to partisan cues.

When one looks at people's willingness to see the candidate get elected, it is once again observed that there are significant differences among party affiliation conditions, $F(2359) = 14.85$, p-value < 0.01.[45] As Figure 4 shows there are significant differences in the proportion of willing voters between the no party label and the other party label conditions ($t(236) = -4.91$, p-value < 0.001) for both the social

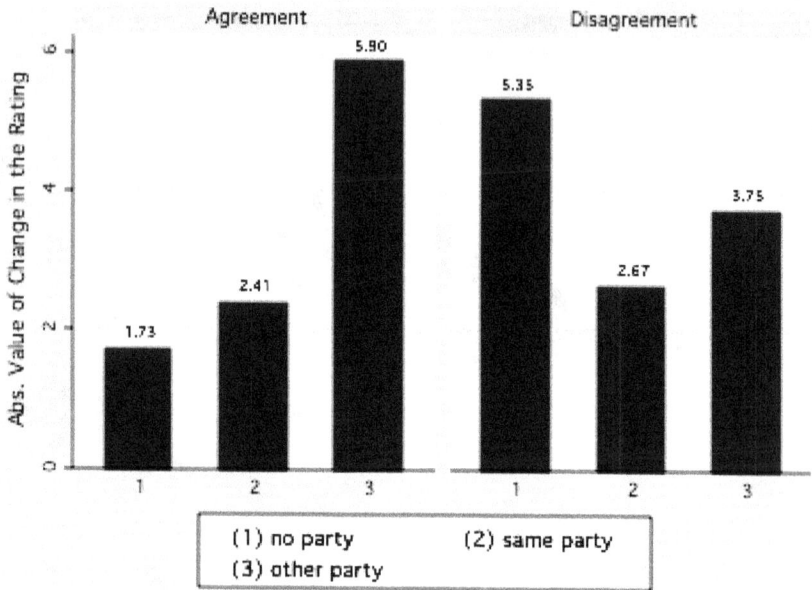

Figure 2. Party Affiliation's Impact on Change in the Ratings.

agreement and disagreement groups. On the other hand, social disagreement is not a significant predictor of this dependent variable, and there is no significant interaction effect of the treatments in the results.

Although the ANOVA indicate whether and how the experimental conditions make a difference in the dependent variables, regression analyses can better illustrate the differences within the conditions and the impact of the sample and personal characteristics. Table 2, Column 2, shows the results for the ordinary least squares (OLS) regression analysis of the candidate thermometer ratings on the experimental treatments, their interaction, and the control variables. Compared to reading a candidate biography with no party label, reading the biography with another party label reduces the feeling thermometer ratings by almost 11 points. Moreover, compared to those who identify with CHP, those who identify with MHP, BDP, and other parties are far less likely to feel warm toward this particular candidate.

The results for the OLS regression of the size of the difference between the before and after treatment thermometer ratings on the same independent variables are reported in Table 2, Column 3. Compared to reading a candidate biography with no party label, reading the biography with another party label increases the size of the changes in candidate evaluations by four points (p-value < 0.10). However, this effect is only valid for the social agreement condition. It is overridden in the social disagreement condition by the significant interaction term between social

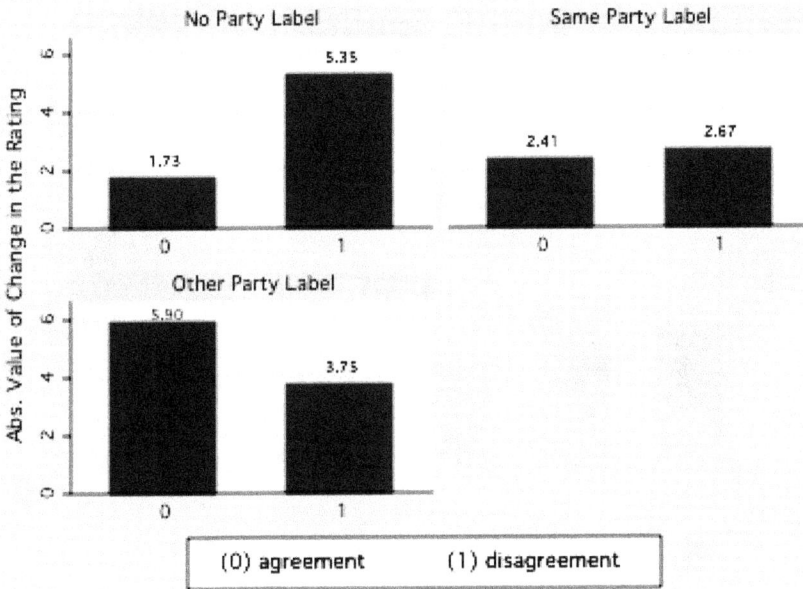

Figure 3. Social Agreement's Impact on Change in the Ratings across Agreement Groups.

disagreement and other party label conditions, which reduces the size of the rating changes by almost seven points.

In addition, social disagreement seems to increase the size of the rating changes in the no party label condition by 4.6 points. However, because of the significant inter-action terms, those who are in the same party label and other party conditions and also receive social disagreement will experience almost no rating change and reduction in the size of the rating change respectively. In brief, compared to those in the no party label condition, those in the other, and to some extent, those in the same party label conditions will experience destabilizing impact of social disagreement. Reading a same party label candidate biography compared to a no label one, however, does not singlehandedly affect the size of the rating changes. Also, MHP and other party identifiers change their ratings significantly more compared to BDP identifiers.

Willingness to see this fictitious candidate as an MP, on the other hand, has a single significant predictor among the experimental independent variables: whether the candidate is from another political party. The odds ratios from the ordered logistic regression results reported in Table 2, Column 4, indicate that those who are in the other party label condition compared to the no party label condition are significantly less likely to approve of the candidate as an MP. The odds are significantly $1-0.25$ that the subject will choose not voting to undecided or undecided to voting in report-ing her willingness to see the candidate get elected. In addition MHP, BDP, and other

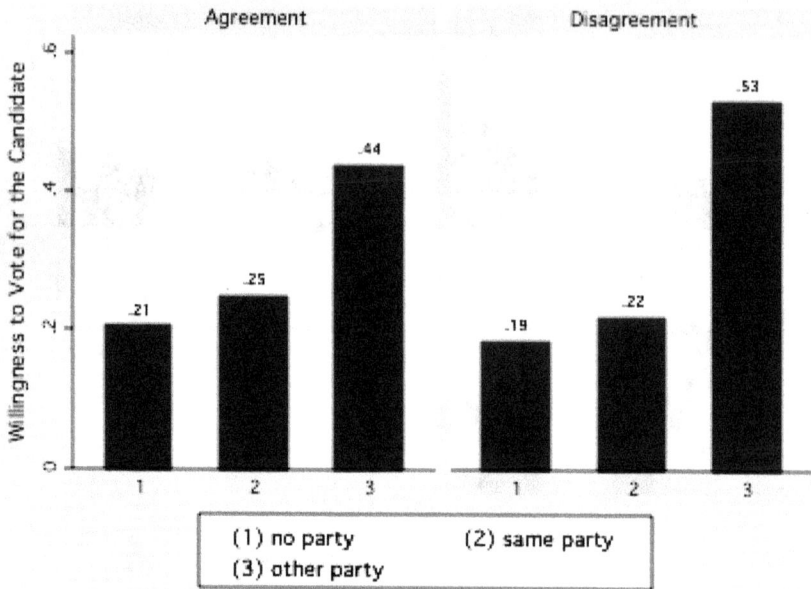

Figure 4. Party Affiliation's Impact on Willingness to Vote for the Candidate.

party identifiers are significantly less willing to approve of the candidate as an MP compared to CHP identifiers, whereas there is once again no significant difference between the CHP and AKP identifiers.

Last, Table 2, Column 5, reports the odds ratios from the ordered logistic regression of one's interest in social and political issues on the independent variables. Interaction of social disagreement with the same party label candidate condition is significant. The results indicate that those who are in the no party label condition and receive social disagreement experience reduction in their likelihood of reporting higher political interest. However, those who are in the same party condition experience an increase in their reported level of political interest. It seems receiving contradictory information from potential social contacts, here people who can be friends, make people more anxious about politics, which triggers more interest in politics. Moreover, the likelihood of reporting higher levels of political interest is significantly less for AKP supporters and more for BDP and other party supporters compared to CHP supporters. In addition, females are significantly less likely to report higher levels of political interest compared to males in this sample. Also, university affiliation of the subject is a significant predictor of neither political interest nor the other dependent variables considered here.

In brief, the results give support to the research hypotheses: political party affiliation determines the attitudes toward the MP hopeful, and in its absence social

Table 2. The Impact of Experimental Treatments on the Dependent Variables, Controlling for the Differences among Sample Universities, Subject Party Affiliation, and Personal Characteristics.

	Feeling thermometer rating on the candidate	Absolute value of change in the feeling thermometer rating	Willingness to see the candidate as an MP	Political interest of the subject
Same party candidate bio	−0.478 (4.284)	0.978 (2.176)	0.656 (0.379)	0.729 (0.330)
Other party candidate bio	−10.769** (4.199)	4.179* (2.190)	0.253** (0.137)	1.155 (0.508)
Social disagreement	−4.165 (3.863)	4.610** (1.957)	1.55 (0.600)	0.407** (0.162)
Same party candidate bio × social disagreement	2.317 (5.244)	−4.466 (2.655)*	0.926 (0.681)	3.252** (1.758)
Other party candidate bio × social disagreement	1.864 (5.157)	−6.651** (2.638)	0.585 (0.394)	1.573 (0.826)
Justice and Development Party	1.037 (3.297)	1.709 (1.713)	0.787 (0.319)	0.529* (0.177)
Nationalist Action Party	−9.842** (5.010)	4.506* (2.514)	0.207*** (0.109)	1.466 (0.759)
Peace and Democracy Party	−9.842** (5.010)	−1.999 (2.663)	0.249** (0.155)	4.820*** (2.710)
Other party	−25.524*** (5.915)	7.164** (2.963)	0.194** (0.131)	4.862** (3.476)
Female	0.824 (2.141)	0.804 (1.087)	0.861 (0.236)	0.516*** (0.115)
Car	−1.292 (2.612)	−0.041 (1.330)	0.916 (0.304)	1.248 (0.332)
Birth-year	−0.355 (0.471)	−0.386 (0.237)	0.980 (0.061)	1.024 (0.052)
Religiosity	1.584 (1.025)	0.216 (0.521)	1.167 (0.154)	1.024 (0.107)
Bilgi	0.524 (3.922)	−0.859 (2.028)	1.228 (0.572)	0.591 (0.237)
ODTU	−0.824 (3.073)	−0.136 (1.578)	0.979 (0.372)	0.680 (0.223)
TOBB ETU	2.199 (3.515)	−0.045 (1.828)	1.175 (0.491)	1.026 (0.283)
Constant	101.853 (42.079)	34.819 (21.166)		
	$N = 319$, $F(16, 302) = 3.66$, Prob $> F = 0.000$, $R^2 = 0.162$	$N = 308$, $F(16, 291) = 1.43$, Prob $> F = 0.124$, $R^2 = 0.073$	$N = 315$, LR $\chi^2(16) = 50.64$, Prob $> \chi^2 = 0.000$, Pseudo $R^2 = 0.098$	$N = 333$, LR $\chi^2(16) = 39.03$, Prob $> \chi^2 = 0.001$, Pseudo $R^2 = 0.049$

Notes: The table reports the regression coefficients from two OLS (the first two columns) and two ordered logit regressions (the last two columns). Standard errors are reported in parentheses. Cut point coefficient estimates from the ordered logistic regressions and their standard errors are not reported here.
*p-Value less then 0.01.
**p-Value less then 0.05.
***p-Value less then 0.10.

disagreement, causes volatility in the attitudes. However, when individuals experience disagreement in their immediate social environment, and also receive party label information, partisan cues are strong enough to override the destabilizing impact of socially supplied disagreement. The latter reduces political interest in the absence of partisan cues, but when disagreement is about a same party candidate political interest is heightened.

Conclusions

The findings point to the significance of party identification for electoral attitudes in Turkey, as well as the impact that social network disagreement can have on the stability of the same attitudes. Regarding the former finding, existing literature documents how party label serves as a filter on political information, giving more credibility to partisan information, and creating distrust toward information from other party sources. This is also valid for candidate evaluation. The experimental formulation of party affiliation as the similarity or difference of party identification between the subject and the attitude object proved useful for illustrating this effect. Subjects seem to use the partisan cue as a heuristic to assess the desirability of making the candidate an MP. Moreover, their assessments of the candidate do not depend on the existence of agreement or disagreement supplied by the potential social contacts.

This is different from what one would expect in a country with weak parties. The argument that weak partisan roots in the electorate make citizens more susceptible to social forces in their electoral decisions has been supported by research that focuses on Latin American cases, and most of these cases are presidential systems. Turkey has a parliamentary system that highlights the party label in voting. This in turn may facilitate and speed up the process of developing a party identification. Hence, further research should address the institutional differences that matter for the development of partisan affiliation in the masses. Such differences might explain the within developing country differences in partisan attachment.

The findings are also telling for the political socialization of the new generation of voters in Turkey. Experimental subjects are undergraduate students of voting age and about 80 percent of them casted a vote in the 2011 general elections. They lived through their teens under AKP rule and the challengers in the political scene have not changed much since 2002. They are from the first generation of voters in Turkey who have been exposed to stable party labels and a relatively stable democracy during their political socialization. Hence, it is only natural that their attitudes toward this fictitious politician do not change by social disagreement, but rather by her party label. This might in turn indicate that the current political parties in Turkey are becoming more rooted in the electorate such that we should expect less electoral volatility in the future.

In the absence of partisan labels, however, socially supplied disagreement causes attitude instability toward candidates, which might underline electoral volatility. If party labels all of a sudden change due to some external shock, candidate choices will depend on political information coming from other sources including social networks. In the Turkish context, because the leader whose party wins the general elections becomes the prime minister, the prime political candidates in Turkey are the party leaders. As a result, when partisan cues become weak, attitudes toward these candidates will become more decisive in electoral outcomes. Those attitudes in turn will become more volatile when there is substantial disagreement in people's social networks. Removing the party label heuristic from the political system means taking away an important tool citizens use in making sense of the labyrinthine world of politics, practically removing an important shield that protects citizen attitudes from the destabilizing effects of information coming from various social contexts.

The results also show that when social disagreement is on a candidate with a known party affiliation, party affiliation's positive impact on attitudinal stability overrides the destabilizing impact of social disagreement among subjects. This once again indicates that partisan cues are relied on in arriving at a judgment about a candidate, although in its absence social disagreement will make those judgments unstable. Hence, from the perspective of the subjects, political party affiliation is strong enough to decisively determine the attitudes toward candidates and those attitudes' stability. Taken together these findings once again point to the possibility that the current political parties in Turkey are taking root in the masses and this is most visible in the new generation of voters.

The findings are also significant for the social networks literature. Network disagreement has been considered a factor that reduces political participation via increasing ambivalence. A different route is suggested here via lessened interest in politics with experimental evidence. In an effort to avoid the discomfort associated with making sense of contradictory political information, people may distance themselves from politics when they are exposed to substantial political disagreement among their contacts. The results indicate that network disagreement causes a reduction in reported levels of political interest unless the party label is accessible. If the latter is the case, political interest increases, adding to the list of benefits that partisan cues provide to the democratic capacity of ordinary citizens.

Acknowledgements

I would like to express my gratitude to Kerem Ozan Kalkan, Emre Erdogan, and Cengiz Erisen whose help contributed greatly to the data collection effort. I would also like to thank Basak Ince, Ioannis Grigoriadis, Zeki Sarigil, and Dilek Cindoglu for allowing me to recruit participants for the study in their undergraduate classes. I truly appreciate the comments from the participants at the TOBB ETU Workshop on Turkish Political Behavior and Political Psychology, in particular Gizem Arikan, Ekrem Karakoc, and the anonymous reviewers, which made this article a better one.

Notes

1. Lau and Redlawsk, "Advantages and Disadvantages," 951–71.
2. Baker, Ames, and Renno, "Social Context and Campaign Volatility," 382–99.

3. Huckfeldt, Johnson, and Sprague, *Political Disagreement.*
4. Mutz, "Cross-Cutting Social Networks," 111–26; Mutz, "Consequences of Cross-Cutting Networks," 838–55.
5. Huckfeldt and Sprague, *Citizens, Politics, and Social Communication.* Huckfeldt and his colleagues have shown in numerous other studies that informal networks of important matters discussion and of political matters discussion overlap to a large extent. Hence, in this article, the terms social network and political discussion network are used interchangeably.
6. Campbell et al., *American Voter*; Rahn, "Role of Partisan Stereotypes," 472–96; Sears et al., "Self-Interest Versus Symbolic Politics," 670–84.
7. Zaller, *Nature and Origins.*
8. Lau and Redlawsk, "Advantages and Disadvantages"; Lodge and Hamill, "Partisan Schema," 505–19.
9. Ibid.
10. Zaller, "Floating Voters in US Presidential Elections, 1948–2000."
11. Blais, "How Many Voters?" 801–3.
12. Converse, "Of Time and Partisan Stability," 139–71.
13. Lawson and McCann, "Television Coverage, Media Effects," 1–30.
14. Popkin, *The Reasoning Voter*; Sniderman, "Taking Sides."
15. Gelman and King, "Why Are American Election?" 409–51.
16. Lawson, *Building the Fourth Estate.*
17. Skidmore, ed., *Television, Politics, and the Transition.*
18. Baker, Ames, and Renno, "Social Context and Campaign Volatility."
19. Ibid.
20. Huckfeldt and Sprague, *Citizens, Politics, and Social Communication.*
21. Granovetter, "Strength of Weak Ties," 1360–80; Granovetter, "Strength of Weak Ties," 201–33.
22. Berelson, Lazarsfeld, and McPhee, *Voting*; Huckfeldt, "Political Loyalties and Social Class," 399–417; Huckfeldt, *Politics in Context*; Huckfeldt and Sprague, "Networks in Context," 1197–216; Huckfeldt, Plutzer, and Sprague, "Alternative Contexts of Political Behavior," 365–81; Huckfeldt and Sprague, *Citizens, Politics, and Social Communication*; Huckfeldt et al., "Political Environments, Cohesive Social Groups," 1025–54; Katz and Lazarsfeld, *Personal Influence*; Lazarsfeld, Berelson, and Gaudet, *People's Choice*; Putnam, "Political Attitudes," 640–54; Weatherford, "Interpersonal Networks and Political Behavior," 117–43.
23. Mutz and Mondak, "Workplace as a Context," 140–55; Mutz, "Cross-Cutting Social Networks," 111–26; Mutz, "Consequences of Cross-Cutting Networks," 838–55; Mutz, *Hearing the Other Side.*
24. Lake and Huckfeldt, "Social Networks, Social Capital," 567–84; McClurg, "Social Networks and Political Participation," 449–64; McClurg, "Electoral Relevance of Political Talk," 737–54.
25. Huckfeld, "Social Communication of Political Expertise," 425–38; Huckfeldt, Ikeda, and Pappi, "Patterns of Disagreement," 497–514.
26. Huckfeldt, Morehouse, and Osborn, "Disagreement, Ambivalence, and Engagement," 65–96; Huckfeldt, Johnson, and Sprague, *Political Disagreement*; Huckfeldt and Mendez, "Moths, Flames, and Political Engagement," 83–96.
27. Barabas, "How Deliberation Affects Policy Opinions," 687–701; Mutz, "Cross-Cutting Social Networks," 111–26; Mutz, "Consequences of Cross-Cutting Networks," 838–55.
28. Lake and Huckfeldt, "Social Networks, Social Capital," 567–84; McClurg, "Social Networks and Political Participation," 449–64; McClurg, "Electoral Relevance of Political Talk," 737–54; Mutz, "Cross-Cutting Social Networks," 111–26; Mutz, "Consequences of Cross-Cutting Networks," 838–55.
29. Klofstad, Sokhey, and McClurg, "Disagreeing about Disagreement."
30. Huckfeld, "Social Communication of Political Expertise," 425–38; Huckfeldt, Johnson, and Sprague, *Political Disagreement*; Huckfeldt and Mendez, "Moths, Flames, and Political Engagement."
31. Festinger, *Theory of Cognitive Dissonance.*

32. Howard, "Electoral Consequences of Ambivalence," 915–29; Zaller, *Nature and Origins*; Mutz, "Cross-Cutting Social Networks," 111–26; Mutz, "Consequences of Cross-Cutting Networks," 838–55; Visser and Mirabile, "Attitudes in the Social Context," 779–95.
33. Huckfeldt and Mendez, "Moths, Flames, and Political Engagement."
34. Erisen and Erisen, "Effect of Social Networks"; Visser and Mirabile, "Attitudes in the Social Context."
35. Erisen and Erisen, "Effect of Social Networks."
36. Redlawsk, "Hot Cognition or Cool Consideration?", 1021–44.
37. Mutz, "Cross-Cutting Social Networks," 111–26; Mutz, "Consequences of Cross-Cutting Networks," 838–55.
38. Lazarsfeld, Berelson, and Gaudet, *People's Choice*.
39. Mutz, "Cross-Cutting Social Networks," 111–26; Mutz, "Consequences of Cross-Cutting Networks," 838–55; Lake and Huckfeldt, "Social Networks, Social Capital," 567–84; McClurg, "Social Networks and Political Participation," 449–64; McClurg, "Electoral Relevance of Political Talk," 737–54.
40. Please refer to the "Methods in Political Psychology" article in this issue for a discussion on the use of experiments in political psychology.
41. Erisen, Erisen, and Redlawsk, "Social Consequences of Incongruency."
42. Supplemental materials for the candidate and potential contact biographies and experimental procedure are available upon request from the author.
43. Druckman and Kam, "Students as Experimental Participants." Unless the causal link between the similarity of the party affiliation and attitudes toward the candidate changes in samples with different political party affiliation composition, sample characteristics should not bias the results. This is also true for other sample characteristics.
44. The effect size for the party affiliation treatment is medium to high (Cohen's f is 0.265).
45. The treatment's effect size is medium to high (Cohen's $f = 0.29$).

References

Baker, Andy, Barry Ames, and Lucio Renno. "Social Context and Campaign Volatility in New Democracies: Networks and Neighborhoods in Brazil's 2002 Elections." *American Journal of Political Science* 50, no. 2 (2006): 382–399.

Barabas, Jason. "How Deliberation Affects Policy Opinions." *American Political Science Review* 98, no. 4 (2004, Nov): 687–701.

Berelson, Bernard R., Paul F. Lazarsfeld, and William N. McPhee. *Voting: A Study of Opinion Formation in a Presidential Campaign*. Chicago: University of Chicago Press, 1954.

Blais, Andre. "How Many Voters Change Their Minds in the Month Preceding an Election?" *PS: Political Science and Politics* 37, no. 4 (2004): 801–803.

Campbell, Angus, Philip E. Converse, Warren E. Miller, and Donald Stokes. *The American Voter*. New York: Wiley Press, 1960.

Converse, Philip E. "Of Time and Partisan Stability." *Comparative Political Studies* 2, no. 2 (1969): 139–171.

Druckman, James N., and Cindy D. Kam. "Students as Experimental Participants: A Defense of the 'Narrow Data Base'." In *Handbook of Experimental Political Science*, edited by James N. Druckman, Donald P. Green, James H. Kuklinski, and Arthur Lupia, 41–57. New York: Cambridge University Press, 2011.

Erisen, Elif, and Cengiz Erisen. "The Effect of Social Networks on the Quality of Political Thinking." *Political Psychology* 33, no. 6 (2012): 839–865.

Erisen, Elif, Cengiz Erisen, and David Redlawsk. "Social Consequences of Incongruency: Motivated Reasoning and Social Networks," Paper presented at the 70th annual conference of the Midwest Political Science Association, Chicago, IL, April, 2012.

Festinger, Leon. *A Theory of Cognitive Dissonance*. Stanford, CA: Stanford University, 1957.

Gelman, Andrew, and Gary King. "Why Are American Election Campaign Polls So Variable When Voters Are So Predictable?" *British Journal of Political Science* 23, no. 1 (1993): 409–451.

Granovetter, Mark S. "The Strength of Weak Ties." *The American Journal of Sociology* 78 (1973): 1360–1380.

Granovetter, Mark S. "The Strength of Weak Ties: A Network Theory Revisited." *Sociological Theory* 1 (1983): 201–233.

Howard, Lavine. "The Electoral Consequences of Ambivalence Toward Presidential Candidates." *American Journal of Political Science* 45, no. 4 (2001): 915–929.

Huckfeldt, Robert. "Political Loyalties and Social Class Ties: The Mechanisms of Contextual Influence." *American Journal of Political Science*, 28, no. 2 (1984, May): 399–417.

Huckfeldt, Robert. *Politics in Context: Assimilation and Conflict in Urban Neighborhoods*. New York: Agathon Press, 1986.

Huckfeld, Robert. "The Social Communication of Political Expertise." *American Journal of Political Science* 45, no. 2 (2001): 425–438.

Huckfeldt, Robert, P. Beck, R. Dalton, and J. Levine. "Political Environments, Cohesive Social Groups, and the Communication of Public Opinion." *American Journal of Political Science* 39, no. 4 (1995): 1025–1054.

Huckfeldt, Robert, K. Ikeda, and F. U. Pappi. "Patterns of Disagreement in Democratic Politics: Comparing Germany, Japan, and the United States." *American Journal of Political Science* 49, no. 3 (2005): 497–514.

Huckfeldt, Robert, Paul E. Johnson, and John Sprague. *Political Disagreement: The Survival of Diverse Opinions within Communication Networks*. New York: Cambridge University Press, 2004.

Huckfeldt, Robert, and J. M. Mendez. "Moths, Flames, and Political Engagement: Managing Disagreement within Communication Networks." *Journal of Politics* 70, no. 1 (2008): 83–96.

Huckfeldt, Robert, J. Morehouse, and T. Osborn. "Disagreement, Ambivalence, and Engagement: The Political Consequences of Heterogeneous Networks." *Political Psychology* 25, no. 1 (2004): 65–96.

Huckfeldt, Robert, E. Plutzer, and J. Sprague. "Alternative Contexts of Political Behavior: Churches, Neighborhoods, and Individuals." *Journal of Politics* 39, no. 2 (1993, May): 365–381.

Huckfeldt, Robert, and J. Sprague. "Networks in Context: The Social Flow of Political Information." *American Political Science Review*, 81, no. 4 (1987, Dec.): 1197–1216.

Huckfeldt, Robert, and J. Sprague. *Citizens, Politics, and Social Communication: Information and Influence in an Election Campaign*. New York: Cambridge University Press, 1995.

Katz, E., and P. F. Lazarsfeld. *Personal Influence: The Part Played by People in the Flow of Mass Communication*. Glencoe, IL: Free Press, 1955.

Klofstad, Casey A., Anand Sokhey, and Scott McClurg. "Disagreeing about Disagreement: How Conflict in Social Networks Affects Political Behavior." *The American Journal of Political Science*, 57, no. 1 (2012): 120–134.

Lake, R., and R. Huckfeldt. "Social Networks, Social Capital, and Political Participation." *Political Psychology* 19, no. 3 (1998): 567–584.

Lau, Richard R., and David P. Redlawsk. "Advantages and Disadvantages of Cognitive Heuristics in Political Decision Making." *American Journal of Political Science* 45, no. 4 (2001): 951–971.

Lawson, Chappell H. *Building the Fourth Estate: Democratization and the Rise of a Free Press in Mexico.* Berkeley: University of California Press, 2002.

Lawson, Chappell H., and James McCann. "Television Coverage, Media Effects, and Mexico's 2000 Elections." *British Journal of Political Science* 35, no. 1 (2005): 1–30.

Lazarsfeld, P. F., B. Berelson, and H. Gaudet. *The People's Choice: How the Voter Makes up His Mind in a Presidential Campaign.* New York: Columbia University Press, 1944.

Lazarsfeld, Paul F., Bernard Berelson, and Hazel Gaudet. *The People's Choice: How the Voter Makes up His Mind in a Presidential Campaign.* New York: Columbia University Press, 1948.

Lodge, Milton, and Ruth Hamill. "A Partisan Schema for Political Information Processing." *American Political Science Review* 80, no. 2 (1986): 505–519.

McClurg, Scott D. "Social Networks and Political Participation: The Role of Social Interaction in Explaining Political Participation." *Political Research Quarterly* 56, no. 4 (2003): 449–464.

McClurg, Scott D. "The Electoral Relevance Of Political Talk: Examining Disagreement and Expertise Effects in Social Networks on Political Participation." *American Journal of Political Science* 50, no. 3 (2006): 737–754.

Mutz, Diana C. "Cross-Cutting Social Networks: Testing Democratic Theory in Practice." *American Political Science Review* 96, no. 1 (2002): 111–126.

Mutz, Diana C. "The Consequences of Cross-Cutting Networks for Political Participation." *American Journal of Political Science* 46, no. 4 (2002): 838–855.

Mutz, Diana C. *Hearing the Other Side: Deliberative Versus Participatory Democracy.* New York: Cambridge University Press, 2006.

Mutz, Diana C., and Jeffrey J. Mondak. "The Workplace as a Context for Cross-Cutting Political Discourse." *Journal of Politics* 68, no. 1 (2006): 140–155.

Popkin, Samuel. *The Reasoning Voter: Communication and Persuasion in Presidential Campaigns.* Chicago: University of Chicago Press, 1991.

Putnam, Robert. "Political Attitudes and the Local Community." *American Political Science Review* 60, no. 3, (1966): 640–654.

Rahn, Wendy. "The Role of Partisan Stereotypes in Information Processing about Political Candidates." *American Journal of Political Science* 37, no. 2 (1993): 472–496.

Redlawsk, David P. "Hot Cognition or Cool Consideration? Testing the Effects of Motivated Reasoning on Political Decision Making." *Journal of Politics* 64, no. 4 (2002): 1021–1044.

Sears, Donald O., Richard R. Lau, Tom R. Tyler, and Harris M. Allen, Jr. "Self-Interest Versus Symbolic Politics in Policy Attitudes and Presidential Voting." *American Political Science Review* 74, no. 3 (1980): 670–684.

Skidmore, Thomas E, ed. *Television, Politics, and the Transition to Democracy in Latin America.* Baltimore: Johns Hopkins University Press, 1993.

Sniderman, Paul M. "Taking Sides: A Fixed Choice Theory of Political Reasoning." In *Elements of Reason: Cognition, Choice, and Elements of Rationality,* edited by Arthur Lupia, Mathew McCubbins, and Samuel L. Popkin, 67–84. Cambridge: Cambridge University Press, 2000.

Visser, Penny S., and R. R. Mirabile. "Attitudes in the Social Context: The Impact of Social Network Composition on Individual-Level Attitude Strength." *Journal of Personality and Social Psychology* 87, no. 6 (2004): 779–795.

Weatherford, M. Stephen. "Interpersonal Networks and Political Behavior." *American Journal of Political Science* 26, no. 1 (1982): 117–143.

Zaller, John R. *The Nature and Origins of Mass Opinion.* Cambridge: Cambridge University Press, 1992.

Zaller, John R. "Floating Voters in US Presidential Elections, 1948–2000." In *Studies in Public Opinion: Attitudes, Nonattitudes, Measurement Error, and Change,* edited by William E. Saris and Paul M. Sniderman, 166–212. Princeton: Princeton University Press, 2004.

Analyzing the Determinants of Group Identity Among Alevis in Turkey: A National Survey Study

ÇİĞDEM V. ŞİRİN

Department of Political Science, University of Texas at El Paso, El Paso, TX, USA

ABSTRACT   *This study systematically explores the factors that affect collective identity associations within the Alevi community in Turkey by employing the social identity approach and examining survey data collected through fieldwork. The results show that Kurdish Alevis express lower levels of attachment to their religious identity as compared to Turkish Alevis. The results also indicate that personal experiences of discrimination tend to increase one's prioritization of Alevi identity. Last, no significant differences are observed regarding group identity between Alevis who reside in urban areas and those who live in rural areas.*

Introduction

Group identity is a key prerequisite for collective political action.[1] The way in which a group's identity is constructed and maintained along with the relative strength of such identity help shape how intergroup conflicts and their resolutions are likely to develop.[2] As such, it is of vital importance to examine the factors that are related to the foundation, essentialization, and solidification of group identity associations in a society.

Although scholars have noted the importance of group identity in political behavior research, most studies have only focused on the USA and Europe. Therefore, it is necessary to extend this field of research to other cross-cultural contexts. In this regard, Turkey provides a rich setting of diverse socio-demographic structure with various combinations of different forms of collective identity, particularly with regard to ethnic and religious origins. Therein, the Alevi community—the largest religious minority group in Turkey with variations in ethnic descent (i.e. members who come from Kurdish and Turkish origins)—offers a unique contextual opportunity for cross-cultural investigations of minority attitudes and behavior. However, to date, there has been a lack of systematic research on Alevis in Turkey. Most works have

74

failed to adopt a theoretical framework to analyze Alevi group identity. Consequently, the literature has been inundated with a myriad of historical descriptive accounts of Alevis that have limited explanatory merit. Furthermore, most studies on the Alevi community have employed qualitative methodologies whereas the literature suffers from a dearth of quantitative works.

In order to address this gap in the literature, this study systematically explores the formation and perpetuation of group identity associations among Alevis by using survey data collected through fieldwork to test a set of hypotheses derived from the social identity approach (a seminal theory of group processes and intergroup relations, which evolved as a merger of social identity theory and self-categorization theory). This study thus constitutes a first endeavor to apply a theoretical framework and quantitatively analyze the determinants of Alevi identity. The key research question is whether and how ethnicity (Kurdish versus Turkish), personal experience of discrimination, and urban/rural residence affect the prioritization and strength of group identification within the Alevi community.

This study proceeds as follows. First, a brief historical overview of the Alevi community in Turkey is provided. Next, the theoretical framework and hypotheses are introduced, followed by a discussion of the empirical data and the research design that the study employs. The findings are then presented, their implications are discussed, and future avenues of research are identified.

The Case of Alevis in Turkey

While the majority population in Turkey is predominantly Sunni Muslim, Alevis are the second largest religious group.[3] "Alevi" etymologically refers to a person who reveres Ali (the son-in-law of the Prophet Muhammed) and his descendants, whom Alevis regard as the prophet's legitimate successors—constituting the historical source of religious rupture for Alevis within the broader Islamic community.[4] That said, it is difficult to categorize Alevis simply as a religious minority since they historically developed as an endogamous group, thereby gradually evolving into a quasi-ethnic community.[5] In fact, most academic sources include ethnic, national, religious, and political criteria in their definitions of Alevi identity.[6]

A vast majority of Alevis are of Turkish origin while approximately 20 percent are estimated to be of Kurdish descent.[7] However, one should note that there is no official demographic information or scholarly consensus concerning the actual number of Alevis in Turkey. This is largely due to the fact that although Kurds and Alevis constitute the largest minority groups in Turkey, the Turkish state does not formally recognize them as minorities or classify them under separate categories in the census.[8] Moreover, due to assimilative state policies dating back to Ottoman times, coupled with ongoing issues of social desirability and other concerns, Alevis have a tendency to hide their identities.[9] These limitations notwithstanding, a number of academic sources estimate that Alevis constitute approximately 30 percent of the total population, which currently stands at around 75 million.[10]

To understand the context behind the formation and development of Alevi identity, a brief historical overview is warranted. Under Ottoman rule, Alevis faced religious persecution as a minority group. During that time, many Alevis retreated into the remote mountainous regions of Anatolia and into the confines of small, local, self-sufficient, and outwardly isolated communities where they developed not only independent theological reasoning but also a specific system of politico-religious institutions.[11] Therein, Alevis practiced *takiye* (dissimulation), refraining from openly identifying as Alevis and even disguising themselves under the pretense of the mainstream population to avoid further persecution and ensure the survival of the community.[12] Consequently, the utterance of "I am Alevi" in the public sphere was virtually absent for centuries.[13]

For many Alevis, the fall of the Ottoman Empire and the founding of the Turkish Republic under the leadership of Mustafa Kemal Atatürk signified an end to religious persecution as the new state embarked on a campaign of secularization and modernization by initiating a series of reforms.[14] The reforms had a radical impact on Alevis: roads were built through formerly isolated areas, compulsory schooling was introduced, and communications improved, each of which helped alleviate Alevi marginalization and allowed for more active engagement in social and political life.[15] Consequently, many Alevis (particularly Turkish Alevis) became fervent supporters of Ataturk and his reforms.[16]

However, following the death of Atatürk, the country experienced a resurgence of religious movements in Turkish society and politics, which undermined previous secularization efforts. As scholars Koçan and Öncü point out, Alevis have often considered such fundamentalist movements as a threat to their existence.[17] The Alevi community's suspicion toward ultra-nationalist religious movements turned into fear as the late-1970s marked an escalation of fundamentalist violence targeting Alevis across various parts of the country, including Maraş (1978), Malatya (1978), Sivas (1978), and Çorum (1980).[18] Such violent attacks against the Alevi community continued into the early 1990s. For instance, during a cultural Alevi festival in Sivas (1993), a fundamentalist mob set fire to a hotel where many Alevi intellectuals and artists had taken refuge.[19] Thirty-seven people were incinerated as a result of this attack.[20] In March 1995, a violent assault on Alevi coffee houses in an Istanbul neighborhood called Gazi killed two people and left several others injured. The mass rally that followed the shooting quickly turned into a violent clash between police forces and protesters, ending with the death of more than 20 civilians.[21] These events contributed to increased fear and anxiety among Alevis and severely hurt their trust toward non-Alevis, the state, and security forces.

In all, centuries of majority persecution, prejudice, and misconceptions resulted in a state of persistent social disparity affecting the Alevi community in Turkish society.[22] The dominant discourse during Ottoman rule depicted Alevism as heretical and impure, thereby encouraging distorted perceptions of Alevis as sectarian "others," branding Alevis with a stigma from which they still suffer today.[23] Consequently, even in the present day, the practice of *takiye* continues to a certain extent among Alevi circles. For instance, Godzińska points out that it is not very common for an Alevi student to openly acknowledge being Alevi out of fear that "a teacher who finds out that he is Alevi will start to discriminate against him."[24] Similarly, many Alevi public officials choose to keep their religious identity undisclosed due to concerns about discrimination and negative reactions in the workplace.

With the start of Turkey's accession efforts to gain European Union membership in the late 1990s, the prospects for making progress on the Alevi issue began to improve. Yet this new period also coincided with a Sunni-based conservative party, Justice and Development Party (*Adalet ve Kalkınma Partisi*, AKP), coming to power in 2002 (and maintaining majority government control for three subsequent election terms to date), which cast into doubt whether any headway could be made concerning Alevi rights. Although AKP has made some gestures in response to the demands and needs of the Alevi community, many Alevis have found them purely symbolic and remain skeptical about the government's intentions.[25]

In March 2012, Alevis' level of trust for the state was further strained when, due to a statute of limitations issue, a court dropped a case against five people charged as perpetrators of the 1993 Sivas massacre. Alevis and civil rights activists argued that the trial process should have been exempt from the statute of limitations (particularly on the grounds that the massacre amounted to crimes against humanity). However, the court proceeded with the release of the defendants, consequently sparking widespread protests across Turkey.[26]

Theoretical Framework and Hypotheses

To examine collective identity associations within the Alevi community, this study employs the social identity approach as its theoretical framework. The social identity approach combines social identity theory and self-categorization theory. Although social identity theory and self-categorization theory share a number of common assumptions, they have different foci and emphases when it comes to self-conception, group membership, group processes, and intra- and intergroup relations.[27] Social identity theory's primary emphasis is on the role that psychological/motivational factors play in shaping the formation of one's group identity and intergroup relations whereas self-categorization theory focuses more on intragroup processes and cognitive/contextual factors underlying the social categorization of oneself as part of a group.[28] By bringing together the arguments of social identity theory and self-categorization theory under the umbrella of the social identity approach, one can effectively analyze collective identity associations as a combination of socio-historical, psychological/motivational, and cognitive/contextual processes.[29]

Social identity theory asserts that individuals yearn to belong to a social group and achieve higher self-esteem via group membership.[30] Acquisition and maintenance of social identity is accompanied by in-group favoritism and out-group bias, hostility, and discrimination. Self-categorization theory adds to these arguments, suggesting that one's self-categorization preferences are primarily contingent on the salience of personal versus group identity in a given social situation.[31] As such, when group identity becomes salient due to certain contextual factors, individuals tend to perceive themselves and their socio-political environment primarily within in-group terms. The salience of group categorization further stimulates intragroup and inter-group comparisons, which leads to the perceptual accentuation of in-group similarities and out-group differences.[32]

In applying this framework, the study analyzes whether and how socio-historical, psychological/motivational, and cognitive/contextual factors influence the prioritization and strength of Alevi identity. More specifically, the following factors are considered:

(1) Ethnic origin (that is, Kurdish versus Turkish Alevis) (as a socio-historical factor).
(2) Personal experience of discrimination (as a psychological/motivational factor).
(3) Urban/rural residence (as a cognitive/contextual factor).

The first factor under consideration is the role that ethnic origin (as a socio-historical factor) plays in shaping the salience of Alevi identity. Exploring this factor is important because no systematic investigation has been conducted on whether there are any significant differences between Kurdish versus Turkish Alevis regarding the prioritization of and attachment to their Alevi identity. Historically, Kurds enjoyed a great extent of autonomy under Ottoman rule, which allowed them to have their own organizations and internal institutions. On the other hand, Turkish Alevis never enjoyed such autonomy. After the founding of the Republic of Turkey, Kurds lost their autonomy due to the state's homogenization policies that emerged as part of the nation-state building process. Consequently, threats to Kurdish rights, language, and culture led to intense grievances, which in turn essentialized Kurdish ethnic group solidarity.[33] Through various in-group socialization processes such as the maintenance of a Kurdish collective memory through ethnocultural discourse, along with continuing efforts for extended recognition of Kurdish rights and demands, the effects of such socio-historical factors are expected to be transferred to and reflected in the psychological state of Kurdish Alevis. With these considerations in mind, the following are hypothesized:

Hypothesis 1a: Kurdish Alevis are more likely to prioritize their ethnic identity over their religious identity as compared to Turkish Alevis.

Hypothesis 1b: Kurdish Alevis are likely to express lower levels of attachment to their religious identity as compared to Turkish Alevis.

Second, the personal experience of discrimination is expected to be a key psychological/motivational factor that influences the salience of Alevi identity. In an early study, political scientist Parenti notes "Few things so effectively assure the persistence of in-group awareness as out-group rejection."[34] As previous research suggests, discrimination against minorities produces grievances and increases the importance of group identity.[35] For instance, analyzing data on US public opinion, scholar Sanchez shows that exposure to discrimination substantially increases Latino group consciousness.[36] More specifically, Sanchez finds that Latinos who have personally experienced discrimination are significantly more likely to believe in group-based concepts (such as linked fate) and have a heightened sense of ethnic identity.[37] In another recent study, political scientists Barreto and Pedraza demonstrate that discrimination increases the strength of social group identity and partisan unity among Latino voters.[38] Several studies substantiate these findings in other cultural contexts. For example, psychologist Dion and his colleagues find that experiences of ethnic discrimination prompted stronger and more favorable feelings of ethnic identity among university students in Canada.[39] These findings suggest that the higher the levels of perceived and real discrimination against a group, the more likely group members are to seek support from their in-group.[40] Subsequently, negative social forces such as racism and discrimination may lead victimized members of a given community to develop a distrustful perception of the society and the political system they live in,[41] which may further compel them to create subcultures to shield their sense of self and identity.[42] With these considerations in mind, the following are hypothesized:

Hypothesis 2a: Members of the Alevi community who have personally experienced discrimination as Alevis are more likely to prioritize their religious identity over their ethnic identity.

Hypothesis 2b: Members of the Alevi community who have personally experienced discrimination as Alevis are likely to express higher levels of attachment to their religious identity.

A third factor that may affect the salience of one's group identity within the Alevi community is urban/rural residence. As mentioned above, under Ottoman rule, Alevis generally hid their identities through the practice of *takiye* (dissimulation) and lived in small, isolated rural communities. However, once the secularization reforms of the modern Turkish state took effect, Alevis felt relatively less threatened by the Sunni majority. Some scholars suggest that the diminution of immediate existential danger coupled with the opening of a once-hidden community to the outside world contributed to the weakening of solidarity ties among Alevis. For example, according to scholar Zeidan, Alevi internal structural changes were accelerated by massive migration into cities wherein

Alevis underwent a process of secularization and modernization, which broke traditional hereditary ties to the religious hierarchy. Religion lost its relevancy and some even practiced intermarriage. A new generation grew up in the 1960s that had not passed through initiation and was not familiar with the Alevi Way.[43]

This socio-historical context may lead one to expect a less salient Alevi identity among those who live in urban areas compared to those who live in a more endogenous rural community.

However, if one considers the effect of urban/rural residence on Alevi identity as a cognitive/contextual factor (in line with self-categorization theory), opposite expectations may ensue. To elaborate, self-categorization theory puts forth the principle of meta-contrast, which asserts that "a given set of stimuli is more likely to be categorized as a single entity if the intraclass differences between those items are seen to be smaller than the interclass differences between those items and others that are included in a given comparative context."[44] In other words, when a given context includes a comparable out-group, the salience of one's in-group identity and perceptions of group homogeneity increase. By comparison, when such context mainly consists of the members of an in-group, the salience of that in-group and perceived group homogeneity decreases such that group identity gives way to personal identity along with accentuated intragroup individual differences. If that is the case, the salience of Alevi identity for urban Alevis is expected to be higher because they are likely to be in social contexts that contain both Alevis and Sunnis as compared to rural Alevis who tend to be generally surrounded by the members of their in-group while having less frequent encounters with the Sunni out-group. Accordingly, based on the insights derived from self-categorization theory, the following are hypothesized:

Hypothesis 3a: Members of the Alevi community who reside in urban areas of Turkey are more likely to prioritize their religious identity over their ethnic identity compared to those who reside in rural areas.

Hypothesis 3b: Members of the Alevi community who reside in urban areas of Turkey are likely to express higher levels of attachment to their religious identity compared to those who reside in rural areas.

Data and Research Design

To explore group identity associations within the Alevi community in Turkey, this study collected survey data compiled through field research across various cities and provinces, including Adıyaman, Ankara, Antalya, Bitlis, Bursa, Diyarbakır, Elazığ, Eskişehir, İstanbul, İzmit, Muş, Ordu, Samsun, Tokat, Tunceli, Urfa, Yalova, and Van. To recruit participants for the survey, the snowball sampling methodology (also known as chain-referral sampling) was employed. More specifically, in visiting local Alevi cultural centers, neighborhoods, and villages within these cities and provinces, survey participants were randomly identified; they then provided access to a wider pool of respondents in order to help increase the number of observations. In all, 1000 surveys were distributed within the Alevi community. The response rate was approximately 58 percent, thus yielding a total of 580 observations.[45]

Ideally, collecting a nationally representative sample through complete random sampling is most desirable in survey research. However, such a sample of the Alevi community is not attainable for a variety of reasons. While there are more than 50 ethnic groups in Turkey, little is known about their size and spatial distribution because the Turkish government does not collect such data.[46] In fact, as mentioned above, the Turkish state neither formally recognizes Kurds and Alevis as minorities nor separately classifies them in its national census.[47] Furthermore, as political scientist Çarkoğlu points out, there exists a tendency among the respondents who belong to these minority groups to hide their true ethnic and religious affiliations.[48] Instead, driven by feelings of distrust, social desirability issues, and safety concerns, members of these minority groups are inclined to publicly claim the dominant Sunni/Turkish identity as a means to avoid discrimination and minimize any possible threats while appearing more socially acceptable.[49] Accordingly, even though private survey companies at times collect national data by employing random selection techniques, empirical investigations that rely on such data can be misleading due to hidden and misreported information that may be given by minority respondents concerned with their security and social well-being.

Given the limitations that are inherent in obtaining a nationally representative randomized sample of minority groups in Turkey, the application of the snowball sampling method (SSM) for collecting data on the Alevi community serves as a fitting alternative. Indeed, many scholars consider the SSM to be the most effective sampling methodology for research conducted with hidden populations and marginalized groups, especially those living in conflict environments. As scholars Cohen and Arieli point out, "In addition to its effectiveness under conditions of conflict, SSM may, in some cases, actually make the difference between research conducted under constrained conditions and research not conducted at all."[50]

While snowball sampling is generally considered the most effective (and often the only available) methodology for studying hidden populations in conflict environments, one should nevertheless acknowledge that this method may raise certain external validity and selection bias concerns. These methodological concerns tend to arise since data collection efforts depend on chain referrals and the willingness of potential participants, which may lead to samples derived from relatively homogenous social networks—particularly when one relies on a single, concentrated residential area.[51] In recruiting participants and compiling the data for this study, these potential drawbacks were minimized by relying on multiple referrals from different social networks across various parts of the country, thereby generating a large sample size with sufficient variation in the socioeconomic backgrounds of the respondents.

Variables

The first dependent variable is the prioritization of Alevi identity versus ethnic identity. To measure this variable, the respondents were asked: "When you think about your religion/sect/belief and ethnicity, which one best describes how you think of yourself most of the time?" The answers were coded as "1" for "my religion/sect/belief" and "0" for "my ethnicity." The second dependent variable is the strength of group identification within the Alevi community. To measure this variable, the following question was asked: "To what extent do you identify with your religion/sect/

belief?" The responses to this question were coded as "5" for "very much, " "4" for "fairly, " "3" for "to some extent," "2" for "very little," and "1" for "not at all."

The first main independent variable is the ethnicity of the respondent, coded as "0" if the respondent is Turkish and "1" if Kurdish. The second main independent variable is personal experience of discrimination. This variable was measured by asking the following question: "How often, if ever, have you felt you were treated unfairly in your personal life because you are Alevi?" The responses were coded as "5" for "just about always," "4" for "very often," "3" for "sometimes," "2" for "not very often," and "1" for "never." The third main independent variable is the urban/rural residence of the respondent coded as "0" if the respondent resides in a rural area and "1" if the location of the respondent is in an urban area.

Apart from these main variables, key demographic, socioeconomic, and political factors were also controlled for. The survey included questions regarding the respondents' age, gender, education level, ideological affiliation, and household income. Gender was coded as "0" if the respondent is female and "1" if the respondent is male. Education level was coded as "1" for "no formal education," "2" for "primary school," "3" for "middle school," "4" for "high school," and "5" for "college." Regarding the variable "ideology," a code of "1" was assigned if the respondent is leaning toward a leftist ideology and "0" otherwise. Household income (i.e. one's average monthly household income for fiscal year 2011) was coded as "1" for "less than 500TL," "2" for "between 500TL and just under 1000TL," "3" for "between 1000TL and just under 2000TL," "4" for "between 2000TL and just under 3000TL," "5" for "between 3000TL and just under 4000TL," "6" for "between 4000TL and just under 5000TL," and "7" for "more than 5000TL." The region that the survey respondents reside in was also controlled for. Specifically, a dummy variable was generated and coded as "1" if the survey was conducted in Western Turkey and "0" otherwise.[52]

As for the statistical models, binary logistic regression analysis was conducted to examine the prioritization of religious versus ethnic identity and ordered logistic regression analysis was employed for examining the strength of group identification within the Alevi community. Robust standard errors were used to avoid any unspecified heteroscedasticity. For both models, the more conservative two-tailed tests of significance were employed.

Results

Table 1 presents coefficients with robust standard errors for the binary logistic regression analysis regarding the prioritization of religious versus ethnic identity. The results indicate that ethnic origin has a statistically significant effect on the prioritization of one's Alevi identity ($p < 0.01$). Specifically, Kurdish Alevis are less likely to prioritize their religious identity over their ethnic identity, which corroborates Hypothesis 1a. As well, one's experience of discrimination as an Alevi exerts a positive and moderately significant effect on the prioritization of Alevi identity ($p < 0.10$), which is in line with Hypothesis 2a.

Table 1. The Prioritization of Religious Versus Ethnic Identity Within the Alevi Community, Binary Logistic Regression

Independent variables	Coefficients (standard errors)	Changes in predicted probabilities (min→max)
Ethnic origin	−1.113*** (0.313)	−0.256
Discrimination	0.159* (0.092)	0.131
Urban/rural residence	−0.421 (0.341)	
Age	−0.005 (0.008)	
Education	−0.023 (0.099)	
Gender	0.161 (0.232)	
Ideology	0.477 (0.434)	
Income	−0.143* (0.079)	−0.181
Region	−0.409* (0.253)	−0.082
Constant	1.308* (0.704)	
N	441	
Log pseudolikelihood	−251.758	

***$p < 0.01$ level.
**$p < 0.05$ level.
*$p < 0.10$ level.

For exploratory purposes, an interaction term for ethnicity and discrimination was included in an additional analysis. The results demonstrate that even when such interaction is included in the model, Kurdish Alevis are still more likely to prioritize their ethnic identity ($p < 0.01$). At the same time, however, the positive and significant coefficient of the interaction variable indicates that Kurdish Alevis are likely to prioritize their religious identity over their ethnic identity if they are frequently subjected to discriminatory treatment as Alevis ($p < 0.01$).

In contrast to the significant results concerning the effects of ethnicity and personal experience of discrimination on the prioritization of Alevi identity, the urban/rural residence variable does not achieve statistical significance. Therefore, no support is found for Hypothesis 3a. One possible explanation for the insignificant results regarding the urban/rural residence variable is that although the principle of meta-contrast (i.e. increased salience of one's in-group identity in the presence of comparable out-groups) may be at work for those living in urban areas, those who reside in more endogenous rural communities may be more frequently practicing Alevism as a religion and thus also have a heightened sense of being Alevi. As such, the effects of high religiosity in the rural context may cancel out the effects of perceived in-group homogeneity (due to out-group contrast) in the urban context, thereby resulting in similar levels of prioritized Alevi identity for both residence types.

Another reason for such diminished differences between urban and rural Alevis may be due to the fact that rural Alevis are no longer living in isolated communities. Specifically, with the expansion of communication and transportation technologies to the rural regions of Turkey, Alevis residing in such areas have increasingly been exposed to the outside world. Indeed, just as urban Alevis may essentialize their in-group identity as they come into contact with out-groups, rural Alevis may also develop similar feelings via exposure to the mainstream media. Therefore, while for urban Alevis the principle of meta-contrast may be at work through *physical* contact with out-groups, the same principle may be applicable to rural Alevis through *virtual* contact with the same out-groups.[53]

Table 1 also presents the changes in predicted probability that a respondent prioritizes his or her religious identity as each variable moves from its minimum to maximum value with all the other variables held constant at their mean or modal values. These values indicate that there is a 26 percent reduction in one's likelihood of prioritizing his or her Alevi identity if the respondent is Kurdish rather than Turkish. By comparison, a shift from no personal experience of discrimination as an Alevi to the highest level of experiencing discrimination increases the likelihood of prioritizing one's Alevi identity by about 13 percent. As such, the results demonstrate that the effects of ethnic origin and discrimination on the prioritization of Alevi identity are not only statistically significant but also substantively important.

Regarding the control variables, the respondents' income and regional residence have a moderately significant influence on the prioritization of religious versus ethnic identity ($p < 0.10$). In particular, the results indicate that respondents with higher levels of income are less likely to prioritize their Alevi identity. This result is consistent with previous research, which finds that lower income individuals tend to express more devotion to their religion as a means to cope with the psychological effects of the financial adversities they often face.[54] Similarly, respondents who reside in Western Anatolia are less prone to prioritize their Alevi identity. One probable reason for such regional differences is because non-Western regions of Turkey tend to be more conservative and may therefore accentuate one's religious identity over his/her ethnic identity.

The results for the ordered logistic regression analysis regarding the strength of group identification within the Alevi community are provided in Table 2. Similar to the results concerning the prioritization of religious versus ethnic identity, Kurdish Alevis tend to identify less strongly with their religious identity than Turkish Alevis ($p < 0.01$). Indeed, the predicted probability of a respondent to identify "very strongly" with the Alevi community decreases by about fourteen percent if the respondent is Kurdish. These results substantiate Hypothesis 1b. However, neither personal experience of discrimination nor urban/rural residence demonstrates a statistically significant effect on the strength of one's identification as an Alevi. Therefore, Hypotheses 2b and 3b are not supported. Further exploratory analyses indicate that there is no significant interaction between ethnicity and discrimination with respect to the strength of religious identification.

The results further indicate that age and education are statistically significant sociodemographic factors in determining the strength of Alevi identification. More specifically, older respondents tend to report weaker attachments to the Alevi identity ($p < 0.10$). This may be partly because ethnicity-based discourses are more prevalent in

Table 2. The Strength of Group Identification Within the Alevi Community, Ordered Logistic Regression

Independent variables	Coefficients (standard errors)	Changes in predicted probabilities (min→max)				
		1	2	3	4	5
Ethnic origin	−0.679*** (0.259)	0.025	0.033	0.092	−0.011	−0.139
Discrimination	0.010 (0.079)					
Urban/rural residence	−0.368 (0.239)					
Age	−0.012* (0.006)	0.024	0.033	0.100	0.005	−0.164
Education	−0.176** (0.079)	0.018	0.026	0.091	0.027	−0.163
Gender	0.035 (0.182)					
Ideology	0.330 (0.473)					
Income	−0.064 (0.074)					
Region	−0.006 (0.193)					
Cut point 1	−4.809 (0.763)					
Cut point 2	−3.842 (0.731)					
Cut point 3	−2.252 (0.720)					
Cut point 4	−0.717 (0.712)					
N	455					
Log pseudolikelihood	−590.51					

***$p < 0.01$ level.
**$p < 0.05$ level.
*$p < 0.10$ level.

Turkish politics and society (particularly due to the ongoing conflict between Turks and Kurds), which may in turn lead to a more heightened sense of one's ethnic identity while lowering the salience of one's religious identity as one's exposure to such discourses increases with age. Meanwhile, respondents with higher levels of education are likely to report lower levels of group identification within the Alevi community ($p < 0.05$). This may be due to the fact that the education system in Turkey is geared toward promoting Turkish identity and national unity. Accordingly, the more one is exposed to such education, the less attached one may feel to his or her religious identity.

Conclusion

This study systematically explored the factors that affect collective identity associations within the Alevi community in Turkey by employing the social identity approach and examining national survey data collected through fieldwork. The results show that Kurdish Alevis are less likely to prioritize their religious identity over their ethnic identity and express lower levels of identification with their religious identity as compared to Turkish Alevis. The results also indicate that personal experiences of discrimination tend to increase one's prioritization of Alevi identity. Last, the results show no significant differences with respect to group identity between Alevis who reside in urban areas and those who live in rural areas.

The findings of this study not only provide new insights concerning key factors that influence the formation and persistence of Alevi identity, but also bear important policy implications for the course of the Alevi political movement, as well as for broader intergroup relations in Turkey. Although strong in-group identity can be a propellant for positive, progressive political action (particularly for voicing key group demands and interests), extreme levels of in-group identification (particularly in reaction to discriminatory treatment) may actually be more traumatizing than empowering and may result in a polarized society that is ripe for intergroup violence. Accordingly, substantive policies should be implemented toward addressing the demands and needs of Alevis as well as other at-risk minority groups.

The findings of this study also shed light on the primary collective identity of Kurdish Alevis. Scholars have had conflicting claims over this issue.[55] Some suggest that Kurdish Alevis demonstrate greater allegiance to their religious affiliation, whereas others argue that Kurdish nationalism presides over their sectarian differences.[56] Up to this point, no previous work had systematically demonstrated whether Alevi or Kurdish identity comes first for Alevi Kurds. However, the empirical evidence brought forth from this study suggests that Alevi Kurds prioritize their ethnic identity over their religious identity. Based on these findings, another implication of this study is that the promotion of Alevism does not necessarily act as a constraint on ethno-nationalist orientations within the Kurdish community.[57]

These exploratory findings encourage further empirical investigations on the subject. As a future avenue of research, one may examine whether and to what extent the prioritization and strength of group identity among the members of the Alevi community can affect their levels of political participation, forms of political action, and intergroup relations. One may also investigate whether and why shifts in the prioritization of ethnic and religious identities may occur between Kurdish and Turkish Alevis. For example, the reason that Kurdish Alevis are more likely to prioritize their ethnic identity over their religious identity may be because they experience more discrimination as Kurds than as Alevis. A future survey study may further explore this possibility by including comparative questions about personal experience of discrimination due to ethnic versus religious origin. Another important avenue would be to extent the scope of the fieldwork by conducting surveys in additional parts of Turkey. One primary location to expand the existing data-set is Hatay with its large Arabic Alevi (a.k.a. Nusayri) community. Expanding the data in such way would provide scholars the opportunity to observe whether ethnic identity presides over religious identity for Arabic Alevis in a manner similar to Kurdish Alevis. One may also carry out further data collection efforts by surveying Alevi immigrants residing in various European countries, particularly in Germany.[58] As for the questions surrounding urban/rural context, more nuanced survey questions may help reveal if the link between urban/rural residence and Alevi identity is mediated through one's level of religiosity and/or contact with out-groups. Conducting survey experiments with innovative scenarios would also be highly useful. In all, further systematic research will help advance the accumulation of our knowledge in this area of study.

Acknowledgements

The author is grateful to Arif and Gül Şirin for their invaluable support throughout her field research in Turkey. The author would also like to thank Leonie Huddy, Kathy Staudt, José D. Villalobos, Cengiz Erişen, Başak Yavcan, Gizem Arıkan, and the anonymous reviewers for their instructive comments and suggestions, as well as Anna Haro for her research assistance.

Notes

1. See, for example, van Zomeren et al., "Exploring Psychological," 353–72.
2. Coy and Woehrle, *Social Conflicts*, 41–63.
3. Koçan and Öncü, "Citizen Alevi in Turkey," 464–89 and Ocak, *Türk Süfiliğine Bakışlar*. Some of the differences that distinguish Alevis from Sunnis include the fact that Alevis (1) use wine and music for religious ceremonial functions, (2) do not observe the five daily prayers, Ramadan, and the Haj, (3) do not segregate women and men during worship, and (4) use *cemevis* instead of mosques as their place of worship. See Zeidan, "The Alevi of Anatolia," 76.
4. Kosnick, "Speaking in One's Own Voice," 979–94; Özalay, "Minorities in Turkey;" and Şener, *Yaşayan Alevilik*.
5. Kosnick, "Speaking in One's Own Voice;" Vorhoff, "Let's Reclaim," 220–52; and Zeidan, "The Alevi of Anatolia." Generally, non-Alevis are not easily admitted to the Alevi community and inter-marriage is not widely tolerated.
6. Kosnick, "Speaking in One's Own Voice."
7. Çelik, "Alevis, Kurds, Hemsehris," 141–57; Güzeldere, "Turkey: Regional Elections," 291–306; and van Bruinessen, "Shifting National," 39–52. As the largest ethnic minority group in Turkey, Kurds constitute approximately 20 percent of the total population in Turkey.
8. Mutlu, "Ethnic Kurds in Turkey," 517–41.
9. Erman and Göker, "Alevi Politics," 99–118.
10. See http://www.turkstat.gov.tr. See also Vorhoff, "Let's Reclaim;" Özalay, "Minorities in Turkey;" and Shindeldecker, *Turkish Alevis Today*.
11. Vorhoff, "Let's Reclaim." See also Canbakal, "An Exercise," 253–71.
12. Ortaylı, "Alevilik, Nusayrilik," 35–47; Vorhoff, "Let's Reclaim;" and Zeidan, "The Alevi of Anatolia."
13. Koçan and Öncü, "Citizen Alevi in Turkey."
14. Kosnick, "Speaking in One's Own Voice."
15. Zeidan, "The Alevi of Anatolia."
16. Vorhoff, "Let's Reclaim."
17. Koçan and Öncü, "Citizen Alevi in Turkey;" see also Erman and Göker, "Alevi Politics" and Ocak, *Türk Süfiliğine Bakışlar*.
18. Çelik, "Alevis, Kurds, Hemsehris."
19. Erman and Göker, "Alevi Politics" and van Bruinessen, "Kurds, Turks and the Alevi," 7–10.

20. Zeidan, "The Alevi of Anatolia."
21. Vorhoff, "Let's Reclaim."
22. Zeidan, "The Alevi of Anatolia."
23. Ibid.
24. Godziñska, "Rituals of Alevi," 57.
25. Soner and Toktaş, "Alevis and Alevism," 419–34.
26. "Turkish Police Fire Teargas After Controversial Court Ruling," *Reuters*, March 13, 2012.
27. Huddy, "From Social to Political," 127–56; Hogg, "Intragroup Processes," 65–93; and Hornsey, "Social Identity Theory," 204–22.
28. Huddy, "From Social to Political."
29. Hornsey, "Social Identity Theory."
30. Tajfel, *Human Groups* and Tajfel and Turner, "An Integrative Theory," 33–47.
31. Turner, "Social Categorization," 77–122; Turner et al., *Rediscovering the Social Group*; Oakes, "The Salience of Social Categories," 117–41; and Oakes et al., *Stereotyping and Social Reality*.
32. Ibid.
33. Gürbey, "Peaceful Settlement," 57–90; Eriten and Romine, "Instrumental and Symbolic Sources;" and Barkey and Fuller, *Turkey's Kurdish Question*.
34. Parenti, "Ethnic Politics," 723.
35. Finke and Harris, "Wars and Rumors;" Fox, *Ethnoreligious Conflict*; and Gurr, "Why Minorities Rebel," 161–201.
36. Sanchez, "The Political Role," 435–46.
37. Ibid.
38. Barreto and Pedraza, "The Renewal and Persistence," 595–605.
39. Dion and Earn, "The Phenomenology," 944–50 and Dion et al., "Personality-Based Hardiness," 517–36.
40. Barreto and Pedraza, "The Renewal and Persistence."
41. Peffley and Hurwitz, *Justice in America*.
42. Davey, "Ethnic Identification" and Kaspar and Noh, "Discrimination and Identity," 1–70. Alternatively, as Kaspar and Noh, "Discrimination and Identity," note, experience or anticipation of discrimination may prompt people to distance themselves from their in-group and develop negative perceptions of their own community. Thus, some individuals may choose to minimize the salience of their ethnic and/or religious identity to escape discriminatory treatment, gain acceptance by the dominant majority, and improve their socioeconomic status. However, individuals who choose this option may face double rejection by the dominant out-group that they seek to acculturate into as well as by their own in-group members who no longer perceive them as part of the community.
43. Zeidan, "The Alevi of Anatolia," p. 77.
44. Turner, "Social Categorization" and Haslam et al., "Social Identity Salience," 810.
45. Mainly due to a number of missing observations within the 580 completed surveys, the final sample sizes dropped to some extent in the statistical analyses. One of the key reasons for such missing observations and the subsequent drop in sample size is that although the participants were informed that their responses would be completely anonymous, some of them were still hesitant to answer certain survey questions (especially questions concerning discrimination as well as questions inquiring about one's socio-demographic information). This is understandable given the fact that the survey was conducted with members of a hidden minority population.
46. Andrews, *Türkiye'de Etnik Gruplar* and Koç et al., "Demographic Differentials," 447–57.
47. Mutlu, "Ethnic Kurds in Turkey," 517–41.
48. Çarkoğlu, "Political Preferences," 273–92.
49. Ibid.
50. Cohen and Arieli, "Field Research," 423.
51. Ibid.
52. The reason that a regional dummy was included as a control is because Western Turkey is generally less conservative, more urbanized, more industrialized, and demographically diverse (due to the high

levels of immigration that this region attracts) as compared to other parts of the country, which may lead to cross-regional differences in collective identity associations among the Alevi community. The Western Turkey regional dummy variable consisted of surveys conducted in Bursa, İstanbul, Eskişehir, İzmit, and Yalova.

53. The author would like to thank İnan Keser, a sociologist from Dicle University, Turkey, for his insightful suggestions regarding this point.
54. See, for example, Rodney, "The Economics of Piety," 483–503 and Schieman, "Socioeconomic Status," 25–51.
55. Çelik, "Alevis, Kurds, Hemsehris" and Stewart, "Modernity and the Alevis," 50–60.
56. See, for example, Çelik, "Alevis, Kurds, Hemsehris;" Erman and Göker, "Alevi Politics;" Stewart, "Modernity and the Alevis;" van Bruinessen, "Kurds, Turks and the Alevi;" and van Bruinessen, "Aslını İnkar Eden," 1–24.
57. The author would like to thank the anonymous reviewer for this important insight.
58. See Özyürek, "The Light of the Alevi," 233–53.

References

Andrews, Peter A. *Türkiye'de Etnik Gruplar* [Ethnic Groups in Turkey]. İstanbul: Ant Yayınları, 1992.
Barkey, Henri J., and Graham Fuller. *Turkey's Kurdish Question.* New York: Rowman and Little Field, 1998.
Barreto, Matt A., and Francisco I. Pedraza. "The Renewal and Persistence of Group Identification in American Politics." *Electoral Studies* 28, no. 4 (2009): 595–605.
van Bruinessen, Martin. "Kurds, Turks and the Alevi Revival in Turkey." *Middle East Report,* 7–10, July/ September 1996.
van Bruinessen, Martin. "Aslını İnkar Eden Haramzadedir! The Debate on the Ethnic Identity of the Kurdish Alevis." In *Syncretistic Religious Communities in the Near East: Collected Papers of the Symposium Berlin 1995,* edited by Krisztina Kehl-Bodrogi, Barbara Kellner-Heinkele, and Anke Otter-Beaujean, 1–24. Leiden: Brill, 1997.
van Bruinessen, Martin. "Shifting National and Ethnic Identities: The Kurds in Turkey and the European Diaspora." *Journal of Muslim Minority Affairs* 18, no. 1 (1998): 39–52.
Canbakal, Hülya. "An Exercise in Denominational Geography in Search of Ottoman Alevis." *Turkish Studies* 6, no. 2 (2005): 253–271.
Çarkoğlu, Ali. "Political Preferences of the Turkish Electorate: Reflections of an Alevi-Sunni Cleavage." *Turkish Studies* 6, no. 2 (2005): 273–292.
Çelik, Ayşe Betül. "Alevis, Kurds, Hemsehris: Resurgence of Alevi Kurdish Identity in the 1990s." In *Turkey's Alevi Enigma: A Comprehensive Overview,* edited by Paul J. White and Joost Jongerden, 141–157. Leiden: Brill, 2003.
Cohen, Nissim, and Tamar Arieli. "Field Research in Conflict Environments: Methodological Challenges and Snowball Sampling." *Journal of Peace Research* 48, no. 4 (2011): 423–435.
Coy, Patrick G., and Lynne M. Woehrle, eds. *Social Conflicts and Collective Identities.* Lanham, MD: Rowman & Littlefield, 2000.

Davey, A. G. "Ethnic Identification, Preference and Sociometric Choice." In *Self-concept, Achievement and Multicultural Education*, edited by Gajendra K. Verma and Christopher Bagley, 60–69. London: MacMillan, 1982.

Dion, Kenneth L., Karen K. Dion, and Anita W. Pak. "Personality-Based Hardiness as a Buffer for Discrimination-Related Stress in Members of Toronto's Chinese Community." *Canadian Journal of Behavioural Science* 24, no. 4 (1992): 517–536.

Dion, Kenneth L., and Brian M. Earn. "The Phenomenology of Being a Target of Prejudice." *Journal of Personality and Social Psychology* 32, no. 5 (1975): 944–950.

Eriten, Nilüfer Duygu, and Jennifer Romine. "Instrumental and Symbolic Sources of Ethnic Conflict: Application to the Kurdish Conflict in Turkey." Unpublished manuscript, University of Illinois, Urbana-Champaign, 2008.

Erman, Tahire, and Emrah Göker. "Alevi Politics in Contemporary Turkey." *Middle Eastern Studies* 36, no. 4 (2000): 99–118.

Finke, Roger, and Jaime Harris. "Wars and Rumors of Wars: Explaining Religiously Motivated Violence." In *Religion, Politics, Society and the State*, edited by Jonathan Fox, 53–71. New York: Oxford University Press, 2012.

Fox, Jonathan. *Ethnoreligious Conflict in the Late Twentieth Century*. Lanham, MD: Lexington Books, 2002.

Godzińska, Marzena. "Rituals of Alevi and Bektashi Religious Minorities – The Religious Relations in the Sunni Majority Environment in Secular Turkey." *Asia & Pacific Studies* 4 (2007): 41–60.

Gürbey, Gülistan. "Peaceful Settlement of Turkey's Kurdish Conflict through Autonomy." In *The Kurdish Conflict in Turkey: Obstacles and Chances for Peace and Democracy*, edited by Ferhad Ibrahim and Gülistan Gürbey, 57–90. New York: St. Martin's Press, 2000.

Gurr, Ted. "Why Minorities Rebel: A Global Analysis of Communal Mobilization and Conflict Since 1945." *International Political Science Review* 14, no. 2 (1993): 161–201.

Güzeldere, Ekrem Eddy. "Turkey: Regional Elections and the Kurdish Question." *Caucasian Review of International Affairs* 3, no. 3 (2009): 291–306.

Haslam, S., Penelope J. Alexander, Katherine J. Oakes, John C. Reynolds, and Turner. "Social Identity Salience and the Emergence of Stereotype Consensus." *Personality and Social Psychology Bulletin* 25, no. 7 (1999): 809–818.

Hogg, Michael A. "Intragroup Processes, Group Structure, and Social Identity." In *Social Groups and Identities: Developing the Legacy of Henri Tajfel*, edited by W. Peter Robinson, 65–93. Oxford: Butterworth-Heinemann, 1996.

Hornsey, Matthew J. "Social Identity Theory and Self-categorization Theory: A Historical Review." *Social and Personality Psychology Compass* 2, no. 1 (2008): 204–222.

Huddy, Leonie. "From Social to Political Identity: A Critical Examination of Social Identity Theory." *Political Psychology* 22, no. 1 (2001): 127–156.

Kaspar, Violet, and Samuel Noh. "Discrimination and Identity: An Overview of Theoretical and Empirical Research." *Paper Series of Multiculturalism Program of Canadian Heritage*, 1–70. Ottawa: Canadian Heritage/Multiculturalism Branch, 2001.

Koç, İsmet, Attila Hancıoğlu, and Alanur Çavlın. "Demographic Differentials and Demographic Integration of Turkish and Kurdish Populations in Turkey." *Population Research and Policy Review* 27, no. 4 (2008): 447–457.

Koçan, Gürcan, and Ahmet Öncü. "Citizen Alevi in Turkey: Beyond Confirmation and Denial." *Journal of Historical Sociology* 17, no. 4 (2004): 464–489.

Kosnick, Kira. "Speaking in One's Own Voice: Representational Strategies of Alevi Turkish Migrants on Open-Access Television in Berlin." *Journal of Ethnic and Migration Studies* 30, no. 5 (2004): 979–994.

Mutlu, Servet. "Ethnic Kurds in Turkey: A Demographic Study." *International Journal of Middle East Studies* 28, no. 4 (1996): 517–541.

Oakes, Penelope J. "The Salience of Social Categories." In *Rediscovering the Social Group: A Self-categorization Theory*, edited by John C. Turner, Michael A. Hogg, Penelope J. Oakes, Stephen D. Reicher, and Margaret S. Wetherell, 117–141. Oxford: Blackwell, 1987.

Oakes, Penelope J., A. Alexander Haslam, and John C. Turner. *Stereotyping and Social Reality*. Oxford: Blackwell, 1994.

Ocak, Ahmet Yaşar. *Türk Süfîliğine Bakışlar*. İstanbul: Iletişim Yayınları, 2002.

Ortaylı, İlber. "Alevilik, Nusayrilik ve Bab-ı Ali." In *Tarihi ve Kültürel Boyutlarıyla Türkiye'de Bektaşiler, Aleviler, Nusayriler*, edited by Irene Melikof, Hakan Yavuz, Hamid Algar, Kais Firro, Karin Vorhoff, David Shankland, İlber Ortaylı, Butrus Abu-Manneh, Mustafa Öz, Niyazi Öktem, İsmail Engin, İlyas Uzum, and Ahmet, Yaşar Ocak, 35–47. İstanbul: Ensar Neşriyat, 1999.

Özalay, Eren. "Minorities in Turkey: The Identity of the Alevis in accordance with the EU Legislation." Unpublished manuscript, University of Göttingen, 2006.

Özyürek, Esra. "The Light of the Alevi Fire Was Lit in Germany and then Spread to Turkey: A Transnational Debate on the Boundaries of Islam." *Turkish Studies* 10, no. 2 (2009): 233–253.

Parenti, Michael. "Ethnic Politics and the Persistence of Ethnic Identification." *American Political Science Review* 61, no. 3 (1967): 717–726.

Peffley, Mark, and Jon Hurwitz. *Justice in America: The Separate Realities of Blacks and Whites*. Cambridge: Cambridge University Press, 2010.

Rodney, Stark. "The Economics of Piety: Religious Commitment and Social Class." In *Issues in Social Inequality*, edited by Gerald W. Thielbar and Saul D. Feldman, 483–503. Boston, MA: Little, Brown, 1972.

Sanchez, Gabriel R. "The Political Role of Group Consciousness in Latino Public Opinion." *Political Research Quarterly* 59, no. 3 (2006): 435–446.

Schieman, Scott. "Socioeconomic Status and Beliefs About God's Influence in Everyday Life." *Sociology of Religion* 71, no. 1 (2010): 25–51.

Şener, Cemal. *Yaşayan Alevilik*. İstanbul: Anadolu Matbaası, 1994.

Soner, Bayram Ali, and Şule Toktaş. "Alevis and Alevism in the Changing Context of Turkish Politics: The Justice and Development Party's Alevi Opening." *Turkish Studies* 12, no. 3 (2011): 419–434.

Shindeldecker, John. *Turkish Alevis Today*. İstanbul: Sahkulu, 1998.

Stewart, Michael. "Modernity and the Alevis of Turkey: Identity, Challenges and Change." *Journal of International Relations* 9, no. 1 (2007): 50–60.

Tajfel, Henri. *Human Groups and Social Categories*. Cambridge: Cambridge University Press, 1981.

Tajfel, Henri, and John C. Turner. "An Integrative Theory of Intergroup Conflict." In *The Social Psychology of Intergroup Relations*, edited by William G. Austin and Stephen Worchel, 33–47. Monterey, CA: Brooks/Cole, 1979.

Turner, John C. "Social Categorization and the Self-concept: A Social Cognitive Theory of Group Behaviour." In *Advances in Group Processes*, edited by E.J. Lawler, 77–122. Greenwich, CT: JAI Press, 1985.

Turner, John C., Michael A. Hogg, Penelope J. Oakes, Stephen D. Reicher, and Margaret S. Wetherell. *Rediscovering the Social Group: A Self-categorization Theory*. Oxford: Blackwell, 1987.

Vorhoff, Karin. "Let's Reclaim Our History and Culture! Imagining Alevi Community in Contemporary Turkey." *Die Welt des Islams, New Series* 38, no. 2 (1998): 220–252.

Zeidan, David. "The Alevi of Anatolia." *Middle East Review of International Affairs* 3, no. 4 (1999): 74–89.

van Zomeren, Martijn, Russell Spears, and Colin Wayne Leach. "Exploring Psychological Mechanisms of Collective Action: Does Relevance of Group Identity Influence How People Cope with Collective Disadvantage?" *British Journal of Social Psychology* 47, no. 2 (2008): 353–372.

Ethnicity and Trust in National and International Institutions: Kurdish Attitudes toward Political Institutions in Turkey

EKREM KARAKOÇ

Department of Political Science, Binghamton University (SUNY), Binghamton, NY, USA

ABSTRACT *As political trust literature has focused on its political and economical determinants, the linkage between ethnicity and trust in domestic and international institutions has been largely overlooked with a few notable exceptions. This study aims to underline this linkage and offer several hypotheses to test them in Turkish context. Using the European Social Survey conducted in 2008, this study finds that, though Kurds have low levels of trust in domestic institutions, their distrust is not uniform across all institutions. Second, it finds that Kurds are pro-international institutions; that is, compared to Turks, they hold higher trust in international institutions. Finally, it finds that, contrary to the studies on the winner/ loser debate in long-standing democracies, winners in general and Kurdish winners, those who voted for the Justice and Development Party, the winning party in the 2007 election— are not distinguishable in their level of trust in political institutions from the rest of society.*

Introduction

The decline in trust in institutions in many established and new democracies has resulted in a significant literature on the determinants of political trust.[1] Concern over declining trust in political institutions is not surprising, given that scholars note that citizens' trust in political institutions enhances the legitimacy and effectiveness of democratic governance, whereas a lack of trust creates concern about the survivability of the regime.[2] So far, the literature on political trust has focused primarily on cultural and institutional factors, growing inequality, the post-communist legacy and other factors such as ideology and government performances in political and economic spheres.[3]

These studies have made an important contribution to our understanding of trust in institutions, but they also have several important shortcomings. First, despite the fact that most countries are composed of different ethnic groups, ethnicity has been side-lined in this literature, with a few notable exceptions. In particular, these studies ignore the fact that ethnic groups may have a positive or negative experience of political institutions, depending on the extent to which those institutions represent these groups' policy preferences and how they perceive the performance of those institutions. Second, these studies focus exclusively on domestic institutions, ignoring attitudes toward international institutions. And finally, and following from the first two shortcomings, they overlook the impact of ethnicity on trust in international organizations. This study aims to fill this gap in the literature by testing a number of hypotheses within the Turkish context, where Turkish Kurds (Kurds from now on) make up around 14–20 percent of the population.[4]

Using the European Social Survey (ESS) conducted in 2008, this study finds that, though Kurds have low levels of trust in domestic institutions, their distrust is not uniform across all institutions. Kurds have little trust in parliament, the judiciary and the police, but more trust in political parties. Second, it finds that Kurds are pro-international institutions; that is, compared to Turks, they hold higher trust in international institutions, especially the European Parliament (EP) and the United Nations (UN). Finally, it finds that, contrary to the studies on the winner/loser debate in long-standing democracies,[5] winners in general and Kurdish winners in particular—that is, those who voted for the Justice and Development Party (AKP, *Adalet ve Kalkınma Partisi*), the winning party in the 2007 election—are not distinguishable in their level of trust in institutions from the rest of society.

This study makes several contributions to the literature on political trust and Turkish studies. First, it contributes to the understanding of the understudied linkage between ethnicity and political trust.[6] Second, its findings suggest that Kurds feel more alienated toward state institutions. Finally, this study provides evidence that ethnic groups such as Kurds for the reasons discussed below are more likely to have higher trust in international organizations.

Determinants of Political Trust

Political trust is a multifaceted concept, and it is important to clarify how it is used in this study. Some define political trust a commodity that political actors use to achieve their goals, while others define it as the willingness of people to follow political leaders. In line with Hetherington and others, this study defines political trust as "the degree to which people perceive that government is producing outcomes consistent with their expectations."[7] Many studies note that the absence of trust in political institutions, ranging from parliament to the judiciary, has deleterious consequences on both citizens' everyday life and effective governance. Citizens who distrust political institutions that are supposed to represent their interests tend to disregard the law by, for example, engaging in tax avoidance, and they have less attachment to democratic governance.[8] In contrast, with increased political trust, citizens will increase their political participation and their support for democratic ideals, ensuring regime stability. High trust also means citizens demonstrate greater compliance to the political authority's laws and regulations. This compliance facilitates the policy-making process[9] because high trust is cost-effective, as governments do not need to utilize their enforcement rules and agencies for other purposes.

One of the dominant approaches in the political trust literature argues that citizens' perception of institutions' performance on political issues affects their levels of political trust. A number of studies find that an assessment of political institutions on the basis of things such as freedom of speech and association and the level of crime significantly affect political trust.[10] Another dominant view emphasizes the role of economic factors in determining the level of political trust among citizens. The basic argument of the latter approach is that those who are satisfied with the governments' handling of economic growth, job creation and corruption are more likely to have higher levels of political trust.[11]

The political-trust literature, emphasizing on political and economic factors, has largely overlooked the relationship between ethnicity and political trust even in countries where ethnic minorities make up a significant percentage of the population.[12] The starting point is straightforward: If ethnic groups perceive as a result of their interaction with political institutions that they are deprived of their political and cultural rights and are economically disadvantaged relative to the ethnic majority, they are more likely to hold low levels of trust in political institutions. If these disadvantages persist—that is, if these minorities do not have a voice or these institutions do not effectively represent their political and economic demands—distrust toward political institutions will be high. In contrast, even if an ethnic minority was discriminated against in the past, if it perceives that a new government and other institutions defend its basic rights and represent its interests, its level of political trust will be the same as, or even higher than, that of the ethnic majority.

Perhaps the most famous case is that of the USA, where African Americans historically faced discrimination in all spheres of life. However, beginning around the time of the Civil Rights Act of 1960, which aimed to remove discriminatory laws and practices, there is a steady increase of trust in institutions among Blacks. Blendon et al. find that Hispanics and African Americans, who look to the federal government to redress historical injustices and inequality, express higher levels of trust in the federal government than do whites.[13] Lawrence, in contrast, using the National Election Study, shows that in the 1960s, when the civil rights movement had begun, Blacks had higher levels of political trust, but that since then their level of political trust has fallen to about that of the general population.[14] Rahn and Rudolph find that the level of political trust among ethnic groups in American cities depends on how ethnic groups are represented by the city political institutions.[15] Hetherington finds no relationship between ethnic minorities and the level of trust in government, while King finds that white Americans are less trusting of government than minorities.[16]

For other countries, the literature is scarce. Despite the fact that ethnic groups in the Baltic countries and Russia make up a significant proportion of the population, to our knowledge only a few studies examine the relationship between ethnicity and political trust. Among these notable exceptions, Dowley and Silver find low levels of trust among Russian ethnic minority groups toward political institutions in the Baltic countries, while for other minorities there is no apparent pattern in other post-communist countries.[17] Ehin supports their finding that in the Baltic countries there is a significant gap in trust in institutions between ethnic Russians and the ethnic majority.[18] This gap may be due to the fact that in the aftermath of the transition to democracy ethnic Russians in the Baltic countries lost their prestigious status during former Soviet Union. Stickley et al. examine the level of trust in Russia in a number of institutions, such as parliament and the president, and find that non-ethnic Russians are not distinguishable from ethnic Russians. In their cross-national study, Elkins and Sides find that minorities at risk have less attachment to the state.[19]

In brief, except in these studies on the Baltic countries and Russia, the relationship between political trust and ethnicity is largely overlooked. The reasons for the degree of trust among ethnic groups are still to be fully understood. This study examines the Turkish case, where political violence still threatens the country as a result of the unresolved Kurdish problem. By doing so, it adds to this neglected but important research area in the political-trust literature.

Political Trust and Ethnicity in the Turkish Context

There are many reasons to believe that political issues are as important as economic ones in affecting political trust in Turkey. In the post-coup era that began in 1983, the country witnessed a substantial economic recovery as it embarked on partial economic liberalization. By the early 1990s, despite the existence of unstable governments and frequent elections, trust in institutions remained relatively high. Distrust in institutions increased significantly in the 1990s. Corruption scandals and the subsequent economic crisis in the 1990s, along with unstable coalition governments, tarnished the image of parliament and political parties. And between 2002 and 2007, as a result of economic growth and stable governance ushered in by the one-party government, political trust has increased noticeably.

To show how political trust changed over the years, the World Values Surveys (WVSs) conducted from 1990 to 2007 in Turkey provide us valuable empirical data.[20] The WVSs ask respondents whether they have confidence in a number of institutions. The options are coded as follows: 1, no trust; 2, not very much trust; 3, quite a lot of trust; and 4, a great deal of trust. Comparison of the last four WVSs in Turkey—the WVS 1990, the WVS 1996, the WVS 2001 and the WVS 2007—shows that confidence in political institutions, including the parliament, political parties and other actors, declined between 1990 and 2001 and then increased by 2007. For example, trust in parliament was about 2.67 out of 4 in 1990. Subsequent economic and political crises decreased the level of trust first to 2.34 in 1996 and then to 2.27 in 2001. After a 5-year single-party government and continuous economic growth, trust in parliament returned to the 1990 level, 2.65, in 2007. Trust in parties decreased from 1.93 in 1996 to 1.87 in 2001, but then later exceeded its 1996 level in 2007, reaching 2.13. Similarly, trust in the justice system increased from 2.86 in 1996 to 3.02 in 2007.[21] The AKP's positive economic performance—

indicated by a significant jump in GDP *per capita*, increased spending on social programs and healthcare reforms—as well as its pro-EU policies, democratizing reforms and other factors were potentially responsible for the increased trust in institutions in 2007, when the last WVS was conducted in Turkey.

Although political trust has increased in Turkey in recent years, the literature suggests strong reasons to doubt that Turkish Kurds hold similar levels of trust in institutions, as do ethnic Turks. Tezcür, using Mann's (2005) terminology, states that "Turkish state policies toward the Kurdish speaking people involved institutional coercion, policed repression, violent repression, and unpremeditated mass killings."[22] Although there have been some improvements in the social and cultural rights of Kurds since the late 1980s, the conflict between the state and Kurdish demands persists. Beginning in the early years of the republic, state authorities saw Kurds not as a separate ethnic group with a distinct language and culture, but as a group that needed to be assimilated into "Turkishness."[23] Starting from the Sheikh Said rebellion in 1925, and especially after the Resettlement Law of 1934, Kurds were resettled into the western part of the country, whereas migrants from the Caucasus and other regions replaced them in formerly Kurdish-dominated areas.[24] This resettlement policy toward Kurds was phased out after 1950, but the backbone of this policy, the rejection the Kurds and their language, remained in effect until the 1990s. The word "Kurds" appeared for the first time in major news outlet only in the early 1990s.[25] Nevertheless, in the post-1980s, the Turkish state has chosen to equate Kurdish demands—such as the recognition of Kurds as a separate ethnic group with a distinct language, as well as including the Kurdish language in the school curriculum—with the Kurdistan Workers' Party (PKK). This strategy worked to solidify Turkish opinion behind the state, but it reduced Kurdish support for the state.[26]

In addition, the economic underdevelopment of Kurdish-dominated region further alienates Kurds toward the state and its institutions. The poverty rate and the unemployment rate, especially among the young are significantly higher among Kurds. Those who find jobs do so in seasonal labor in neighboring cities or beyond. In addition to the poverty rate, compared to non-Kurds, Kurds have lower levels of education; about 26 percent of Kurds have no schooling whatsoever, while the same is true for six percent of the rest of the population.[27]

A recent survey research confirms that Kurds have developed an attitude different from that of other Turks toward the Kurdish problem in general and state institutions in particular. When asked about the causes of Kurdish problem, Kurds point to their region's economic backwardness, the state's discriminatory policies toward Kurds and the denial of Kurdish identity as most important. Similarly to the Turkish state's position, ethnic Turks treat the Kurdish problem as having resulted from interference by foreign powers, the PKK and Kurds' desire to separate from Turkey.

In sum, based on the discussion above, one expects that Kurds' historical political exclusion and economic underdevelopment—whether they have resulted from geographic reasons or past and current governments' economic policies—have led Kurds to believe that political institutions do not treat them fairly and do not represent their policy preferences on Kurdish problem.[28] Thus, this study suggests[29]:

Hypothesis 1: Kurds are likely to hold lower levels of political trust than Turks.

However, political trust among Kurds may differ depending on whether they voted for the governing party or another party. Those who voted for an election's winners show much more satisfaction with democracy and develop positive attitudes toward the political system.[30] In particular, winners feel that their policy preferences will be represented by the government for which they have voted, and the party in government, as a rational actor that wants to keep its electoral base in the next election, is obliged to keep its promises. The AKP governments have permitted broadcasting in Kurdish, founded a new Kurdish public channel, TRT-6 (Turkish Radio-Television Channel 6), and lifted the emergency law in the southeast.[31] They have also launched many social programs, such as increasing the number of green cards, which allow families in need to use hospitals for free and to have their medicine paid for by the government. In addition, needy families in the region receive monthly paychecks, provided that they send their children to primary school. As a result of these policies, which matched the preferences of most Kurdish voters, the AKP has garnered significant votes in the Kurdish region, sharing Kurdish votes with the Kurdish ethnic party.

Therefore, second hypothesis suggests that Kurds who voted for the AKP will have much higher levels of political trust than Kurds who voted for other parties.

Hypothesis 2: Kurds who voted for the AKP should have much higher levels of political trust than Kurds that vote for other parties.

Trust in International Institutions and Ethnicity

The linkage between trust in national and international institutions has recently received some attention.[32] The Transfer Heuristic approach argues that those who are cynical about domestic political institutions "transfer" their distrust to international institutions. The reasoning is that if their own government cannot fulfill their expectations, international bodies will also be less capable or trustable to function as desired.[33] Although the main focus of the studies that examine this linkage has been on EU enlargement, similar findings have been found with regard to other international organizations such as the UN. Trust in domestic political institutions is strongly associated with trust in the UN; a recent study on Turkey shows that political trust is positively associated with trust in both the UN and the EU.[34] Brewer et al. find that political trust boosts trust in other nations. Other studies examine trust in international bodies but ignore the linkage between trust in domestic institutions and trust in international organizations. For example, Hessami examines trust in the World Bank, the International Monetary Fund and the World Trade Organization but overlooks the importance of political trust and focuses instead on demographic variables and globalization.[35] Others challenge this view. In particular, the proponents of Substitution approach argue that those with low trust, who are skeptical of domestic political institutions, can instead place their trust in international institutions because they believe that those international institutions will compensate for "unaddressed domestic national shortcomings or failings."[36] Nevertheless, the empirical evidence based on studies above favors the former approach, which leads to offer following hypothesis:

Hypothesis 3: Those who have higher levels of trust in domestic institutions will have higher levels of trust in international organizations.

Insofar as these hypotheses have been tested in regards to ethnicity, studies on the Baltic countries suggest that Russian ethnic minorities are less trusting of international institutions, while ethnic minorities in Central and Eastern Europe are more trusting.[37] The Turkish context also offers some important insights into the nature of this relationship. The high number of applications by Kurds to the European Court of Human Rights (ECJR) may provide evidence that citizens distrustful of domestic institutions seek justice in international bodies.[38] As a result of the democratic deficit in Turkey for Kurds, Kurds tend to support Turkey's EU-membership process more than does the rest of the population.[39] Not surprisingly, Pro-BDP (Peace and Democracy Party, *Barış ve Demokrasi Partisi*) Kurds have been pressing the EU to make the resolution of the Kurdish problem a condition for Turkish EU membership.[40] This may suggests that rather than Transfer Heuristic approach, Substitution approach may be relevant to the Kurdish case as a significant number of Kurds tend to turn their faces to international organizations whether ECJR or EU in case they feel that domestic institutions cannot be a remedy to their problems.

Trusting international organizations, more than domestic ones is not surprising given that international institutions, in particular those associated with the EU, have also been critical of human-rights violations in Turkey and sympathetic toward Kurdish social and cultural demands. During the 1990s, the EP condemned the loss of human life when the police or army clashed with and killed Kurdish protestors.[41] It issued numerous statements that urged Turkey to democratize its laws and improve its human-rights records. Although the EP is an ineffective body within the EU, its statements resonated favorably among the Kurdish population. In sum, the discussion above leads to the following hypothesis:

Hypothesis 4: Kurds will hold higher levels of trust in international organizations, compared to Turks.

Data and Methods

This study uses the 2008 round (Round 4) of the ESS to test the hypotheses offered above.[42] The survey was conducted in Turkey in the fall 2008, about 1 year after the election. The sample size of this nation-wide survey for this study ranges from 1750 to 1056, depending on the model.[43] For robustness check, this study replicated the analysis using Round 2 of the ESS, conducted in 2002/2003.[44]

Dependent Variable

The ESS asks how much one trusts given political institutions. The institutions are parliament, political parties, the judiciary and the police for domestic institutions, and the EP and the UN for international institutions. These questions measure diffuse support for the regime rather than support for the specific government.[45] For each institution, the variable ranges from 0 (lowest trust) to 10 (highest trust). The factor analysis tests whether trust in individual domestic institutions measures one underlying concept. The factor analysis in Table 1 shows that there are two underlying concepts, trust in state institutions (*Devlet Kurumları*) and trust in political parties. This conclusion contrasts with that of Mishler and Rose, who found that trust in political parties, parliament, the judiciary and other institutions is highly interdependent.[46] This difference suggests that citizens in Turkey distinguish between the state (*Devlet*) and political parties, mostly likely the governing party. In addition, trust in international organizations is highly loaded. Listhaug and Wiberg found that trust in order institutions such as the army, the police and legal institutions differs from trust in political institutions such as parliament.[47] In sum, there are three dependent variables, two for domestic institutions and one for international institutions. The variables for trust in state institutions and trust in international institutions are created as additive index, 0–30 and 0–20, respectively. And trust in political parties ranges from 0 to 10.

Independent Variables

The main independent variable is ethnicity, measured by the language spoken at home. This measure does not include Kurds who cannot speak their mother language and therefore underestimates the percentage of Kurds. However, in the absence of an ethnic-identity question in the ESS, it is one of the best proxies to measure ethnicity. Those who speak Kurdish are coded as 1, and those who speak Turkish are coded as 0. The sample includes 9.4 percent Kurdish-speaking citizens.[48]

The study also includes a number of individual-level variables in our models that have been found to be important determinants of political trust.[49] The first set of variables is political in nature. First is political interest variable, a measure that asks

Table 1. Factor Loadings for Institutions

National	Loadings	Uniqueness	International	Loadings	Uniqueness
Parliament	0.74	0.40	EP	0.84	0.28
Judiciary	0.76	0.37	UN	0.84	0.28
Police	0.75	0.42			
Parties	0.35	0.82			

N:2118; rotated orthogonal varimax.

whether the respondent is interested in politics, and answers can range from 1 (not at all interested) to 4 (very interested). In addition, three variables out of the left–right scale to control for partisanship are introduced. Zero to four are recoded as the left (20 percent), 5 as the center (40 percent) and 6–10 as the right (39 percent). The center is the reference category. Given that this scaling can be considered arbitrary, for the robustness test this study has used the original scaling, from 0 to 10.[50]

Perception of government performance and the degree of satisfaction with the current economic situation matter for trust in domestic institutions because those who have higher satisfaction with government and the economy carry over their satisfaction to other domestic political institutions. Both variables range from 0 to 10. Literature suggests that income and gender are important determinants of trust in international institutions such as the UN or the EP, while social trust, education and political interest have weak impacts on trust in international institutions.[51] Anderson et al. argue that winners have a different attitude toward democracy and political institutions than do those who voted for the party that remained in the opposition or out of parliament.[52] Therefore, one expects that, those voters, including Kurdish voters, who vote for the AKP are more likely to have higher levels of trust.

Social trust is another control variable, despite the fact that its relation to political trust has been controversial. For example, one study shows that those who reside in less trusting societies are more likely to have less trust in governments, while other studies find a weak association between the two.[53] The variable ranges from 0 to 10. Zero amounts to no trust and 10 amounts to complete trust in people.[54]

The study also includes two opinion variables: satisfaction with one's household income and religiosity. The former is measured by the degree to which a respondent views his or her current household income as satisfactory. The variable ranges from 1, which represents a comfortable living, to 4, which represents significant difficulty living on his or her current income. Self-reported religiosity is measured on a scale of 0 (not at all religious) to 10 (very religious). Finally, the last control variables are *the respondent's education, age, and sex* (coded 1 for men) because of their significance to previous analyses of political attitudes and behavior.[55] The impact of education on political trust is controversial. Almond and Verba see its role as more positive, Dalton, in contrast, asserts that high levels of education lead to critical attitudes toward political institutions while Listhaug and Wiberg argue that its positive impact varies depending on the institution.[56]

Results

Figure 1 displays trust in domestic and international institutions by ethnicity, which suggests that there is a substantial difference between Kurds and Turks. The mean trust level in parliament is 5.90 for ethnic Turks and 5.57 for Kurds, while ethnic Turks trust the police more than all other institutions (6.57) and Kurds trust them the least (5.45). Put differently, between the two groups, the mean difference for trust in legal institutions and the police are 15 and 20 percent, respectively, while it is only 5 percent for trust in parliament. Of all political institutions, political

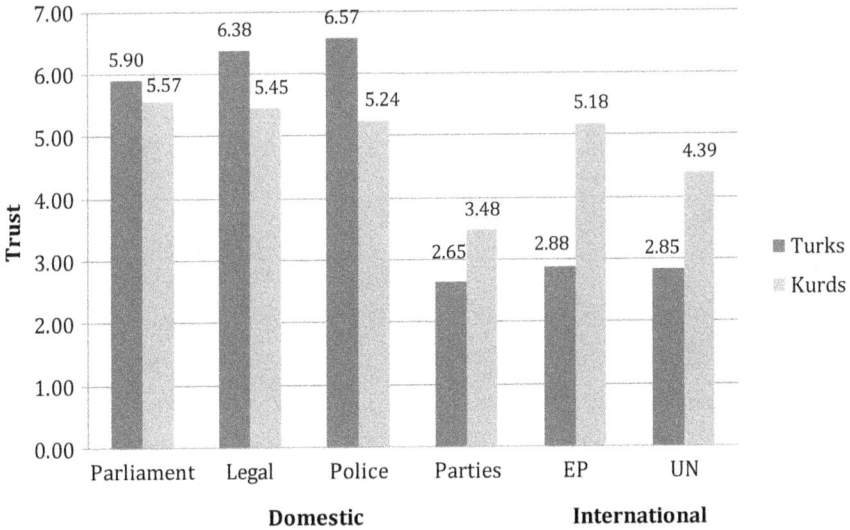

Figure 1. Trust in Domestic and International Institutions by Ethnicity.
Note: Trust index ranges from 0 (lowest) to 10 (highest).

parties garner the lowest level or trust. Nevertheless, it is interesting to note that although Kurds have much lower trust in parliament than do Turks, Kurds exceed Turks in their trust of political parties, 3.48 versus 2.65. The mean difference in trust in political parties between Kurds and Turks shows that Kurds' trust is 24 percent higher than is that of Turks.[57]

As for trust in international institutions, a clear difference emerges between Kurds and Turks. The mean level of trust in the EP for Kurds is 5.18, while it is only 2.88 for Turks, suggesting the Kurds' mean trust level for the EP is 95 percent higher than it is for Turks. Similarly, the mean trust in the UN is 4.39 for Kurds, while it is much lower for Turks (2.85).[58]

Following Anderson and Guillery, Anderson et al. and related studies on the winner/loser consent debate, the expectation is that those who voted for the governing party in the elections should hold higher levels of trust.[59] Figure 2 shows winners' trust in domestic and international institutions among Kurds. Those Kurds who voted for the AKP show much higher levels of trust in parliament, legal institutions, the police and political parties. Trust in international institutions does not vary significantly between Kurdish AKP and non-AKP voters. Losers, mostly BDP voters, hold higher levels of trust in the EP and the UN, while the difference in trust for international institutions between Turkish winners and losers is much smaller.[60]

Having presented the descriptive results, this study turns to multivariate analyses that take into account a number of important variables. In order to test our hypotheses on trust in domestic institutions, Table 2 presents six models. Model 1 suggests that Kurds indeed have much lower levels of trust in national institutions, and that this

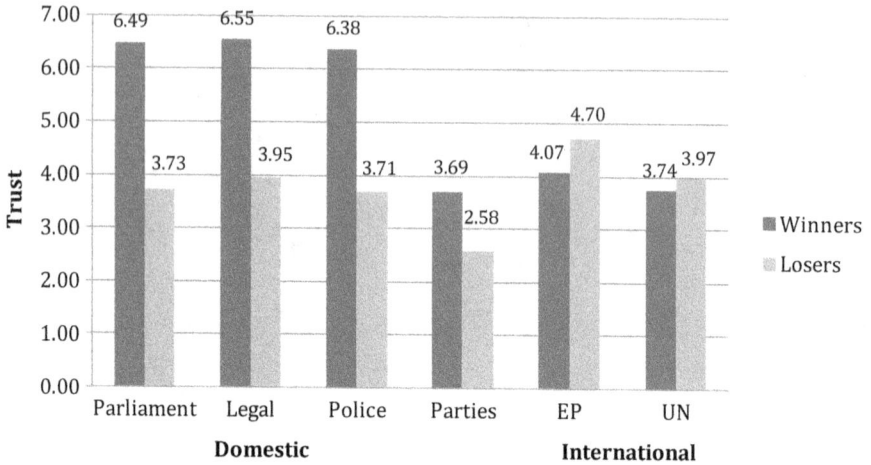

Figure 2. Trust in Institutions among Kurds.
Note: The trust index ranges from 0 (lowest) to 10 (highest). "Winners" refers to those who voted for a governing party and "losers" to those who voted for other parties.

level of trust does not change even if the winner variable in Model 2 is included.[61] Model 3 tests whether Kurds who vote for the election winner are likely to hold higher levels of trust in state institutions. The statistically significant coefficient shows that those Kurds who vote for the AKP hold higher trust in state institutions. The interpretation of the interaction variable is always tricky, and its coefficient should be interpreted by taking into account two main variables as well. For this reason, a marginal-effect figure, Figure 1, is created, which suggests that although the mean for Kurdish winners is higher than it is for Kurdish losers, the confidence interval that overlaps both suggests that the marginal effect for the coefficient is not statistically significant (Figure 3).[62]

Other variables—satisfaction with the government, political interest, religiosity and rural voters—have a positive impact on the first dimension of political trust: trust in state institutions. Following Sarigil, this study has also considered the impact of religiosity on ethnicity by first creating an interaction of Kurdish and religiosity and dividing the sample by ethnicity, and then running the same models for Kurds and ethnic Turks.[63] The results suggest that religious Kurds and religious Turks behave similarly, both holding higher levels of political trust.[64] In contrast, compared to centrist voters, leftist voters are less likely to hold positive attitudes toward state institutions. This should be not surprising for two reasons. First, compared to the right, the left has historically been more critical toward political institutions. Second, the right-wing AKP is in power, so it is not surprising that the left may associate it with political institutions. Similarly, higher education is negatively associated with trust in state institutions. Gender and age do not have statistically significant impacts on political trust. Satisfaction with the economy is statically

Table 2. Ethnicity and Trust in Domestic Institutions

	Political trust					
	State institutions			Political parties		
	Model 1	Model 2	Model 3	Model 4	Model 5	Model 6
Kurdish	−3.846	−5.946	−7.544	0.439	0.293	0.154
	*0.690***	*0.910***	*1.285***	*0.239**	*0.331*	*0.470*
Winner	–	0.785	0.558	–	0.137	0.117
		0.595	*0.608*		*0.218*	*0.223*
Kurdish*winner	–		3.002	–		0.259
			*1.706**			*0.621*
Economic Satisfaction	0.200	0.163	0.169	0.118	0.070	0.070
	*0. 087***	*0.108*	*0.108*	*0.030***	*0.039**	*0.039**
Government Satisfaction	0.502	0.569	0.560	0.183	0.221	0.221
	*0.082***	*0.104***	*0.104***	*0.028***	*0.038***	*0.038***
Political interest	1.226	1.215	1.200	−0.055	−0.065	−0.066
	*0192***	*0.239***	*0.239***	*0.067*	*0.087*	*0.087*
Right	0.191	−0.051	−0.033	−0.244	−0.234	−0.233
	0.440	*0.565*	*0.565*	*0.153*	*0.206*	*0.206*
Left	−3.562	−2.681	−2.592	−0.292	−0.117	−0.110
	*0.544***	*0.721***	*0.722***	*0.189*	*0.262*	*0.263*
Social trust	0.153	0.158	0.169	0.106	0.108	0.108
	*0.074***	*0.091**	*0.091**	*0.026***	*0.033***	*0.033***

(Continued)

Table 2. (Continued).

	Political trust					
	State institutions			Political parties		
	Model 1	Model 2	Model 3	Model 4	Model 5	Model 6
Income	−0.232	−0.344	−0.352	−0.120	−0.115	−0.116
	0.239	*0.299*	*0.299*	*0.083*	*0.108*	*0.108*
Age	−0.004	−0.001	−0.002	−0.002	0.001	0.001
	0.013	*0.017*	*0.017*	*0.004*	*0.006*	*0.006*
Religious	0.482***	0.438***	0.443***	0.170***	0.122***	0.123**
	*0.092***	*0.116***	*0.116***	*0.032***	*0.042***	*0.042***
Education	−0.370**	−0.372*	−0.409*	−0.028	−0.034	−0.037
	*0.181**	*0.227*	*0.228*	*0.063*	*0.083*	*0.083*
Female	−0.089	−0.011	−0.002	−0.238	−0.124	−0.124
	0.388	*0.487*	*0.486*	*0.135*	*0.178*	*0.178*
Rural	0.899***	1.335***	1.330***	0.154	0.151	0.151
	*0.233***	*0.292***	*0.292***	*0.081*	*0.107*	*0.107*
Constant	9.520	8.680	8.916	0.900	0.960	0.982
	*1.455***	*1.851***	*1.854***	*0.506*	*0.675*	*0.677*
N	1750	1056	1056	1767	1066	1066
Adjusted R^2	0.212	0.251	0.252	0.137	0.128	0.123

Notes: The reference category for the partisanship variables, the left and the right, is the center. Entries are unstandardized coefficients with robust standard errors (italics).
*$p < 0.1$.
**$p < 0.05$.
***$p < 0.01$.

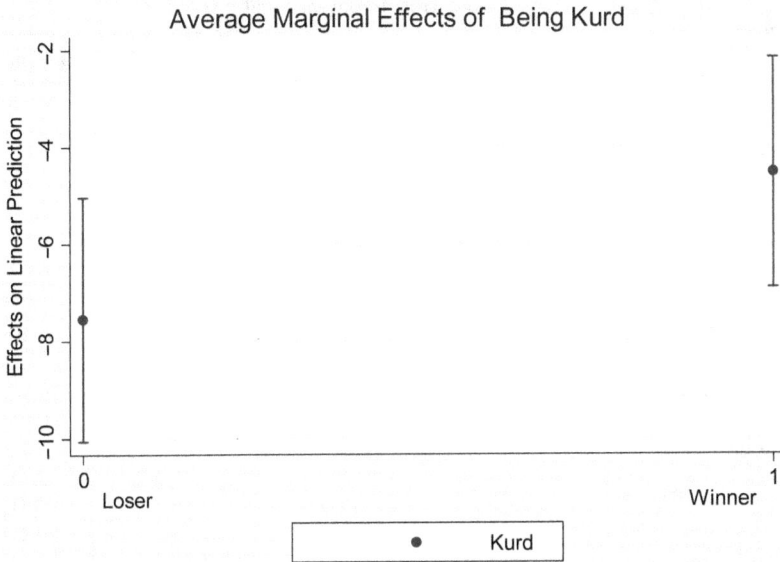

Figure 3. The Marginal Effects of Being a Kurd/Winner on Trust in State Institutions.

significant only in Model 1, but when the winner variable is introduced, it is no longer significant.

Models 4–6 test the second dimension of political trust: trust in political parties. Model 4 suggests that the trust level among Kurds is much higher than it is among Turks, but this significance disappears once the winner variable is included. This suggests that higher trust in the parties occur among Kurdish voters, and thus that voting for AKP significantly increases trust in political parties among Kurdish voters. Model 5 suggests that election winners are not distinguishable by their level of trust from the rest of the sample. Model 6 tests the impact of Kurdish election winners. Its statistically insignificant coefficient indicates that there is no statistical distinction between Kurdish and Turkish election winners. As for other variables— satisfaction with the economy and government and social trust—religious voters hold higher trust in political parties while the other control variables do not have statistically significant impacts.

Do Kurds hold higher trust in international organizations, as Figure 1 suggests? Model 1 in Table 3 confirms that Kurds are more likely to hold higher trust in international institutions than are Turks. And the size of the coefficient suggests that as moved from Turks to Kurds; trust in international organizations increases by 4.2 out of 10. One may argue that the Sèvres syndrome—the idea that the West has a long-run policy of destroying the country, a view that emerged in reaction to the 1920 Treaty of Sèvres—runs deep among Turkish speakers, but the same is not true for Kurds. As a ramification of this syndrome, while Turks believe that

Table 3. Ethnicity and Trust in International Institutions

	Trust in international organizations	
	Model 1	**Model 2**
Kurdish	4.167 *0.505****	3.991 *0.880****
Political trust	0.207 *0.017****	0.205 *0.019****
Kurdish*political trust	–	0.011 0.045
Economic satisfaction	0.108 *0.064**	0.108 *0.064**
Government satisfaction	0.123 *0.061***	0.123 *0.061***
Political interest	0.085 *0.143*	0.085 *0.143*
Right	−1.226 *0.324****	−1.219 *0.325****
Left	0.157 *0.403*	0.165 *0.404*
Social trust	0.027 *0.054*	0.027 *0.054*
Income	0.052 *0.176*	0.052 *0.176*
Age	−0.017 *0.009**	−0.017 *0.009**
Religious	0.057 *0.067*	0.058 *0.067*
Education	−0.116 *0.132*	−0.117 *0.132*
Female	−0.229 *0.285*	−0.229 *0.285*
Rural	−0.727 *0.172****	−0.726 *0.172****
Constant	2.960 *1.083****	2.980 *1.086****
N	1618	1618
Adjusted R^2	0.153	0.153

Notes: The reference category for the partisanship variables, the left and the right, is the center. Entries are unstandardized coefficients with robust standard errors (italics).
*$p < 0.1$.
**$p < 0.05$.
***$p < 0.01$.

international organizations are one of the root causes of Kurdish problem, Kurds put the blame more on domestic institutions and actors.[65] Another interesting finding is that, as the coefficient of the political-trust variable suggests, citizens transfer their trust or distrust of domestic institutions to international organizations. Model 2 shows that Kurds and Turks are not distinguishable in terms of transferring political trust to trust in international organizations. This indifference between Kurds and Turks also means that for the former, there are peculiar reasons other than (dis)trust in domestic institutions, which leads to higher trust in international organizations. Given the data limitation this study has, rather than speculating the causes of this finding, it leaves this interesting puzzle to future studies.

The findings on control variable suggest that ideological and performances of government variables account for trust in international bodies while the impact of other variables varies. Satisfaction with the economy and government boosts trust in international organizations, while rightist, senior and rural voters hold less trust in them. Seven out of 12 control variables do have statistically significant coefficients. Religiosity, education, female, income satisfaction and left voters are not statistically significant.

Conclusion

This study aims to contribute to a neglected relationship between ethnicity and trust in institutions. The findings suggest that, unlike in post-communist countries, political trust in Turkey can be divided into two dimensions: trust in state institutions (*Devlet Kurumları*)—namely parliament, legal institutions and the police—and political parties. The findings suggest that voting for the winning party does not affect individuals' confidence in state institutions in general and for Kurds. Further diagnostic analysis shows that those Kurds who vote for the AKP tend to link themselves to the political system more while the rest of Kurds, mainly pro-BDP voters hold the lowest trust level in state institutions. Moreover, the results also suggest that there is also a positive relationship between trust in state institutions and trust in international organizations. This finding is consistent with earlier studies.[66] However, Kurds' trust in international institutions cannot be explained by their distrust in national ones, which suggest that other socioeconomic and political causes shape the way Kurds evaluate international institutions.

The findings speak to several studies on other countries as well. First, unlike studies on the USA, it is found that an ethnic minority has a lower level of trust in national institutions in a country where political violence due to ethnic conflict has cost thousands of lives. This finding is similar to studies on Russian ethnic minorities in the Baltic countries, but for a different reason.[67] While Russians once held prestigious positions in these societies and then lost their socioeconomic status after the breakdown of the Soviet Union, Kurds have always resided at the bottom of the socioeconomic ladder. Russians blamed international actors such as the EU, the UN or others for their deteriorating socioeconomic and political position in these countries. Survey research shows that in contrast to Kurds, a significant percentage of the Turkish population believes international organizations are one of the main causes of the Kurdish problem because of their "covert support" for the PKK.[68] Kurds tend to look to international organizations more than do Turks; in part this may be because while Kurds feel more discriminated by state institutions, and the anti-imperialistic and anti-international organization discourse did not permeate into Kurds as much as the rest of Turkish society.[69]

When considered only as Turkish citizens, Kurds have equal rights in all aspects; however, the right to care for and develop their ethnicity, culture and language is not included in this understanding of equality.[70] The results suggest that past and current state policies have created a significant degree of alienation toward state institutions among Kurds, eroding the belief that Kurds have the same rights and opportunities with Turks in Turkey. This calls for policy makers to attempt policy measures to increase political trust among Kurds and lessen the gap between Kurds and Turks. Otherwise, Kurds and Turks will continue to have two distinct perspectives toward domestic and international institutions, whose persistency cannot be perceived as a good omen for the future.

Acknowledgements

I thank Kemal Karakoç, Süryal Karakoç, Fatih Mehmet Sula, Ceren Belge, Elif Erişen, Gizem Arıkan, Sema Akboğa, Başak Yavcan, Emre Erdoğan, Zeki Sarıgil, Cengiz Erişen and the participants of the workshop for this special issue as well as an anonymous reader for their insightful comments.

Notes

1. See Pharr and Putnam, *Disaffected Democracies*; Hetherington, *Why Trust Matters*; and Mishler and Rose, "What are the Origins of Political Trust?," 30–62.
2. Hetherington, *Why Trust Matters* and Marien and Hooghe, "Does Political Trust Matter?," 267–91.
3. Chanley, Rudolph, and Rahn. "The Origins and Consequences," 239–56; Hetherington, *Why Trust Matters*; and Mishler and Rose, "What are the Origins of Political Trust?," 30–62.
4. KONDA, "Kürt Meselesi'nde Algı ve Beklentiler Araştırması. Bulgular Raporu" and Koç, Hancıoğlu, and Çavlin, "Demographic Differentials and Demographic," 447–57.
5. Anderson and Guillory, "Political Institutions and Satisfaction," 66–81; Anderson et al., *Losers' Consent*; Anderson and Lotempio, "Winning, Losing, and Political Trust in America," 335–51; and Anderson and Tverdova, "Winners, Losers, and Attitudes Toward Government," 321–338.
6. Dowley and Silver, "Support for Europe," 315–37; Dowley and Silver, "Social Capital, Ethnicity and Support," 505–27; and Ehin, "Political Support in the *Baltic* States 1993–2004," 1–20.
7. Hetherington, *Why Trust Matters*, 9.
8. Scholz and Lubell, "Trust and Taxpaying," 398–417.
9. Marien and Hooghe, "Does Political Trust Matter?," 267–91.
10. Mishler and Rose, "Trust, Distrust and Skepticism," 418–51 and Mishler and Rose, "What are the Origins of Political Trust?," 30–62.
11. MacKuen, Erikson, and Stimson, "Peasants or Bankers?," 597–611.
12. See, for example, Mishler and Rose, "What are the Origins of Political Trust?," 30–62. For notable exceptions, see Dowley and Silver, "Support for Europe," 315–37 and Dowley and Silver, "Social Capital, Ethnicity and Support," 505–27.

13. Blendon et al., "Changing Attitudes in America," 205–16 (208).
14. Lawrence, "Is It Really the Economy Stupid?," 127.
15. Rahn and Rudolp. "A Tale of Political Trust," 530–60.
16. King, "The Polarization of American Parties and Mistrust" and Hetherington, *Why Trust Matters*, 17.
17. Dowley and Silver, "Support for Europe," 523.
18. Ehin, "Political Support in the *Baltic* States 1993–2004," 1–20.
19. Stickley et al., "Institutional trust *in* Contemporary Moscow," 779–96 and Elkins and Sides. "Can Institutions Build Unity in Multiethnic States?," 693–708.
20. Data can be found at http://www.worldvaluessurvey.org/
21. Please note that the WVS 2001 did not have the justice-system question and the WVS 1990 did not include confidence in political parties.
22. Tezcür, "Kurdish Nationalism and Identity in Turkey".
23. Aslan, "Everyday Forms of State Power," 75–93.
24. Yeğen, "The Kurdish Question in Turkish State Discourse," 555–68.
25. Somer, "Resurgence and Remaking of Identity," 591–622; van Bruinessen, *Agha, Shaikh and State, the Social and Political Structures*.
26. Barkey, "Under the Gun," 114–32 and Aydınlı and Ozcan, "The Conflict Resolution and Counterterrorism Dilemma," 438–57.
27. Smits and Gündüz-Hosgör, "Linguistic Capital," 829–53; KONDA, "Kürt Meselesi'nde Algı ve Beklentiler Araştırması. Bulgular Raporu".
28. There is an extensive literature on ethnicity and social trust in the political-psychology literature that suggests that minority groups feel excluded and marginalized from the decision-making process (e.g. Huddy, "From Social to Political Identity," 127–56; Huddy, "Group Identity and Political Cohesion," 65–93; Hogg, "Intragroup Processes, Group Structure, and Social Identity," 65–93; and Hornsey, "Social Identity Theory and Self-categorization Theory," 204–22. Building from this literature, we can argue that minority groups can view institutions as representative of the interests of the main ethnic group, and not of their own interests. For an extensive literature, we direct the reader to the social identity literature and Çiğdem V. Şirin's article in this special issue.
29. The gradual change from the denial of Kurds as an ethnic group toward the recognition of Kurds and their language, together with other reforms, may create positive attitudes toward political institutions among Kurds. One may argue that the economic and social policies of the AKP government have been influential in creating a bond between Kurds and both the government in particular and political institutions, leading no difference of trust in political institutions among Kurds and Turks.
30. Anderson and Guillory, "Political Institutions and Satisfaction," 66–81 and Anderson et al., *Losers' Consent*.
31. Bengio, "The 'Kurdish Spring'," 619–32. In addition, as of the Fall, 2012, Kurdish language has also been offered as an elective course in high schools.
32. Bellucci, Sanders, and Serricchio. "Explaining European Identity".
33. Bellucci, Sanders, and Serricchio, "Explaining European Identity"; Brewer et al., "International Trust and Public Opinion," 93–109; and Torgler, "Trust in International Organizations," 65–93.
34. Torgler, "Trust in International Organizations," 65–93 and Erdoğan, "Determinants of Turkish Citizens' Attitudes," 131–60.
35. Brewer, et al., "Do Americans Trust Other Nations?," 36–51. Sanchez-Cuenca, "The Political Basis of Support for European Integration," 147–72. See Hessami, "What Determines Trust in International Organizations?". See Fischer and Hahn (*Determinants of Trust in the European Central Bank*) look at trust in the European Central Bank. http://nbn-resolving.de/urn:nbn:de:bsz:352-opus-74646
36. See Bellucci, Sanders, and Serricchio, "Explaining European Identity".
37. Dowley and Silver, "Support for Europe," 315–37.
38. Yeğen, "Turkish Nationalism and the Kurdish Question," 119–51 and Keck and Sikkink *Activists Beyond Borders*.
39. Casier, "Designated Terrorists," 393–413.

40. Eccarius-Kelly, "Political Movements and Leverage Points," 91–118 and Casier, "Designated Terrorists," 393.
41. Robins, "More Apparent than Real," 114–32 (127) and Saylan, "The Europeanization Process and Kurdish Nationalism in Turkey," 185–202.
42. The most recent survey released is that of 2008, as Turkey was included in the ESS in 2002 and 2008, where similar sets of questions were asked. This study uses the most recent ESS survey for this analysis. More information about the ESS's sample, methodology and other important issues can be found on its website.
43. Due to the number of missing observations as regards the winner variable, which requires that the political-party choice of the respondents be specified, the sample shrinks significantly for some models. We also run our models using the design weight. The substantial interpretation of the results were the same.
44. All our main results are confirmed using Round 2 of the ESS. The only major difference is that the interaction variable for the Kurdish-winners variable is statistically significant. The results are available upon request.
45. Listhaug and Wiberg, "Confidence in Political and Private Institutions," and Miller et al., "Type-set Politics," 67–84.
46. Mishler and Rose, "What are the Origins of Political Trust?," 30–62.
47. Listhaug and Wiberg, "Confidence in Political and Private Institutions," 306.
48. About 1.5 percent of the people marked Arabic, English, German and other languages. They are excluded from the analysis. For the robustness check, we created another variable in which Arabic-speaking Turkish citizens are coded as Turks. The results are robust over different specifications. The results are available upon request.
49. Mishler and Rose provide an extensive summary on the determinants of political trust, and for the sake of space we refer the reader to the literature on these independent variables. See Mishler and Rose, "Trust, Distrust and Skepticism," 418–451 and "What are the Origins of Political Trust?," 30–62.
50. The results are robust over this scaling as well.
51. Erdoğan, "Determinants of Turkish Citizens' Attitudes," 131–60.
52. Anderson et al., Losers' Consent.
53. Putnam, Bowling Alone; Mishler and Rose, "What are the Origins of Political Trust?," 30–62 and Newton, "Social and Political Trust in Established Democracies," 169–87.
54. Levi ("Social and Unsocial Capital," 45–55) argues that the direction goes from political trust to social trust, while Brehm and Rahn argue that the relationship between political and social trust is reciprocal. Others are ambiguous about the relationship between the two. In the Turkish context, persistent low social trust despite changes in political trust suggests that the causality is a major concern. The low correlation between social trust and trust in state institution (0.09) and trust in parties (0.18) suggests a weak relation between the two concepts in the Turkish context.
55. Verba, Schlozman, and Brady, Voice and Equality.
56. Almond and Verba, The Civic Culture, 1963; Listhaug and Wiberg, "Confidence in Political and Private Institutions"; and Dalton, Citizen Politics.
57. We employed t-test to see whether Kurds and Turks differ in their attitudes toward domestic institutions. T-test suggests these two groups are statistically different in their mean scores (p 0.001) except for trust in parliament (p 0.1)
58. T-test suggests these two groups are statistically different in their mean scores (p 0.001).
59. Anderson and Guillory, "Political Institutions and Satisfaction," 66–81 and Anderson et al., Losers' Consent.
60. T-test suggests these two groups in their trust in domestic institutions are statistically different in their mean scores (p 0.001) except for trust in parliament (p 0.1). On the other hand, t-test suggests that these two groups (Kurdish winners versus Kurdish losers) are not statistically different.
61. For the robustness check, other relevant variables, such as whether you are discriminated against because of your ethnicity, are added to the model. The results were robust over different model specifications. However, following Norris ("Conclusions," 257–72), an alternative hypothesis is

that high expectations among Kurds, resulting from the recent policies, have led them to become more critical of institutions, thereby reducing their trust in them. Although this is a realistic assumption, our data limitation does not allow us to test this possibility.

62. Running the model only Kurdish sample yields the same substantial result.

63. Sarıgil, "Curbing Kurdish Ethno-nationalism in Turkey," 533–53.

64. The results are available upon request.

65. We thank the reviewer for reminding us of this important point.

66. Erdoğan, "Determinants of Turkish Citizens' Attitudes," 131–60 and Hessami, "What Determines Trust in International Organizations?".

67. Dowley and Silver, "Support for Europe," 315–37 and Ehin, "Political Support in the *Baltic* States 1993–2004," 1–20.

68. KONDA, "Kürt Meselesi'nde Algı ve Beklentiler Araştırması. Bulgular Raporu".

69. Given the limitations of the data, we could not control for whether Kurds' high levels of trust in international organizations are also affected by other factors such as the anti-imperial discourse in schools and media, to which ethnic Turks may be more receptive. Nevertheless, despite a number of control variables (not shown here), the significant difference in the levels of trust between the two groups suggests that any omitted variable will not affect the results substantially.

70. Gürbey, "The Development of the Kurdish Nationalism Movement in Turkey since the 1980s," 10.

Bibliography

Almond, G., and S. Verba. *The Civic Culture: Political Attitudes in Five Western Democracies*. Princeton, NJ: Princeton University Press, 1963.

Anderson, Christopher J., and C. A. Guillory. "Political Institutions and Satisfaction with Democracy: A Cross-national Analysis of Consensus and Majoritarian Systems." *American Political Science Review* 91, no. 1 (1997): 66–81.

Anderson, Christopher J., and A. Lotempio. "Winning, Losing, and Political Trust in America." *British Journal of Political Science* 32, no. 2 (2002): 335–351.

Anderson, Christopher J., and Y. V. Tverdova. "Winners, Losers, and Attitudes toward Government in Contemporary Democracies." *International Political Science Review* 22, no. 4 (2001): 321–338.

Anderson, Christopher J., Andre Blais, Shaun Bowler, Todd Donovan, and Ola Listhaug. *Losers' Consent: Elections and Democratic Legitimacy*. Oxford: Oxford University Press, 2005.

Aslan, Senem. "Everyday Forms of State Power and the Kurds in the Early Turkish Republic." *International Journal of Middle East Studies* 43, no. 1 (2011): 75–93.

Aydınlı, Ersel, and Nihat Ali Ozcan. "The Conflict Resolution and Counterterrorism Dilemma: Turkey Faces its Kurdish Question." *Terrorism and Political Violence* 23, no. 3 (2011): 438–457.

Barkey, Henri. "Under the Gun: Turkish Foreign Policy and the Kurdish Question." In *The Kurdish Nationalist Movement in the 1990s: Its Impact on Turkey and the Middle East*, edited by Robert Olson, 114–132. Lexington: University Press of Kentucky, 1996.

Bellucci, Paolo, David Sanders, and Fabio Serricchio. "Explaining European Identity." In *The Europeanization of National Polities? Citizenship and Support in a Post-enlargement Union*, edited by Paolo Bellucci, David Sanders, Gabor Toka, and Mariano Torcal, 61–90. Oxford: Oxford University Press, 2012.

Bengio, Ofra. "The 'Kurdish Spring' in Turkey and its Impact on Turkish Foreign Relations in the Middle East." *Turkish Studies* 12, no. 4 (2011): 619–632.

Blendon, Robert J., John M. Benson, Richard Morin, Drew E. Altman, Mollyann Brodie, Mario Brossard, and Matt James. "Changing Attitudes in America." In *Why People Don't Trust Government*, edited by Joseph S. Nye, Jr. Philip D. Zelikow, and David C. King, 205–216. Cambridge, MA: Harvard University Press, 1997.

Brewer, P. R., K. Gross, S. Aday, and L. Willnat. "International Trust and Public Opinion about World Affairs." *American Journal of Political Science* 48, no. 1 (2004): 93–109.

Brewer, P. R., S. Aday, and K. Gross. "Do Americans Trust Other Nations? A Panel Study." *Social Science Quarterly* 86, no. 1 (2005): 36–51.

van Bruinessen, Martin. *Agha, Shaikh and State, the Social and Political Structures of Kurdistan*. London: Zed Books, 1992.

Casier, Marlies. "Designated Terrorists: The Kurdistan Workers' Party and its Struggle to (Re)Gain Political Legitimacy." *Mediterranean Politics* 15, no. 3 (2010): 393–413.

Chanley, Virginia A., Thomas J. Rudolph, and Wendy M. Rahn. "The Origins and Consequences of Public Trust in Government: A Time Series Analysis." *Public Opinion Quarterly* 64, no. 3 (2000): 239–256.

Dalton, Russell J. *Citizen Politics: Public Opinion and Political Parties in Advanced Industrial Democracies*. New York: Oxford University Press, 2002.

Dowley, Kathlen, and Brian Silver. "Social Capital, Ethnicity and Support for Democracy in the Post-Communist States." *Europe-Asia Studies* 54, no. 4 (2002): 505–527.

Dowley, Kathlen, and Brian Silver. "Support for Europe among Europe's Ethnic, Religious, and Immigrant Minorities." *International Journal of Public Opinion Research* 23, no. 3 (2011): 315–337.

Eccarius-Kelly, Vera. "Political Movements and Leverage Points: Kurdish Activism in the European Diaspora." *Journal of Muslim Minority Affairs* 22, no. 1 (2003): 91–118.

Ehin, P. "Political Support in the Baltic States 1993–2004." *Journal of Baltic Studies* 38, no. 1 (2007): 1–20.

Elkins, Zachary, and John Sides. "Can Institutions Build Unity in Multiethnic States?" *American Political Science Review* 101, no. 4 (2007): 693–708.

Erdoğan, Emre. "Determinants of Turkish Citizens' Attitudes towards International Institutions." *Turkish Policy Quarterly* 6, no. 4 (2007): 131–160.

Fischer, Justina A. V., and Volker Hahn, *Determinants of Trust in the European Central Bank*. Working Paper Series in Economics and Finance 695, Stockholm School of Economics, 2008.

Gürbey, Gülistan. "The Development of the Kurdish Nationalism Movement in Turkey since the 1980s." In *The Kurdish Nationalist Movement in the 1990s*, edited by Robert Olson, 9–37. Lexington: University Press of Kentucky, 1996.

Hessami, Zohal. "What Determines Trust in International Organizations? An Empirical Analysis for the IMF, the World Bank, and the WTO," 2011. Accessed May 1, 2012. http://mpra.ub.uni-muenchen. de/34550

Hetherington, M. J. *Why Trust Matters: Declining Political Trust and the Demise of American Liberalism*. Princeton, NJ: Princeton University, 2005.

Hogg, Michael A. "Intragroup Processes, Group Structure, and Social Identity." In *Social Groups and Identities: Developing the Legacy of Henri Tajfel*, edited by W. Peter Robinson, 65–93. Oxford: Butterworth-Heinemann, 1996.

Hornsey, Matthew J. "Social Identity Theory and Self-categorization Theory: A Historical Review." *Social and Personality Psychology Compass* 2, no. 1 (2008): 204–222.

Huddy, Leonie. "From Social to Political Identity: A Critical Examination of Social Identity Theory." *Political Psychology* 22, no. 1 (2001): 127–156.

Huddy, Leonie. "Group Identity and Political Cohesion." In *Oxford Handbook of Political Psychology*, edited by D. O. Sears, L. Huddy, and R. Jervis, 65–93. Oxford: Oxford University Press, 2003.

Keck, Margaret E., and Kathryn Sikkink. *Activists beyond Borders: Advocacy Networks in International Politics*. Ithaca, IL: Cornell University Press, 1998.

King, David C. "The Polarization of American Parties and Mistrust of Government." In *Why People Don't Trust Government*, edited by Joseph Nye, Jr Philip D. Zelikow, and David C. King, 155–178. Cambridge, MA: Harvard University Press, 1997.

Koç, İ., A. Hancıoğlu, and A. Çavlin. "Demographic Differentials and Demographic Integration of Turkish and Kurdish Populations in Turkey." *Population Research and Policy Review* 27, no. 4 (2008): 447–457.

Lawrence, Robert. "Is It Really the Economy Stupid?" In *Why Americans Mistrust Government*, edited by Joseph Nye, Philip Zelikow, and David King, 111–132. Cambridge, MA: Harvard University Press, 1997.

Levi, Margaret. "Social and Unsocial Capital: A Review Essay of Robert Putnam's Making Democracy Work." Politics & Society 24, no. 1 (1996): 45–55.

Listhaug, Ola, and Matti Wiberg. "Confidence in Political and Private Institutions." In *Citizens and the State*, edited by Hans-Dieter Klingermann and Dieter Fuchs, 298–322. Oxford: Oxford University Press, 1995.

MacKuen, Michael B., Robert S. Erikson, and James A. Stimson. "Peasants or Bankers?: The American Electorate and the U.S. Economy." *American Political Science Review* 86, no. 3 (1992): 597–611.

Marien, Sofie, and Marc Hooghe. "Does Political Trust Matter? An Empirical Investigation into the Relation between Political Trust and Support for Law Compliance." *European Journal of Political Research* 50, no. 2 (2011): 267–291.

Miller, Arthur H., Edie N. Goldenberg, and Lutz Erbring. "Type-set Politics: Impact of Newspapers on Public Confidence." *American Political Science Review* 73, no. 1 (1979): 67–84.

Mishler, William, and Richard Rose. "Trust, Distrust and Skepticism: Popular Evaluations of Civil and Political Institutions in Post-communist Society." *Journal of Politics* 59, no. 2 (1997): 418–451.

Mishler, William, and Richard Rose. "What are the Origins of Political Trust? Testing Institutional and Cultural Theories in Post-communist Societies." *Comparative Political Studies* 3, no. 4 (2001): 30–62.

Newton, Kenneth. "Social and Political Trust in Established Democracies." In *Critical Citizens: Global Support for Democratic Governance*, edited by Pippa Norris, 169–187. Oxford: Oxford University Press, 1999.

Norris, Pippa. "Conclusions: The Growth of Critical Citizens and its Consequences." In *Critical Citizens: Global Support for Democratic Governance*, edited by Pippa Norris, 257–272. Oxford: Oxford University Press, 1999.

Pharr, Susan, and Robert D. Putnam, eds. *Disaffected Democracies*. Princeton, NJ: Princeton University Press, 2000.

Putnam, Robert D. *Bowling Alone*. New York: Simon & Schuster, 2000.

Rahn, Wendy, and Thomas J. Rudolp. "A Tale of Political Trust in American Cities." *Public Opinion Quarterly* 69, no. 4 (2005): 530–560.

Robins, Philip. "More Apparent than Real: The Impact of the Kurdish Issue on Euro-Turkish Relations." In *The Kurdish Nationalist Movement in the 1990s: Its Impact on Turkey and the Middle East*, edited by Robert Olson, 114–132. Lexington: University Press of Kentucky.

Sanchez-Cuenca, Ignacio. "The Political Basis of Support for European Integration." *European Union Politics* 1, no. 2 (2000): 147–172.

Sarıgil, Zeki. "Curbing Kurdish Ethno-nationalism in Turkey: An Empirical Assessment of Pro-Islamic and Socio-economic Approaches." *Ethnic and Racial Studies* 33, no. 3 (2010): 533–553.

Saylan, Ibrahim. "The Europeanization Process and Kurdish Nationalism in Turkey: The Case of the Democratic Society Party." *Nationalities Papers: The Journal of Nationalism and Ethnicity* 40, no. 2 (2012): 185–202.

Scholz, J. T., and M. Lubell. "Trust and Taxpaying: Testing the Heuristic Approach to Collective Action." *American Journal of Political Science* 42, no. 2 (1998): 398–417.

Smits, J., and A. Gündüz-Hosgör. "Linguistic Capital: Language as a Socioeconomic Resource among Kurdish and Arabic Women in Turkey." *Ethnic and Racial Studies* 26, no. 5 (2003): 829–853.

Somer, Murat. "Resurgence and Remaking of Identity: Civil Beliefs, Domestic and External Dynamics, and the Turkish Mainstream Discourse on Kurds." *Comparative Political Studies* 8, no. 6 (2005): 591–622.

Stickley, A., S. Ferlander, T. Jukkala, P. Carlson, O. Kislitsyna, and I. H. Mäkinen. "Institutional Trust in Contemporary Moscow." *Europe-Asia Studies* 61, no. 5 (2009): 779–796.

Tezcür, Güneş Murat. "Kurdish Nationalism and Identity in Turkey: A Conceptual Reinterpretation." *European Journal of Turkish Studies* 10. Accessed December, 2012. http://ejts.revues.org/index4008.html

Torgler, Benno. "Trust in International Organizations: An Empirical Investigation Focusing on the United Nations." *The Review of International Organizations* 3, no. 1 (2008): 65–93.

Verba, Sidney, Kay Lehman Schlozman, and Henry E. Brady. *Voice and Equality: Civic Voluntarism in American Politics*. Cambridge, MA: Harvard University, 1995.

Yeğen, Mesut. "The Kurdish Question in Turkish State Discourse." *Journal of Contemporary History* 34, no. 4 (1999): 555–568.

Yeğen, Mesut. "Turkish Nationalism and the Kurdish Question." *Ethnic and Racial Studies* 30, no. 1 (2007): 119–151.

Emotions as a Determinant in Turkish Political Behavior

CENGİZ ERİŞEN
Department of Political Science, TOBB University of Economics and Technology, Sögütözü, Ankara, Turkey

ABSTRACT *This article provides an experimental analysis of the role emotions play in Turkish voters' political attitudes and behavior with respect to the Syria crisis. By examining the political effects of emotions, this article contributes to the discussion on Turkish voters' political attitudes and political behavior. Through an experimental design, this study shows how incidentally raised emotions on the Syria issue can influence individual attitudes on foreign policy, interest in seeking more information about the issue, and evaluations of Turkish Prime Minister Recep Tayyip Erdoğan's performance. This article aims to stimulate further research in the literature on the potential effects of emotions in Turkish political behavior.*

Despite the wide range of research on Turkish politics and public opinion, there has been insufficient focus on understanding differences in individual preferences. Whilst previous research has shown some interest in individual level dynamics in understanding public opinion, analysis of the psychological underpinnings of attitudes and behavior is lacking in previous studies conducted in the Turkish context. Motivated by the fast-growing research on emotions in the international literature, the particular aim of this study is to explore the role and influence of emotions in forming political attitudes, preferences, and judgments of Turkish voters. The current study examines political attitudes and preferences on a foreign policy topic from a political psychology perspective through experimental data.

The scholarly quest to understand the role of emotions in politics is a thriving domain of research in political psychology. Over the last two decades, the discipline has examined the many ways that emotions effect and influence political attitudes,[1] political preferences,[2] political decisions,[3] and information processing.[4] A multifaceted and fast-growing research literature on emotions has produced a well-cited scholarly work and strengthened the prominent position of political psychology in the political science discipline.

Given this importance of emotions in political life, it seems valuable to investigate their effects in the Turkish context. Yet, no prior scholarly research (let alone empirical work) has done so, and current scholarly research has largely neglected individual determinants of citizen behavior in the Turkish context. Instead, it has mostly focused on aggregate analysis of electoral behavior, leaving individual differences and the psychological determinants of political behavior unexplored. This article posits that affect and emotions are integral to several aspects of political behavior, and that scholars need to control for their potential effects. It, therefore, aims to explore how emotions can influence public behavior on political issues in Turkey.

To investigate this research question, the article focuses on a particularly relevant current political issue: the Syria crisis. This conflict has been a major and influential topic in recent Turkish domestic and foreign policy. So far, it has affected Turkish politics in several ways, as well as the perception of Turkey in international platforms. Given the level of violence and human rights violations, and the links to Turkish domestic affairs and security, this crisis has evoked strong emotional reactions in the Turkish public. These qualities thus provide fertile ground to test the effects of emotions in political attitudes and behavior.

The organization of the article is as follows. It first provides a theoretical framework and a discussion on the conceptualization of emotions. These sections are followed by the presentation of research hypotheses and the introduction of the research design. Finally, the findings are presented and implications are discussed.

Theoretical Framework

Earlier research in political psychology primarily relied on cognitive, rationalistic assumptions about individual behavior. Through this lens, thinking more, engaging in cognitive calculations, and making cost-and-benefit analyses about a decision were considered to assist an individual to reach the best choice possible in political life. By selecting the best choice, the individual is expected to increase the utility from the decision by achieving the best possible outcome.[5] In this cognitive paradigm, reason-based decision-making was considered as "cold," cognitive, and deliberative, in complete contrast to "hot processes," which were viewed as biases that lead to irrational choice behavior.[6] That is, reason was allocated a key role in the political heaven of ideal citizens, while the role of emotion was denigrated as representing a major obstacle that prevents citizens from engaging in rational political behavior and fulfilling their civic duties.

More recently, following a struggle over reason and emotion, scholars began to argue that considering feelings and emotions as the source of irrational behavior is a mistake.[7] The previously accepted argument that utilitarian reasoning and cognition are by default prior and superior to emotions had to be revised. A series of well-designed experiments, replicated findings, and established strands of emotion research have led scholars to appreciate the influence of emotions in all aspects of political life. A growing body of literature now indicates that emotional states and reactions can influence thoughts, cognitive processing and social behavior in several ways.[8] The overall message from the current literature on emotions is that we cannot deny the strength of emotions (i.e. affect or feelings) in political behavior and judgments.

A number of seminal works in political behavior also contain hints of an interest in emotions. For example, in his seminal work, *The Economic Theory of Democracy*, Downs argued that rational citizen behavior entails cognitive calculation and decisions reached in favor of the best utility. Down's theory accounts for one's civic duty in the process of casting a vote, which component in fact indirectly integrates emotions into the decision process. Similarly, authors of the *American Voter* analyzed the nature of emotions at a general level, but not as an important component of political behavior.[9] In stark contrast to these seminal studies relying on the rationalist paradigm, work on the simple influence of feeling thermometers initiated the momentum in the literature on emotions.[10] Studies on the general effects of affect and emotions raised interest but did not initially attract further concerted research. Rather, it was the introduction of theory-based emotions research into the literature that was more important. Primarily motivated by findings in social psychology and neuroscience,[11] several studies established a strong theoretical structure that led to a thriving research domain in political psychology.[12]

Current research in political science on emotions and affect has motivated a new perspective on attitude formation, reasoning, and decision-making in politics. As Damasio's seminal work on the interaction of cognition and emotion shows, politics is as much about emotions as it is about cognition and thinking.[13] Existing research confirms that the interaction of cognition and emotion can be a constructive force shaping individual behavior. Although the potency of affect on behaviors was once conceived of as a byproduct of cognition,[14] it is now viewed as both a motivational component underlying information processing strategies and a direct source of information that individuals consult in making social judgments.[15]

Conceptualization of Emotions

A contentious point in the literature is how to accurately conceptualize emotions. Discussion has revolved around three possible ways. The first common approach has been to label emotions as valence where classification is made in terms of simple positivity or negativity of the emotional response.[16] The gist of this approach is that the initial affective reaction to an external target (e.g. a political candidate, event, issue, or policy), which is fast, basic, and automatic, generates the initial motivation of consecutive information processing steps.

The valence approach claims that political judgments and decisions appear to be made through an answer to one simple question: "How do I feel about it?" Instead of engaging in a deliberative and effortful process of listing the pros and cons of a decision, individuals simply reach their preferences by consulting their feelings about the object.[17] Thus, the individual's judgment on a like–dislike continuum may strongly correlate with their preference for a political choice, implying that political choices may result from simple like–dislike judgments.[18]

The valence approach is conceptually very strong. Negative and positive emotions are separated from each other and linked to the basic motivational systems of approach and avoidance. Those who feel positive about an event, issue, or political candidate are more likely to be attracted by the target and wish to approach it. On the other hand, those who feel negative wish avoid it, aiming to protect themselves from potential negative outcomes. In turn, a basic division of negative and positive feelings determines one's appraisal of a political event.

A second way of conceptualizing emotions, promoted by Marcus and his colleagues, is a two-dimensional approach, with the first dimension referring to valence and the second to arousal (strength of emotion). It is known as the affective intelligence model (AIM).[19] As one of the most cited theories of emotion in political science, AIM posits that emotion can be conceptualized in terms of two relatively independent systems that influence an individual's use of effortful versus disposition-based processing. The disposition system refers to using emotions to provide direct guidance and facilitate approach-oriented behaviors. In this state, in making political decisions, individuals tend to rely on political heuristics and habits (e.g. prior political partisan preferences, a focus on personally important issues, and a tendency to vote for incumbents). The surveillance system, on the other hand, motivates individuals to scan their environment and rely less on prior beliefs and habits. Specifically, the second system refers to emotions that warn the individual to focus their attention on threatening stimuli in order to learn and seek more information about them. Thus, according to AIM, when individuals feel anxious about politics and political candidates, they seek out more information about the targeted political issue. In contrast, when individuals feel positive or enthusiastic, they are more likely to rely on their habitual political behaviors and involvement in politics.

Third, distinct from the valence and two-dimensional approaches is the discrete conceptualization of emotions that draws on the notion that emotions are constituent experiences: that is, for example, fear is not the same as anger, which in turn is not the same as sadness. In discrete emotions research, the goal is to predict behavioral differences (also known as action tendencies) that each emotion promotes.[20] In this way, the theory predicts, distinct emotions may promote distinct behavioral outcomes.

Previous studies have demonstrated the distinct nature of emotions. In one of those studies, two political scientists, Conover and Feldman provide several important inferences about the role of emotions in political evaluations.[21] First, this study shows the general effects of emotions on political judgments, with its results supporting the hypothesis that emotional reactions are important in understanding political evaluations. The second finding is that positive and negative emotions have distinct influences on political evaluations. Third, and most importantly, the findings reveal that feelings of fear and anger about the economy differentially influence individual political evaluations. When people perceive that economic indicators (e.g. inflation and unemployment) are controllable by accountable individuals, they strongly respond to events with anger. On the other hand, when people perceive economic indicators to be uncontrollable, they feel afraid about these events and react with less anger. The conclusion from this is that, although both are considered as negative emotions, anger and fear promote distinct political evaluations.

An extension to this finding comes from the psychological and appraisal-tendency approach. Stemming from earlier research on risk behavior,[22] psychologists, Lerner and Keltner focus on how individual assessments of risk may differ between negative emotions of anger and fear.[23] In several experimental studies, they find that, although having the same valence, anger and fear differ profoundly in generating distinct behavioral outcomes regarding risk assessments. They find that fearful people make pessimistic risk assessments (of higher risk), whereas angry people make optimistic risk assessments (of lower risk). Extending these findings to political issues, the authors were able to show the distinct effects of anger and fear on the perceived risks of terrorism in the aftermath of 9/11. They found that subjects who were experimentally manipulated to be angry were more optimistic about potential terror events and were more likely to give punitive responses concerning policies for dealing with terrorism. In contrast, subjects who were experimentally manipulated to be afraid and anxious were more pessimistic about terrorism and more conciliatory in their policy judgments.

In a similar study, Huddy, Feldman, Taber, and Lahav emphasize how threat perceptions and anxiety promote distinct behavioral outcomes with respect to the object of terrorism.[24] Heightened anxiety induces risk aversion, which in turn increases the public preference for conciliatory policies through diplomacy, combined with disapproval of presidential performance. On the other hand, threat perceptions enhance support for military action, punitive policies, and curtailment of civil liberties. These effects are also moderated by gender and education. Women and less educated people feel higher levels of anxiety coupled with perceptions of a greater risk of terrorism and war, whereas men and highly educated people show the reverse pattern.

Huddy, Feldman, and Cassese have extended these findings to present clear evidence of the distinct behavioral effects of anger and anxiety on political preferences and political thinking.[25] They not only replicated previous research about these effects but also extended the findings on differing behavioral outcomes of anxiety and anger. More specifically, they found that anxious individuals oppose military action and its risky and potentially dangerous outcomes, whereas angry individuals strongly support all military and other measures against terrorists and potential threats. Overall then, these studies have shown that anger and fear (although both are considered as negatively valenced) promote distinct attitudinal and behavioral outcomes within the paradigm of discrete conceptualization of emotions.

Hypotheses

In light of the discussion above, the principal expectation in this study is to observe an effect of emotions on political attitudes and decisions. The critical point is to test the relative explanatory power of emotions in comparison with other indicators. It is, therefore, relevant to evaluate the role of emotions in political behavior, particularly in the Turkish context.

This study aims to test the distinct effects of discrete emotions on attitudes regarding the continuing tensions in Syria. Syria has been facing an uprising since the spring of 2011. Compared to other social movements of the Arab Spring, the Syrians have faced strong resistance from the Assad regime, which has been unwilling to improve human rights and democratize the country. As a neighboring country to Turkey, events in Syria have been closely observed by the current Justice and Development Party (AKP, *Adalet ve Kalkınma Partisi*) government. Prime Minister (PM) Recep Tayyip Erdogan, in particular, has voiced his concerns about Syria in national and international platforms, and has aimed to take a role as an important actor in the development of events.

Recent Turkish foreign policy has been shaped to stress the importance of public uprising in Syria. The downing of a Turkish jet by Syria in June 2012 increased tensions to such a level that neither side will be able to maneuver politically and militarily without further conflict. Since then, Syrian government enmity toward Turkey has increased as a result of the latter's foreign policy activities against the Assad regime. Turkish domestic security is also a factor in Turkish involvement in the events. For instance, the Turkish media has repeatedly reported that the Syrian government has given greater freedom to PKK (Kurdistan Workers' Party) supporters in Syria, which may partly explain the increasing PKK terrorist attacks in the summer of 2012 in Turkey. Meanwhile, international platforms have been ineffective in resolving the crisis, due to the strong blocking by Russia and China in the UN Security Council. The lack of a definitive international message to the Assad government appears to have motivated it to increase the degree of force it has used in the conflict. As a result, tens of thousands of Syrians have sought refuge in neighboring states, while the conflict remains far from a settlement. In Turkey, it is evident that the Syria crisis has directly influenced the Turkish public, the political actors' agenda, and Turkish foreign policy.

One can form several hypotheses concerning this political issue about the influence of emotions on political attitudes and behavior. First, based on the previous discussion on the distinct effects of anger and fear, we can predict that the angrier the individuals feel, the more they will be willing to support stricter policies toward Syria, and the more they will support military action against Syria. Second, we can predict that fear will promote risk-averse behavior, including support for fewer restrictions against Syria coupled with the use of diplomacy through international organizations. Third, we can predict that individuals who feel frightened or threatened by the situation and experience increased anxiety about the issue will be more likely to favor diplomacy and a more risk-aversive Turkish foreign policy. Thus, the following hypothesis is proposed concerning these expectations:

Hypothesis 1: Individuals who are angry about the Syria crisis will favor risk-seeking policies as opposed to those who feel threatened by it.

Anger and fear can also be expected to promote distinct evaluations with respect to risk. One of the important findings of previous research is that fear and positive emotions promote similar behavior, particularly with respect to risk assessments. Although a distinction between the two negative emotions is expected, we can also expect to see an opposite effect of anger compared to a positive emotion, hope. Hope (closely associated with happiness and enthusiasm) is a positive feeling experienced when an individual perceives himself/herself to be in a positive mood, or sees the positive aspects of an event. Thus, feelings of hope should promote thoughts and considerations that are positively related to an event. In the context of the Syria crisis, we can predict that individuals who feel hopeful and positive will be more likely to have positive policy evaluations and preferences. In particular, this positive feeling will promote support for risk-averse Turkish foreign policy and fewer restrictions on Syria, similarly to those who experience fear due to the situation. The following hypothesis posits this expectation:

Hypothesis 2: Individuals who are positive about the Syria crisis will be risk-averse and behave differently from those who are angry about it.

A secondary issue in this discussion, in addition to the attitudinal outcomes, concerns behavior about political information. Previous research suggests that individuals who feel anxious and afraid are more likely to seek further information on a political topic, whereas those who feel positively will not.[26] Given this expectation, it is also relevant to test whether individuals who feel threatened by the Syrian crisis are more likely to (wish to) learn more about events in Syria compared to others. To that end, the following hypothesis is proposed:

Hypothesis 3: Individuals who are afraid as a result of the Syria crisis will show greater interest in seeking further political information than those who are positive about it.

Another important issue in this debate concerns the public evaluations of PM Recep Tayyip Erdoğan. Since Erdoğan is the most important actor in defining Turkish foreign policy, particularly with respect to Syria, it is relevant to test whether experimentally induced emotions could alter individuals' approval of the PM and his way of handling foreign and domestic policies. Here, positive emotions, as well as the general likability of the leader, are expected to positively influence his approval ratings. The following hypothesis is proposed accordingly:

Hypothesis 4: Individuals who have positive emotions will show greater approval of the prime minister.

Finally, gender differences may also be a factor in risk estimations and threat perceptions with respect to Syria. Previous studies found that men tend to be more risk acceptant, angrier, and less afraid compared to women.[27] In line with this argument, the prediction in this study is that there will be differences in experienced levels of fear and anger, with women perceiving greater risks than men.

Research Design

An experiment was designed to collect data in the spring of 2012, specifically the last two weeks of April 2012. The experiment was conducted with university students studying at TOBB University of Economics and Technology, Middle East Technical University, Bilkent University and Istanbul Bilgi University. In total, 243 students participated in the study. Given the experimental design of this study, conducted with a convenience student sample, it was expected that there would be no potential challenges of inference and threats to the validity of the results.[28] That is, a convenience sample does not hinder experimentally testing the hypotheses posited in this study about the effects of emotions.

The study procedure was as follows. First, participants reported their attitudes regarding current foreign policy events, in addition to reporting their party identification and political ideology. Next, every participant was randomly assigned to one of four experimental conditions. To manipulate emotion, participants in each group were shown the text below (in Turkish), which differed only in the word capitalized in this example.

Current events in Syria evoked a lot of emotion for many people. We are particularly interested in what makes you most ANGRY about the events in Syria. Please describe in detail the one thing that makes you most ANGRY about these events. Write as detailed a description of that thing as possible. If you can, write your description so that someone reading it might even get ANGRY from learning about the situation.

Below are two questions that you may answer in your discussion:

- What aspect of the events in Syria makes you the ANGRIEST?
- Why does it make you so ANGRY?

While those in the anger condition read the above instructions, for those in the other two emotion conditions, the word "anger" was replaced with "fear" or "hopeful." Participants in the neutral group simply reported three to five activities that they had engaged in during the day before the study. The neutral group thus functioned purely as a control condition to provide a benchmark to compare the experimental treatment conditions. Given these conditions, this study is a single-factor between-subject experimental design.

Emotion induction through a self-reflective writing procedure is an effective method of producing discrete emotions.[29] The writing process is intended to produce the particular emotion that the researcher wants to evoke. In this case, participants in the anger condition should be more likely to report things indicating negativity, such as the increasing violence, and strong opposition to the Assad regime. Those in the fear condition should also be more likely to report negativity, but at the same time think more about the potential threats that the Syrian crisis could have for Turkish security, particularly considering the possible extensions of the crisis to PKK terrorism and the potential spillover of the conflict into Turkey.

Those in the hope condition should be more likely to report things that could pull Turkey back from the conflict, be more optimistic that the violence could end soon, and strongly promote solutions in international platforms (e.g. the United Nations or European Union) and through multilateral policies.

To prepare the data for analysis, a research assistant, who was unaware of the research hypotheses, first coded the written responses as to whether participants had engaged in the experimental exercise or not. Eleven participants, who wrote less than three sentences in the response box, were judged not to have engaged in the treatment process sufficiently. These participants were, therefore, dropped from the study.[30]

After each participant had received the experimental treatment, they completed a questionnaire in five sections. The first asked specific questions about the Syria crisis (the main dependent variables). The second included a battery of political participation questions. The third asked participants to report their emotions regarding the Syria crisis. The fourth tested their political knowledge, while the fifth section gathered demographic information and provided an experimental manipulation check.

Results: Differentiating Anger, Fear, and Hope

First, it was necessary to ensure that the experimental conditions had truly evoked the targeted three emotions (anger, fear, and hope) to show that the participants in each experimental condition were more likely to experience the experimentally manipulated emotion compared both to the control group and the other emotions. Next, it was critical to be able to show that the results differentiated between the three emotions, such that anger was different to fear, or that anger and fear were both different to hope.

In the study, participants reported their level of anger (angry, hostile, and disgusted), fear (nervous, scared, and afraid), and positive emotions (enthusiastic, proud, and hopeful) in response to the Syria crisis. Participants reported the degree to which events in Syria make them feel each emotion on a scale of 1 (not at all) to 5 (very). An explanatory factor analysis of these nine emotions revealed that there were three distinct emotions (eigenvalues $Factor_1 = 2.14$; $Factor_2 = 1.70$; and $Factor_3 = 1.36$). All planned emotion items scaled very well together ($\alpha_{anger} = 0.80$; $\alpha_{fear} = 0.89$; and $\alpha_{hope} = 0.74$). As a result, three discrete emotion scores were generated by taking the average scores of the three respective emotion items.[31]

The next step was to check whether the experimental conditions to induce fear, anger, and hope had actually promoted the respective emotions. Individual analysis of variance tests on the reported levels of anger ($F_{1,232} = 8.81$; $p < 0.01$), fear ($F_{1,232} = 5.70$; $p < 0.01$), and hope ($F_{1,232} = 12.15$; $p < 0.01$) proved that the expected emotional effects had been induced for all three experimental manipulations compared to the neutral group. That is, participants in the anger condition felt significantly more angry than those in the neutral condition ($p < 0.01$). Similarly, participants in the fear condition felt significantly more afraid than those in the neutral condition ($p < 0.02$). Finally, participants in the hope condition felt significantly more positive than those in the neutral condition ($p < 0.05$).

These results show that the intended emotion was evoked for each participant as a result of the experimental manipulation. In other words, because of the experimental treatment that asked participants to report their thoughts and ideas that make them, respectively, angry, afraid, or hopeful about the Syria crisis, the participants felt the targeted emotion more depending on their experimental condition. Those in the anger condition were angrier about events in Syria; those in the fear condition were more afraid; those in the hope condition felt more hopeful and positive about the events. Obviously, those in the control group were supposed to be neutral in their evaluations and expected to be different in their political evaluations and preferences compared to participants in the emotion-evoking experimental groups.

Political Consequences of Emotions

This section provides the results on the political consequences of experimentally induced different emotions on the Syria crisis.

Threat Perception

Given the literature, anger and fear were both likely to promote higher threat perceptions, whereas positive emotions would do the opposite. Whilst anger and fear were expected to generate a stronger perception of external threat, a positive emotion (like hope or enthusiasm) should decrease the level of perceived threat. Accordingly, the next section reports whether particular emotions evoked distinct evaluations of threat stemming from the Syria crisis.

Three questions were asked in the study to measure the level of threat perception as a result of the Syria crisis: "Do you think the Syria crisis is a threat for Turkey" ($1 =$ strongly disagree; $7 =$ strongly agree); "How worried are you that the events in Syria threaten Turkey's security" ($1 =$ not at all; $7 =$ very much); and "How worried are you that the Syria crisis threatens Turkey's economy" ($1 =$ not at all; $7 =$ very much). These three items scaled well together ($\alpha_{threat\ perception} = 0.60$), justifying the generation of a single measure.

In order to fully analyze the effects of the experimental conditions, a dummy variable was created for each experimental treatment with the neutral group as the baseline. Thus, all results for the experimental treatment groups were compared to the neutral condition, which represented the normal conditions for an individual's daily political evaluations and considerations on the Syria issue. Because the dependent measure was continuous, an ordinary-least squares analysis was used for estimation with robust standard errors.

The first column in Table 1 reports the findings on the level of threat perception depending on the experimental condition, and the control variables of political knowledge,[32] gender,[33] income,[34] and political ideology.[35] The first finding from this model is that those in the anger and fear conditions perceive a significantly

Table 1. The Effect of Emotions on Political Evaluations

	Threat perception	Risk engagement	Turkey's role in Syria
Anger condition	0.38** (0.18)	0.41* (0.23)	0.64** (0.26)
Fear condition	0.55*** (0.19)	0.42* (0.22)	0.62** (0.28)
Hope condition	0.04 (0.19)	0.24 (0.23)	0.63*** (0.26)
Female	0.27* (0.14)	−0.34* (0.18)	−0.42** (0.20)
Income	−0.03 (0.07)	0.27*** (0.10)	0.19 (0.12)
Political knowledge	−0.29** (0.14)	−0.09 (0.18)	−0.13 (0.21)
Political ideology	0.06** (0.03)	0.21*** (0.03)	0.24*** (0.04)
Constant	2.73*** (0.26)	1.86*** (0.34)	2.24*** (0.39)
	$N = 231$	$N = 232$	$N = 232$
	$F_{7,223} = 4.76$	$F_{7,224} = 7.94$	$F_{7,224} = 7.74$
	Prob. $> F = 0.0001$	Prob. $> F = 0.0001$	Prob. $> F = 0.0001$
	$R^2 = 0.12$	$R^2 = 0.12$	$R^2 = 0.20$

Note: All entries are unstandardized regression coefficients with standard errors in parentheses.
$^*p < 0.10$.
$^{**}p < 0.05$.
$^{***}p < 0.01$.

higher threat associated with the Syria crisis than the control group. That is, experimentally evoked anger and fear made participants become significantly more cautious in their political judgments.

In contrast, the threat perceptions of participants in the hope condition were no different to those in the neutral condition, suggesting that participants who were induced to feel positive and hopeful about the future of Syria made similar evaluations of the potential threat from Syria to people's normal perceptions. However, both females and those reporting a more right-wing political ideology were much more likely to perceive the Syria crisis as threatening, while politically knowledgeable individuals were less likely to perceive those events as threatening. This could suggest that political knowledge is a factor that could moderate the degree of threat individuals perceive from a neighboring foreign conflict.

Risk Engagement and Support for Punitive Policies against Syria

One of the major political consequences of emotions is that individuals differ in the degree to which they support risky policies. To that end, the study included five questions on a scale of 1 (strongly oppose) to 7 (strongly support) asking whether the individual wants governmental policies on Syria to be conciliatory or stricter, whether sanctions on Syria should be decreased or increased, whether Turkey should force the Syrian regime to change through international organizations, whether they would oppose or support the establishment of a buffer zone in Syria, and whether they would oppose or support a war against Syria. These questions, intended to measure the underlying construct of risky policies of engagement with Syria, all scaled well together ($\alpha_{\text{risk engagement}} = 0.82$). At this level of reliability, it was possible to generate a single continuous measure in which lower ratings indicated support for conciliatory policies while higher ratings indicated support for punitive policies.

The second column in Table 1 presents the results on the level of risk engagement that participants supported, depending on the experimental condition, while controlling for other explanatory variables as before. The first finding is that participants in the anger and fear conditions showed significantly greater preferences for stricter and punitive policies against Syria than those in the neutral condition. Having showed that the experimental conditions evoked the targeted emotions, and that angry and anxious individuals were more likely to perceive the events in Syria as threatening, these results demonstrate that both induced anger and fear generate support for punishment of the Assad regime. A particular implication of this finding is that angry and fearful individuals will be more likely to push for policies that are risky and that directly involve Turkey in the growing conflict between the two states. That is, individuals made to feel angry or frightened by the conflict in Syria will show greater risk-acceptance and willingness for Turkey to engage in militarized conflict in Syria. Thus, contrary to expected difference between these two negative emotions regarding the level of support they would induce for risky policies, the results indicate similar policy preferences for both angry and frightened individuals.

In addition, females were more likely, as expected, to oppose risky policies, whereas those who perceive themselves as more right wing ideologically were more likely to support stricter policies. Interestingly, those with higher income were also more likely to support pursuing risky policies against Syria, even though this could entail engagement in a militarized conflict.

Turkey's Role in the Syria Crisis

Another point of interest is the degree to which individuals are willing to support Turkey's active role in the Syria crisis. For a long time, the AKP government has regarded the issue as a central political issue and strongly engaged with it, not only in domestic politics but also in foreign affairs. PM Erdoğan has repeatedly voiced his concerns and opposition to the Assad regime's repression of the Syrian people. One can predict that the Turkish government's strong position on the issue is likely to be divisive, with some citizens supporting such active policies on Syria while others do not. Similarly, the AKP government's general priority on pursuing an active foreign policy in the Middle East is another issue that one can associate with the Syria crisis. In both cases, taking a more active role in the region is obviously not a risk-averse policy. Thus, we can investigate how induced emotions influence participants' degree of support for Turkey's leadership role on Syria and the Middle East region in general.

To that end, four questions were asked to measure how participants wished to see Turkey, both on the issue of Syria and in the region: "Do you support Turkey's active role on the Syria issue?," "Do you support the government's taking a more active role on the Syria issue?," "Do you support Turkey's playing a leading role on the issue of Syria?," and "Do you support Turkey's taking an active role in the Middle East?" All questions had the same response options from 1 (strongly oppose) to 7 (strongly support). Responses to these four questions scaled very well together ($\alpha_{\text{Turkey's role in Syria}} = 0.87$) and a single measure is created. The results are shown in the final column of Table 1.

The primary finding is that, compared to the control group, both negative and positive emotion treatment conditions equally and significantly promoted support for a stronger leadership role for Turkey, not only on the issue of Syria but also in the Middle East in general. That is, participants who were manipulated to feel angry, afraid, and hopeful about events in Syria all positively supported the idea of Turkey taking a leading role to solve the unfolding and increasingly bloody events in Syria. These findings suggest that inducing any higher level of emotion about events in Syria, whether positive or negative, makes people more likely to want Turkey to do something about it.

In conclusion, this study's results on perceived threat, risk engagement and Turkey's role in the conflict present supporting evidence for the second hypothesis but not the first. It is clear that the political evaluations generated by inducing the two negative emotions are distinct from the positive emotion, but also that negative emotions have significantly different effects to the neutral condition. However, the predicted distinct evaluative outcomes of fear and anger with respect to threat perception and risk-acceptance were not confirmed. This finding suggests that even when experimentally manipulated, anger and fear do not promote distinct evaluations; rather that they primarily evoke emotions on a bipolar (negative and positive) scale. In other words, although fear and anger are distinct as two discrete emotions, the political outcomes that they evoke for an individual are similar with respect to the Syria crisis.

Political Interest and Seeking More Information

Another aspect of these analyses deals with participants' degree of interest in seeking more information about the issue. The study included two items asking whether participants would like to receive information bulletins and updates about parliamentary decisions concerning the Syria crisis. Response options for these questions were 1 (not at all interested) to 4 (very much interested). Because the items are on an ordinal scale, an ordered logistic regression was conducted with robust standard errors on each item. Table 2 reports the results.

The results for both items supported Hypothesis 3. That is, participants who felt fear as a result of their experimental treatment had more interest in learning official information with respect to the events in Syria than those in the neutral group. In other words, participants who were asked to briefly discuss the things that make them anxious and afraid about the Syria crisis were significantly more likely to wish to seek information about the issue compared to those in the control group. The results for the anger condition were similar, showing that participants were more interested in new information when they experienced induced anger with

Table 2. Political Interest and Seeking Information

	Information bulletin	Predicted probabilities (min. → max.)	Information from the parliament	Predicted probabilities (min. → max.)
Anger condition	0.85** (0.41)	0.03 → 0.44	1.07*** (0.43)	0.01 → 0.66
Fear condition	0.80** (0.42)	0.03 → 0.43	0.89** (0.46)	0.01 → 0.63
Hope condition	0.20 (0.39)	–	0.34 (.40)	–
Female	0.70** (0.31)	–	0.56* (0.33)	–
Income	0.24 (0.20)	–	0.12 (0.20)	–
Political knowledge	0.68** (0.33)	–	0.58* (0.34)	–
Political ideology	−0.05 (0.07)	–	−0.05 (0.06)	–
Cut 1	−1.27 (0.60)		−2.50 (0.74)	
Cut 2	0.65 (0.57)		−0.99 (0.66)	
Cut 3	2.246 (0.62)		1.49 (0.66)	
N	231		231	
Wald χ^2 (7)	14.56		14.02	
Prob. > χ^2	0.04		0.05	
Pseudo R^2	0.04		0.04	

Note: All entries are ordered logistic regression coefficients with standard errors in parentheses.
*$p < 0.10$.
**$p < 0.05$.
***$p < 0.01$.

respect to the Syria crisis. Predicted probability values suggest that being in the fear condition (compared to the control group and hope condition) make individuals 40 percent more likely to request an information bulletin and approximately 60 percent more likely to request information from parliament about the issue, while holding other variables at their mean values.[36] Similarly, being in the anger condition makes one seek further information about the issue with almost equal probability. Evidently, self-reflective writing on the things that make people afraid or angry about events in Syria is strong enough to alter individuals' reported willingness to seek information. Finally, as expected, compared to the neutral group, the positive emotion (hope condition) did not induce any greater interest to learn more about the subject of Syria.

The analysis also demonstrated that both politically knowledgeable individuals and women were more likely to express a desire to learn more about the issue. Given that it is likely that individuals who know more about politics will be more interested to learn about the Syria issue in particular, these results are an expected behavior. Overall, these results provide significant support for the hypothesis that experimentally induced emotions can motivate individuals to seek information.

Evaluating PM Erdoğan's Performance

The next focus of analysis concerns the interesting question of how induced emotions may affect evaluations of political leaders' performance. In general, it can be expected that individuals rate important political figures in line with their ideological preferences and particular political attitudes, such that ideologically right-wing individuals will be more likely to support leaders from right-wing political parties and vice-versa. This experimental study, in which emotions are manipulated, provides a valuable opportunity to investigate how evaluations of Turkey's principal political actor differ across the conditions. Given that PM Erdoğan is the most important individual in forming and conducting Turkey's policy on Syria,[37] it is worthwhile testing whether emotional manipulations did in fact alter individual evaluations of his political performance.

The study included four items on PM Erdoğan's performance. The first three items directly measured levels of approval/disapproval of the way PM Erdoğan is handling his job: "How strongly do you approve or disapprove of the way Recep Tayyip Erdoğan is handling his job as the prime minister," "...handling the economy...," and "...handling foreign affairs with other countries...?" These items had the same response options, ranging from 1 (strongly disapprove) to 7 (strongly approve). The fourth item was a "feeling thermometer" generally employed to gauge affective (like–dislike) reactions to individuals, groups, political institutions, or other relevant object. The rating scale ranges from 0 (very cold feelings for the target) to 100 (very warm feeling for the target) with a neutral rating option of 50. Here, the participants were asked to rate Recep Tayyip Erdoğan on this scale. Table 3 reports the findings.

The main result of this analysis was that participants in the hope condition gave significantly higher ratings of the way that PM Erdoğan handles his job, the economy, and foreign affairs than those in the neutral group. Even controlling for political ideology (which was also consistently significant in these models), participants that were induced to feel positive and hopeful about events in Syria tended to show greater support for PM Erdoğan. A possible behavioral mechanism explaining this effect could be that people associate the Syria issue directly with PM Erdoğan, so the emotions they were induced to feel as a result of the experimental treatment motived them to show greater support for his performance. The combined results from this analysis provide supporting evidence for Hypothesis 4.

Participants in the fear condition also showed greater approval of the way the PM handles his job and liked him more than the neutral group. A possible explanation for this interesting (but not unexpected) finding is that when people feel afraid and anxious about a situation, they seek refuge in supportive evaluations of important political actors and their policies to feel safer. Thus they may like and give greater support for the political leader currently handles both that particular issue and manages policies in general. In line with this expectation, we see those who were experimentally felt fearful about the Syria issue approved of PM Erdoğan's way of handling his job and liked him more.

Table 3. The Effect of Emotions on Premiership Approval

	Job approval	Handling the economy	Handling foreign affairs	Affective evaluations
Anger condition	0.41 (0.32)	0.20 (0.39)	0.26 (0.34)	7.59 (5.03)
Fear condition	0.69** (0.34)	0.32 (0.36)	0.55 (0.34)	9.33** (4.90)
Hope condition	0.72*** (0.30)	0.62* (0.35)	0.74** (0.33)	11.88** (5.09)
Female	−0.59*** (0.23)	−0.91*** (0.27)	−0.22 (0.25)	−6.95* (3.57)
Income	0.09 (0.15)	−0.09 (0.18)	0.02 (0.17)	2.52 (2.44)
Political knowledge	0.46* (0.24)	0.29 (0.28)	0.05 (0.26)	4.58 (3.73)
Political ideology	0.46*** (0.05)	0.48*** (0.06)	0.42*** (0.05)	7.52*** (0.78)
Constant	0.72* (0.42)	1.59*** (0.52)	1.31*** (0.52)	−7.02 (6.06)
	$N = 231$	$N = 231$	$N = 231$	$N = 224$
	$F_{7,223} = 24.14$	$F_{7,223} = 18.29$	$F_{7,223} = 12.07$	$F_{7,216} = 27.12$
	Prob. $> F =$ 0.0001	Prob. $> F =$ 0.0001	Prob. $> F =$ 0.0001	Prob. $> F =$ 0.0001
	$R^2 = 0.39$	$R^2 = 0.43$	$R^2 = 0.26$	$R^2 = 0.38$

Note: All entries are unstandardized regression coefficients with standard errors in parentheses.
*$p < 0.10$.
**$p < 0.05$.
***$p < 0.01$.

As predicted from previous scholarly studies, political ideology strongly influenced levels of support for the way PM Erdoğan does his job in general and handles the economy and foreign affairs in particular. Participants reporting themselves politically right wing were significantly more approving of Erdoğan's performance. However, while ideology is an important variable, its effect in this study was not substantially different from the effect of particular emotions. This finding suggests that emotions are in fact an integral part of the way Turkish voters define their support for political leaders. In turn, this means that scholars should include emotion reactions to certain political targets and policies to properly model Turkish citizens' political behavior. In addition, female participants in this study consistently disapproved of the way PM Erdoğan handles his job and the economy, and also felt cooler toward him than male participants.[38]

Overall, these results show that experimentally manipulated emotions significantly influence individual political attitudes, behavior, and evaluations. There is clear evidence that the three experimentally evoked emotions had distinct effects to the neutral condition, and that the negative emotions had different effects to the positive emotions. Although these analyses did not find the predicted distinct influences of anger and fear, they do show, at the very least, that experimentally induced emotions can strongly influence voters' political attitudes and behavior.

Conclusion

This study examined the role of emotions in Turkish political attitudes. It provided consistent and strong evidence that emotions alter political evaluations, attitudes, and behavior with respect to the important foreign policy topic of the Syria crisis. Specific experimentally manipulated emotions (although quite subtle) changed, in distinct ways, participants' risk assessments, threat perceptions, policy evaluations, behavior on information seeking, and premiership approval and performance evaluations. These findings indicate that, as in other countries, emotions cannot be ignored in the Turkish political context, and that emotions should be included in models of political behavior and individual level analysis in future research.

Although Turkish foreign policy toward Syria was the topic of interest in this study, we should not forget that the theory and hypotheses investigated here are equally applicable to other cases and policies. Events in Syria and the resulting recently increased tensions have provided a valuable ground for research to detect if emotions influence political attitudes and preferences. However, other cases of interest in Turkey (such as the effect of emotions on the level of support for European Union membership in Turkey,[39] emotions with respect to domestic social, ethnic, and religious issues in Turkey, the consequences of emotions for political attitudes and behavior evoked as a result of terrorist attacks, or foreign policy-making during the Arab Spring) should be investigated by future scholarly research. Thus, there are many important topics to explore with respect to the many facets of emotions in political life within the Turkish context, and future research could valuably focus on these unexplored areas of Turkish political attitudes and behavior in relation to emotions.

This study also contributes to the wider emotions literature in political psychology by supporting previous theoretical predictions in a different location. In turn, this study improves the external validity of results on emotions, given that the current literature on emotions in political science primarily relates to inquiry in the US context. By conducting research in distinct cultures, locations, and publics, it is possible to test and improve theoretical inferences and external validity. With respect to experimental studies, improving external validity is critical for future development, not only of methodology but also of scholarly research in the discipline. Among future directions, one could first suggest that emotions and individual psychological indicators should be accounted for in understanding the determinants of Turkish political behavior. An important particular goal is to seek theoretically driven arguments and employ hypothesis testing. Second, different research methods should be used for hypothesis testing. While every method has strengths and drawbacks, experimental design is the strongest one to infer causal associations between indicators, and is the approach that is currently most needed in the Turkish political science discipline. Strengthened methods could eventually improve the quality of research and theory building in the discipline.

Acknowledgements

I thank Emre Erdoğan, Kerem Ozan Kalkan, and Zeki Sarıgil for allowing me to collect data in their courses for this study. I am also indebted to Elif Erişen and

POLITICAL PSYCHOLOGY OF TURKISH POLITICAL BEHAVIOR

Çiğdem V. Şirin for their extremely useful comments on an earlier draft of this article. I also appreciate Zeliha Çetinkaya's research assistantship in data collection and preparation.

Notes

1. Redlawsk, *Feeling Politics* and Erisen and Erisen, "Cognitive vs. Emotional Evaluations."
2. Erisen, Lodge, and Taber, "Affective Contagion in Effortful Political Thinking" and Lodge and Taber, "The Primacy of Affect," 455–82.
3. Marcus, Neuman, and MacKuen, *Affective Intelligence and Political Judgment*.
4. Lodge and Taber, "The Primacy of Affect"; Redlawsk, Civettini, and Lau, "Affective Intelligence and Voting: Information Processing and Learning," 152–79; and Cassino and Erisen, "Priming Bush and Iraq in 2008," 372–94.
5. Lupia, McCubbins, and Popkin, eds., *Elements of Reason*.
6. Shafir, Simonson, and Tversky, "Reason-based Choice," 11–36.
7. Elster, *Alchemies of the Mind*.
8. Sears, Huddy, and Jervis, eds., *Oxford Handbook of Political Psychology*; Redlawsk, *Feeling Politics*; Neuman et al., eds., *Affect Effect*; and Lodge and Taber, *The Rationalizing Voter*.
9. Campbell et al., *American Voter*.
10. An example would be Sniderman, Brody, and Tetlock, *Reasoning and Choice*.
11. LeDoux, *The Emotional Brain*; Forgas, "Mood and Judgment," 39–66; Lazarus, *Emotion and Adaptation*; and Zajonc, "Feeling and Thinking," 151–75.
12. Lodge, McGraw, and Stroh, "An Impression-driven Model," 399–419; Lodge and Taber, "The Primacy of Affect"; and Marcus, Russell Neuman, and MacKuen, *Affective Intelligence and Political Judgment*.
13. Damasio, *Descartes' Error*.
14. Smith and Lazarus, "Appraisal Components, Core relational Themes and Emotions," 233–69.
15. Lodge and Taber, "The Primacy of Affect." For a distinct view on emotions within social networks see Erisen and Erisen, "The Effect of Social Networks," 839–65.
16. Lodge and Taber, "The Primacy of Affect."
17. Schwarz and Clore, "Mood, Misattribution, and Judgments of Well-being," 513–23 and Schwarz and Clore, "Mood as Information," 294–301.
18. Sniderman, Brody, and Tetlock, *Reasoning and Choice*.
19. Marcus, Russell Neuman, and MacKuen, *Affective Intelligence and Political Judgment* and Marcus, "The Psychology of Emotion and Politics," 182–221.
20. Frijda, *The Emotions* and Elster, *Alchemies of the Mind*.
21. Conover and Feldman, "Emotional Reactions to the Economy," 50–78.
22. Johnson and Tversky, "Affect, Generalization, and the Perception," 20–31.
23. Lerner and Keltner, "Beyond Valence," 473–93 and Lerner and Dacher. "Fear, Anger, and Risk," 146–59.
24. Huddy et al., "Threat, Anxiety, and Support," 593–608.
25. Huddy, Feldman, and Cassese, "On the Distinct Political Effects," 202–330.
26. Marcus, Russell Neuman, and MacKuen, *Affective Intelligence and Political Judgment* and Brader, *Campaigning for Hearts and Minds*.
27. Lerner et al., "Effects of Fear and Anger on Perceived Risks of Terrorism," 144–50.
28. For more discussion on student samples, see the methods section in this special issue. It should also be remembered that earlier studies have demonstrated that student samples and representative samples provide similar results on the effects of emotions, e.g. Lerner et al., "Effects of Fear and Anger on Perceived Risks of Terrorism." The theoretical and methodological reasoning for these assumptions are also discussed elsewhere Druckman and Kam, "Students as Experimental Participants," 70–101.

29. Lerner and Keltner, "Beyond Valence"; Lerner et al., "Effects of Fear and Anger on Perceived Risks of Terrorism"; and Small and Lerner, "Emotional Policy," 149–68.
30. Considering the small number of participants dropped for the data analysis (less than 5 percent), this does not raise concerns over the rate of non-compliance with the study.
31. None of the correlations across the emotions were above thresholds that could cause concern over inference ($r_{anger-fear} = 0.50$; $r_{anger-positive} = 0.12$; $r_{fear-positive} = -0.02$).
32. Eight open-ended items were asked to measure levels of political knowledge: Identification of the Speaker of Grand National Assembly, President of the Constitutional Court of the Republic of Turkey, a minister from the current government, the current Minister for EU Affairs, the US President, and the UK Prime Minister. Another item asked participants to name an MP from his/her voting district. The final question asked the number of years before general elections must be held in Turkey. A research assistant unaware of the research hypotheses coded all responses as correct or incorrect. Summing up the correct responses then generates a single variable of political knowledge.
33. One question determined whether the participant was female or male.
34. Participants were asked to report their total family income in 2011. The response options included 14 categories from 5,000TL to 90,000TL or more.
35. Political ideology was measured with a single item asking the individual to report his or her political position on a scale ranging from 0 (strongly left) to 10 (strongly right).
36. Because the coefficients in ordered logit models are not directly interpretable, I calculated the predicted probabilities. The probabilities show the change in predicted probability when each independent variable moves from its minimum to maximum value, while holding other variables at their mean values. I used CLARIFY software to calculate the predicted probabilities. King, Tomz, and Wittenberg, "Making the Most of Statistical Analyses," 347–61.
37. One cannot ignore the importance of Ahmet Davutoğlu as Minister of Foreign Affairs in generating Turkish foreign policy. However, PM Erdoğan makes final decisions regarding critical foreign policies and the public tends to vote for or against AKP with him in mind in the elections.
38. One should be careful about generalizing this finding since this could be an artifact of the convenience sample. We can only suggest that for this sample, women were more likely than men to disapprove premiership performance.
39. Erisen and Erisen, "Cognitive vs. Emotional Evaluations."

References

Brader, Ted. *Campaigning for Hearts and Minds: How Emotional Appeals in Political Ads Work.* Chicago: University of Chicago Press, 2006.
Campbell, Angus, Phillip E. Converse, Warran E. Miller, and Donald E. Stokes. *American Voter.* Chicago: University of Chicago Press, 1960.
Cassino, Dan, and Cengiz Erisen. "Priming Bush and Iraq in 2008: A Survey Experiment." *American Politics Research* 38, no. 2 (2010): 372–394.
Conover, Pamela Johnston, and Feldman Stanley. "Emotional Reactions to the Economy: I'm Mad as Hell and I'm Not Going to Take it Anymore." *American Journal of Political Science* 30, no. 1 (1986): 50–78.

Damasio, Antonio R. *Descartes' Error: Emotion, Reason, and the Human Brain*. New York: Putnam, 1994.

Druckman, Jamie N., and Cindy D. Kam. "Students as Experimental Participants: A Defense of the Narrow Data Base." In *Cambridge Handbook of Experimental Political Science*, edited by Jamie N. Druckman, Donald P. Green, James H. Kuklinski, and Arthur Lupia, 70–101. New York: Cambridge, 2011.

Elster, Jon. *Alchemies of the Mind: Rationality and the Emotions*. New York: Cambridge University Press, 1999.

Erisen, Elif, and Cengiz Erisen. "The Effect of Social Networks on the Quality of Political Thinking." *Political Psychology* 33, no. 6 (2012): 839–865.

Erisen, Cengiz, and Elif Erisen. "Cognitive vs. Emotional Evaluations as the Foundations of the Public Perception of the EU in Turkey." In *The Great Catalyst: European Union Project and Lessons from Greece and Turkey*, edited by Bulent Temel. New York: Lexington Books, forthcoming.

Forgas, Joe P. "Mood and Judgment: The Affect Infusion Model (AIM)." *Psychological Bulletin* 11, no. 1 (1995): 39–66.

Frijda, Nico H. *The Emotions*. New York: Cambridge University Press, 1986.

Huddy, Leonie, Stanley Feldman, and Erin Cassese. "On the Distinct Political Effects of Anxiety and Anger." In *Affect Effect: Dynamics of Emotion in Political Thinking and Behavior*, edited by W. Russell Neuman, George E. Marcus, Ann N. Crigler, and Michael MacKuen, 202–330. Chicago: Chicago University Press, 2007.

Huddy, Leonie, Stanley Feldman, Charles Taber, and Gallya Lahav. "Threat, Anxiety, and Support of Anti-terrorism Policies." *American Journal of Political Science* 49, no. 3 (2005): 593–608.

Johnson, Eric J., and Amos Tversky. "Affect, Generalization, and the Perception of Risk." *Journal of Personality and Social Psychology* 45, no. 1 (1983): 20–31.

King, Gary, Michael Tomz, and Jason Wittenberg. "Making the Most of Statistical Analyses: Improving Interpretation and Presentation." *American Journal of Political Science* 44, no. 2 (2000): 347–361.

Lazarus, Richard S. *Emotion and Adaptation*. New York: Oxford University Press, 1991.

LeDoux, Joseph E. *The Emotional Brain: The Mysterious Underpinnings of Emotional Life*. New York: Simon and Schuster, 1995.

Lerner, Jennifer S., and Dacher Keltner. "Beyond Valence: Toward a Model of Emotion-Specific Influences on Judgment and Choice." *Cognition and Emotion* 14, no. 4 (2000): 473–493.

Lerner, Jennifer S., and Dacher Keltner. "Fear, Anger, and Risk." *Journal of Personality and Social Psychology* 81, no. 1 (2001): 146–159.

Lerner, Jennifer S., Roxana M. Gonzalez, Deborah A. Small, and Baruch Fischhoff. "Effects of Fear and Anger on Perceived Risks of Terrorism: A National Field Experiment." *Psychological Science* 14, no. 2 (2003): 144–150.

Lodge, Milton, Kathleen McGraw, and Paul Stroh. "An Impression-Driven Model of Candidate Evaluation." *American Political Science Review* 83, no. 2 (1989): 399–419.

Lodge, Milton, and Charles Taber. "The Primacy of Affect for Political Candidates, Groups, and Issues: An Experimental Test of the Hot Cognition Hypothesis." *Political Psychology* 26, no. 3 (2005): 455–482.

Lodge, Milton, and Charles Taber. *The Rationalizing Voter*. New York: Cambridge University Press, forthcoming.

Lupia, Arthur, Mathew D. McCubbins, and Samuel L. Popkin, eds. *Elements of Reason: Cognition, Choice, and the Bounds of Rationality*. New York: Cambridge University Press, 2000.

Marcus, George E. "The Psychology of Emotion and Politics." In *Oxford Handbook of Political Psychology*, edited by David O. Sears, Leonie Huddy, and Robert L. Jervis, 182–221. London: Oxford University Press, 2003.

Marcus, George E., W. Russell Neuman, and Michael MacKuen. *Affective Intelligence and Political Judgment*. Chicago: University of Chicago Press, 2000.

Neuman, W. Russell, George E. Marcus, Ann N. Crigler, and Michael MacKuen, eds. *Affect Effect: Dynamics of Emotion in Political Thinking and Behavior*. Chicago: Chicago University Press, 2007.

Redlawsk, David. *Feeling Politics: Emotion in Political Information Processing*. New York: Palgrave, 2006.

Redlawsk, David P., Andrew CivettiniJ. W., and Richard Lau. "Affective Intelligence and Voting: Information Processing and Learning in a Campaign." In *The Affect Effect: Dynamics of Emotion in Political Thinking and Behavior*, edited by W. Russell Neuman, George E. Marcus, Ann Crigler, and Michael MacKuen, 152–179. Chicago: University of Chicago Press, 2007.

Schwarz, Norbert, and Gerald L. Clore. "Mood, Misattribution, and Judgments of Well-being: Information and Directive Functions of Affective States." *Journal of Personality and Social Psychology* 45, no. 3 (1983): 513–523.

Schwarz, Norbert, and Gerald L. Clore. "Mood as Information: 20 Years Later." *Psychological Inquiry* 14, no. 3–4 (2003): 294–301.

Sears, David O., Leonie Huddy, and Robert L. Jervis, eds. *Oxford Handbook of Political Psychology*. London: Oxford University Press, 2003.

Shafir, Eldar, Itamar Simonson, and Amos Tversky. "Reason-based Choice." *Cognition* 49, nos. 1–2 (1993): 11–36.

Small, Deborah A., and Jennifer S. Lerner. "Emotional Policy: Personal Sadness and Anger Shape Judgments about a Welfare Case." *Political Psychology* 29, no. 2 (2008): 149–168.

Smith, Craig A., and Richard S. Lazarus. "Appraisal Components, Core Relational Themes and Emotions." *Cognition and Emotion* 7, nos. 3–4 (1993): 233–269.

Sniderman, Paul, Richard E. Brody, and Philip A. Tetlock. *Reasoning and Choice: Explorations in Political Psychology*. New York: Cambridge University Press, 1991.

Zajonc, Robert. "Feeling and Thinking: Preferences Need No Inferences." *American Psychologist* 35, no. 2 (1980): 151–175.

Leadership Traits of Turkey's Islamist and Secular Prime Ministers

BARIŞ KESGİN

Department of Political Science, Susquehanna University, Selinsgrove, PA, USA

ABSTRACT   *Leaders are influential in Turkish politics; since early Republican years under Atatürk and İnönü, the dominance of omnipotent leaders continued, if not escalated, under democratic elections. Menderes or Demirel or Erbakan, and presently Erdoğan, each leader assumed office with different personal and political backgrounds, worldviews, and personality characteristics. Nonetheless, a systematic study of political leaders in Turkish politics and foreign policy has rarely been a concern to scholars of Turkey. This lack of attention to Turkey's political leaders affects not only a nuanced understanding of its domestic politics but also its foreign policy. How do Turkish leaders' idiosyncratic traits affect their politics? How does the common phrase "secular and religious leaders" capture differences among Turkey's leadership? Utilizing a method of leadership assessment at-a-distance, this piece provides answers to such questions with respect to foreign policy profiles of all post-Cold War prime ministers of Turkey. It illustrates that Turkish leaders have distinct leadership traits but cannot be reduced to "seculars" and "Islamists."*

Turkish politics has always been "a stage for leader-based politics."[1] In the domestic political arena, party leaders—often the chairperson directly—decide who is going to make the party list in general elections, who is going to run for office in local elections, and who will participate in the decision-making bodies of their party. Hence, political scientist Hakan Yavuz argues that in Turkey "personalities are always more important than party programs or institutions."[2] Likewise, in matters of foreign policy, prime ministers have been important actors in Turkish foreign policy-making.[3] Leaders such as Turgut Özal (particularly during his presidency) and Necmettin Erbakan (during his short one-year tenure as head of government) did have substantial influence over Turkish foreign policy. Similarly, the present Turkish Prime Minister Recep Tayyip Erdoğan has made a significant impact on Turkey's foreign policy since coming to power in November 2002.[4] However, scholars of Turkish politics and foreign policy have rarely chosen to study leaders' personalities and trace their potential effects on foreign policy.

Until recently, there were only two exceptions to this trend. First, published in 2002, the Heper and Sayarı volume is a very informative collection of essays on Turkish leaders and their contributions (or lack thereof) to Turkey's democratization.[5] Although it has rather limited engagement with foreign policy issues, this book provides valuable information about leader personalities as each chapter has a section on leader personality. Another book, edited by political scientist Ali Faik Demir, focuses exclusively on foreign policy and leadership, and it is (most likely) the only such study in the Turkish foreign policy literature.[6] Then, most recently, the first published study of a Turkish leader, applying leadership traits analysis, appeared in *Turkish Studies*.[7] Still, as of mid-2012, there is no study that covers all major political actors (e.g. prime ministers in the past two decades) in Turkey and assesses their personalities in a systematic and replicable manner.

Instead, Turkish leaders have often been portrayed simply as secular or religious individuals in both domestic and foreign media. This dichotomous interpretation of Turkish leaders then is utilized in interpreting their policy choices. For example, in the fall of 2010, the Turkish and world media often depicted Erdoğan and his government as Islamic. Even academics may resort to differences between secular and Islamic groups.[8] While these perceptions derive from the political history of the country and personal backgrounds of leaders concerned, it is controversial that the label Islamic or religious by itself would explain a leader's (Erbakan or Erdoğan or Gül) approach to the world or their foreign policy motivations. Such a poor understanding is so prevalent that it shapes the minds of the public and the policy-makers, questioning this simplistic perception of Turkish leadership is more than warranted. Religion may very well be a more important factor for some leaders than others; then, a plausible question is if there would be any differences among the so-called religious and secular prime ministers of Turkey, and their foreign policies. The findings here will offer answers in that regard.

This study is based on the premise that effects of leadership personalities on Turkish foreign policy can be found in the post-Cold War era. Such influences are not confined to one or a few Turkish leaders, nor can they be reduced to a dichotomous interpretation, explaining Turkish prime ministers' individual characteristics help understand foreign policy behavior of Turkey. After briefly reviewing methods of assessment of political leadership and more specifically political scientist Margaret Hermann's Leadership Traits Analysis (LTA), the paper highlights Turkish prime ministers' role in the making of the country's foreign policy. Then, all post-Cold War prime ministers of Turkey are profiled and a discussion about how their leadership characteristics influenced Turkish foreign policy follows. According to the findings here, Turkish leaders exhibit different leadership styles beyond a simplistic account of secular and religious leaders; also, the norming group used to assess leadership style matters (yet, does not challenge or contradict the first conclusion). Furthermore, the so-called secular and religious leaders differ among themselves. Of all Turkish prime ministers in the post-Cold War era, Erbakan stands out as a unique leader. The essay concludes with a call for attending to how individual actors can influence political outcomes and psychological factors in Turkey's foreign policy.

At-a-Distance Assessment of Political Leaders

Former US Secretary of State Henry Kissinger once said, "As a professor, I tended to think of history as run by impersonal forces. But when you see it in practice, you see the difference personalities make."[9] The scholarly study of foreign policy reflects Kissinger's observation; in this line of research, the individual constitutes the heart of international politics.[10] In particular, those who follow the tradition of Snyder, Bruck, and Sapin assume that individual features of political leaders influence state behavior. According to those, personality characteristics (such as beliefs, motives, decision style, and interpersonal style) affect personal orientation to behavior, which in turn shapes one's general orientation to foreign affairs.[11] In other words, for scholars of foreign policy decision-making, individuals or, groups of individuals, are the source of all state actions.[12]

The study of individuals in the field of foreign policy analysis has benefited from and is closely connected with the literature and research in psychology.[13] However, unlike a psychological examination of a person, the study of political leaders requires unique methods—because leaders are not available or willing to interview for psychological analysis. However, one can infer leaders' personality traits or beliefs from their public speeches and/or other spontaneous utterances.[14] "At-a-distance" techniques overcome this problem of access to political leaders. These methods help profile political leaders based on their publicly available verbal records (speeches, interviews, letters, etc.). In essence, these techniques are adaptations from conventional personality measurements in psychology and they require meticulously designed procedures of coding and operationalization of selected personality measures.[15]

Since the introduction of ProfilerPlus, developed at Social Science Automation, in 2001, "at-a-distance" methods of political leadership assessment have been computerized. ProfilerPlus has been widely used in personality assessment of various political leaders. Automated content analysis is important not only for significantly reducing the time spent for analysis but also for developing systematic, objective, and replicable results. Moreover, it is also advantageous for making use of a wealth of materials available, thanks to the Internet. This also constitutes a major milestone in conducting similar research since automated content analysis allows researchers to expand the study of political leaders beyond Western countries. While there are many documents available for studies of non-Western political leadership, systematic studies of non-Western leaders remain relatively scarce.[16]

Leadership Traits Analysis

In a survey of research programs about leaders' cognition, political scientists Michael Young and Mark Schafer identify LTA as one of the most significant methods.[17] Indeed, LTA has led to multiple, fruitful lines of research and has been applied to many leaders around the world.[18] This technique claims that leaders' choices of certain words reflect their personalities. As Margaret Hermann, the pioneer of this method, explains, "In effect, the trait analysis is quantitative in nature and employs frequency counts. At issue is what percentage of the time in responding to interviewers' questions when leaders could exhibit particular words and phrases are they, indeed, used."[19] Each leadership trait is calculated according to a coding scheme and can take a value between 0 and 1; the higher the value, the more a leader exhibits one trait. As such, LTA involves a careful content analysis of leaders' discourse and its quantification into seven traits:

(1) Belief in ability control events.
(2) Conceptual complexity.
(3) Distrust of others.
(4) In-group bias.
(5) Need for power.
(6) Self-confidence.
(7) Task focus.

Broader implications of any trait score, for a leader's behavior and leadership style, are judged by comparisons to a group.

A leader's profile is assessed via a comparison of his traits' scores to those of a meaningful group of other leaders, that is, the norming group. When a leader's scores are a standard deviation below the norming group's mean, then he profiles *low* in that trait. Accordingly, when a score is one standard deviation above the norming group's, then the leader has a *high* score for the trait in question. When a leader's score is close to the norming group's mean, the leader is *moderate* in that particular trait. A leader's ranking in comparison to this group (high or low) then suggests how leaders react to constraints, are motivated toward the world, their openness to information, etc. These, in turn, imply leaders' leadership style. Leaders have different styles of decision-making because they "relate to those around them-whether constituents, advisers, or other leaders- and how they structure interactions and the norms, rules, and principles they use to guide such interactions" in different manners.[20]

First, how a leader ranks according to his scores in belief in one's own ability to control events and need for power help determine the leader's responsiveness to constraints. Here, leader personality is assessed as to

how important it is for them to exert control and influence over the environment in which they find themselves, and the constraints that environment poses, as opposed to being adaptable to the situation and remaining open to responding to the demands of domestic and international constituencies and circumstances.[21]

Then, a leader's conceptual complexity and self-confidence scores together indicate his openness to new information. This assessment is important because the two ends suggest distinct approaches to decision-making.[22] Leaders who are open to contextual information act as "cue-takers" and seek information both supportive of and contrary to their own. Leaders who are less open to new information, on the other hand, act as advocates of their own agendas and ideas; they seek support for their position and work to persuade others along the way. A leader whose conceptual complexity score is higher than his self-confidence score—hence, who is open to new information—is able to get others to do things because others perceive that the leader is interested in what happens to them and that he is concerned about helping them.[23]

In relation to the third question about why leaders seek their positions, there are two issues that must be accounted for assessing a leader's motivations: one is why the leader sought the office, and the other is the leader's motivations in leading and securing their group (also, their position within).[24] These motives are so important that they "shape [leaders'] character—what is important in their lives and what drives them to act."[25] Based on the conclusions from relevant literature, one can identify two types of motivation in political leaders. One is a leader driven by an internal focus such as an ideology, a set of specific interests, problems, or a cause that force them to act. The latter group of leaders are motivated by a desired relationship with others in their environment and they take action because of these factors other than themselves. Task focus score can help profile a leader for his/her motivation for seeking office. Based on conclusions from these comparisons, leadership styles are determined according to Table 1.

In recent years political scientist Stephen Dyson's research has significantly contributed to the leadership traits analysis. One of Dyson's recent works can be illustrative of this line of research. For instance, comparing Tony Blair's traits scores (British prime minister, 1997–2007) with all other British prime ministers since 1945, Dyson studied how Blair's personality affected British decisions in the 2003 Iraq war. According to Dyson's analysis, Tony Blair has a high belief in ability to control events, a low conceptual complexity, and a high need for power compared to all 12 British prime ministers in the post-1945 era.[26] First, Blair's significantly higher belief in ability to control events score suggests that Blair strongly believes in his ability to control events in the political environment, and he perceives Britain as an influential actor in world politics. Second, a low conceptual complexity score signals a worldview of binary categories such as good vs. evil and us vs. them. Blair's conceptual complexity score, which is one standard deviation below other British prime ministers, indicates that he would have a decisive decision-making style where other significant factors outside his black-and-white view are not evaluated properly or may go unnoticed. Lastly, Dyson shows that Blair is high in the need for power trait hence would be actively involved in policy formulation and work with small groups of hand-picked individuals. In addition, a combined high belief in ability to control events and high need for power score suggests that Blair would likely challenge constraints in the international system. This leadership traits analysis of Tony Blair shows how his preferences and behavior explain Britain's choice in Iraq. As the Iraq war unfolded, Blair "demonstrated a proactive policy orientation, internal locus of control in terms of shaping events, a binary information processing and framing style, and a preference to work through tightly held processes in policy making."[27]

Table 1. Leadership Style as a Function of Responsiveness to Constraints, Openness to Information, and Motivation

Responsiveness to constraints	Openness to information	Motivation	
		Problem focus	**Relationship focus**
Challenges constraints	Closed to information	Expansionistic (focus of attention is on expanding leader's, government's, and state's span of control)	Evangelistic (focus of attention is on persuading others to join in one's mission, in mobilizing others around one's message)
Challenges constraints	Open to information	Actively independent (focus of attention is on maintaining one's own and the government's maneuverability and independence in a world that is perceived to continually try to limit both)	Directive (focus of attention is on maintaining one's own and the government's status and acceptance by others by engaging in actions on the world stage that enhance the state's reputation)
Respects constraints	Closed to information	Incremental (focus of attention is on improving state's economy and/or security in incremental steps while avoiding the obstacles that will inevitably arise along the way)	Influential (focus of attention is on building cooperative relationships with other governments and states in order to play a leadership role; by working with others, one can gain more than is possible on one's own)
Respects constraints	Open to information	Opportunistic (focus of attention is on assessing what is possible in the current situation and context given what one wants to achieve and considering what important constituencies will allow)	Collegial (focus of attention is on reconciling differences and building consensus—on gaining prestige and status through empowering others and sharing accountability)

Source: Hermann (2003), p. 185.

Other recent works in LTA also explored decision-making processes in Western governments during the Iraq War. In one such study, political scientists Vaughn Shannon and Jonathan Keller look at leadership traits of the members of the George W. Bush administration and their positions regarding the 2003 Iraq War.[28] They show that against some constructivist and realist propositions about how international norms violated due to global social pressures or self-interest and the anarchic nature of world politics—respectively, leaders' beliefs and their decision-making styles have significant impact on why and how leaders may defy international norms.[29] Shannon and Keller argue that particular leadership traits (such as high belief in ability to control events, need for power, distrust of others, and in-group bias) can predict a leader's propensity to respect or challenge international norms. Dyson's research on Blair, Shannon, and Keller's work on the US administration illustrate the significance of LTA as a method of explaining foreign policy behavior and linking it with the personalities of decision-makers.

Obviously, LTA has not been void of criticism. One of the main criticisms against this method has been that it was unable to capture the leader's personality; instead, it was offering a snapshot at a certain moment.[30] Nonetheless, LTA as method does not discard that personality can be contextually dependent, which can be determined by studying diverse material.[31] Notwithstanding such criticisms, many leader profiles that were assessed using the LTA technique match well with the image of those leaders in the eyes of other leaders, advisers, and journalists.[32] Such validation is proof that a leader's general profile can be assessed with a certain number of word count and a variety of issues covered across time and space. It is also argued that LTA scores would become less stable when they are calculated at smaller units of time, or across different issues.[33] Finally, as mentioned earlier, LTA could be criticized for its limitation to Western context. Then, a challenge is still ahead of LTA to test to what extent it could offer explanations cross culturally in profiling leadership in other countries.

Data

The independent variables of interest are the leadership traits of Turkey's prime ministers in the post-Cold War era. In order to measure these variables, all the spontaneous foreign policy remarks of Turkish prime ministers are under investigation here. More specifically, the whole universe of readily available, spontaneous foreign policy statements made by Turkey's contemporary prime ministers are collected. The texts of these statements were accessed from various databases such as *LexisNexis*, *Factiva*, and *Foreign Broadcasting and Information System*. In addition, some online documentation on the Internet was readily available for analysis. Hence, only those "readily available" materials are incorporated in this study. It is, however, assumed that most if not all spontaneous foreign policy statements (as defined here) Turkey's leaders made were accessed. These texts required only minor editing as they were prepared for processing in ProfilerPlus. All the text was already translated into English, or sometimes the leader already spoke in English.[34] For LTA, a response/

record of at least 100 words is expected to produce a meaningful result—granted that it would be complemented with other materials that bring up the total number of words to at least 5000 words. An accurate LTA profile requires at least 5000 words analyzed, which is met for all the leaders studied here.[35]

Table 2. LTA: Trait Conceptualization and Coding Scheme

Trait	Description	Coding
Belief can control events	Perception of the world as an environment leader can influence. Leader's own state is perceived as an influential actor in the international system	Percentage of verbs used that reflect action or planning for action of the leader or relevant group
Conceptual complexity	Capability of discerning different dimensions of the environment when describing actors, places, ideas, and situations	Percentage of words related to high complexity (i.e. "approximately," "possibility," "trend") vs. low complexity (i.e. "absolutely," "certainly," "irreversible")
Distrust of others	Doubt about and wariness of others	Percentage of nouns that indicate misgivings or suspicions that others intend harm toward speaker or speaker's group
In-group bias	Perception of one's group as holding a central role, accompanied with strong feelings of national identity and honor	Percentage of references to the group that are favorable (i.e. "successful," "prosperous," "great"), show strength (i.e. "powerful," "capable") or a need to maintain group identity (i.e. "decide our own policies," "defend our borders")
Need for power	A concern with gaining, keeping, and restoring power over others	Percentage of verbs that reflect actions of attack, advise, influence the behavior of others, concern with reputation
Self-confidence	Personal image of self-importance in terms of the ability to deal with the environment	Percentage of personal pronouns used such as "my," "myself," "I," "me," and "mine," which show speaker perceives self as the instigator of an activity, an authority figure, or a recipient of a positive reward
Task focus	Relative focus on problem solving vs. maintenance of relationship to others. Higher score indicates greater problem focus	Percentage of words related to instrumental activities (i.e. "accomplishment," "plan," "proposal") vs. concern for other's feelings and desires (i.e. "collaboration," "amnesty," "appreciation")

Source: Dyson (2006), p. 292.

Table 3. Turkey's Prime Ministers in the Post-Cold War Era

	Prime minister	Term in office
"Secular"s	Süleyman Demirel	November 20, 1991–May 16, 1993
	Tansu Çiller	June 25, 1993–March 6, 1996
	Mesut Yılmaz	March 6, 1996–June 28, 1996, and June 30, 1997–January 11, 1999
	Bülent Ecevit	January 11, 1999–November 18, 2002
"Islamist"s	Necmettin Erbakan	June 28, 1996–June 30, 1997
	Abdullah Gül	November 18, 2002–March 14, 2003
	Recep Tayyip Erdoğan	March 14, 2003–present

By selecting the spontaneous foreign policy utterances of leaders, this study follows Hermann's principle.[36] Spontaneity here means that these statements were made either in an interview or in a press conference setting where the leader responded to the questions from the media members.[37] In addition, given the aim of this study to match foreign policy with leader characteristics, it is appropriate to analyze political leaders' foreign policy statements only during their tenure in office and not for the entirety of their political careers.[38]

The leadership traits are generated by automated-coding of these materials by the software designed specifically for this purpose: the ProfilerPlus program.[39] Profiler-Plus generates LTA scores following its coding procedures as summarized in Table 2, and coding schemes for LTA in ProfilerPlus are developed specifically for this sort of research. Instead of an individual reading the text line by line and coding himself/ herself, the program concludes the coding based on the grammatical and coding rules, as well as the vocabularies it is given. For LTA, ProfilerPlus recognizes the words associated with measuring each trait.[40] For the Turkish prime ministers studied here, each leader's statements are aggregated monthly; ProfilerPlus, using its LTA schemes, then codes these verbal outputs.

Turkey's Post-Cold War Prime Ministers and Reference Groups for Analyses

In order to understand if Turkey's "secular" and "religious" prime ministers are significantly different between themselves, this paper reports leadership traits scores of all seven Turkish prime ministers who served since November 1991. These leaders are listed secular or religious following their widely accepted, popular images in the media and among the public. Accordingly, then, Table 3 shows Turkey's prime ministers and their terms in office.[41]

Since earlier norming groups rely on hand-coded averages of heads of state and political leaders from around the world, these results cannot serve as reference for LTA results generated from automated analysis. As Table 4 shows, this study utilizes

Table 4. Norming Groups

Leadership trait	214 political leaders (SSA)	83 Middle Eastern leaders (SSA)	104 political leaders (Hermann 2012)	44 Arab/Islamic leaders (Hermann 2012)	Turkish prime ministers since 1991
Belief can control events	Mean = 0.34 Low < 0.30 High > 0.38	Mean = 0.33 Low < 0.29 High > 0.37	Mean = 0.344 Low < 0.303 High > 0.385	Mean = 0.329 Low < 0.287 High > 0.372	Mean = 0.351 Low < 0.319 High > 0.383
Conceptual complexity	Mean = 0.65 Low < 0.61 High > 0.69	Mean = 0.64 Low < 0.60 High > 0.68	Mean = 0.586 Low < 0.543 High > 0.630	Mean = 0.583 Low < 0.543 High > 0.623	Mean = 0.564 Low < 0.527 High > 0.601
Distrust of others	Mean = 0.01 Low < 0.01 High > 0.01	Mean = 0.01 Low < 0.01 High > 0.01	Mean = 0.171 Low < 0.101 High > 0.241	Mean = 0.187 Low < 0.118 High > 0.256	Mean = 0.138 Low < 0.097 High > 0.179
In-group bias	Mean = 0.51 Low < 0.44 High > 0.58	Mean = 0.50 Low < 0.43 High > 0.57	Mean = 0.144 Low < 0.112 High > 0.176	Mean = 0.137 Low < 0.108 High > 0.167	Mean = 0.142 Low < 0.114 High > 0.170
Need for power	Mean = 0.26 Low < 0.22 High > 0.30	Mean = 0.25 Low < 0.22 High > 0.28	Mean = 0.253 Low < 0.223 High > 0.283	Mean = 0.256 Low < 0.225 High > 0.287	Mean = 0.287 Low < 0.243 High > 0.331
Self-confidence	Mean = 0.36 Low < 0.27 High > 0.45	Mean = 0.37 Low < 0.26 High > 0.48	Mean = 0.368 Low < 0.276 High > 0.461	Mean = 0.360 Low < 0.258 High > 0.462	Mean = 0.400 Low < 0.320 High > 0.480
Task focus	Mean = 0.73 Low < 0.67 High > 0.79	Mean = 0.71 Low < 0.65 High > 0.77	Mean = 0.616 Low < 0.546 High > 0.685	Mean = 0.594 Low < 0.525 High > 0.664	Mean = 0.637 Low < 0.572 High > 0.702

Notes: SSA refers to Social Science Automation's data (publicly available). Data from Margaret Hermann, personal communication (April 2012). Turkish prime ministers' scores come from the author's research.

two sets of available norming groups from Social Science Automation and Margaret Hermann, each with a comprehensive reference group for world's leaders and another for Middle Eastern leaders. In addition, based on the results generated in this piece, a norming group of Turkish prime ministers is reported here. The discussion to follow constructs profiles of Turkey's prime ministers based on the average profile of a Turkish prime minister and briefly compares them to each reference group separately.

Discussion

In order to understand any prime minister's role in Turkish foreign policy making, first it is necessary to assess the bureaucratic organization and cultural practices in which the Turkish prime minister works. Historically speaking, Turkish foreign policy-making has included other actors along with the prime minister: the civilian Ministry of Foreign Affairs bureaucracy, the Turkish military, the president, as well as the parliament.[42] The role of Turkey's prime minister in the foreign policy-making establishment as the chief executive is arguably constrained by these institutional and historical factors in Turkey.[43] For instance, all the prime ministers here, but Gül and Erdoğan, were the head of a coalition cabinet and hence dealt with decision-making processes in coalitions.[44] In addition, one could anticipate that Turkish prime ministers have also been limited by international constraints such as Turkey's dependence on the USA in economic (particularly in the 1990s) and security matters as well.

Table 5 displays the averages for all Turkish prime ministers under investigation here. Before a discussion about leadership styles of the seven leaders, first an overview of their individual traits is in order. To start with, belief in ability to control events and the need for power scores for Turkish prime ministers indicate that Çiller, Ecevit, Gül, and Yılmaz respect constraints and Demirel, Erdoğan, and Erbakan challenge constraints. Second, all Turkish prime ministers have higher conceptual complexity scores than their self-confidence scores; hence, they all are open to information. However, a rank ordering of the difference between conceptual complexity and self-confidence reveals that there are significant differences among the

Table 5. LTA Scores for Turkish Prime Ministers

Leadership Trait	Demirel	Çiller	Yılmaz	Erbakan	Ecevit	Gül	Erdoğan
Belief can control events	0.408	0.348	0.339	0.337	0.309	0.339	0.378
Conceptual complexity	0.591	0.538	0.573	0.523	0.603	0.516	0.595
Distrust of others	0.136	0.143	0.139	0.224	0.098	0.112	0.121
In-group bias	0.152	0.170	0.133	0.187	0.120	0.136	0.113
Need for power	0.342	0.278	0.245	0.355	0.259	0.277	0.258
Self-confidence	0.312	0.305	0.377	0.502	0.487	0.444	0.395
Task focus	0.572	0.610	0.692	0.542	0.660	0.722	0.662

leaders in this regard. Specifically, Erbakan's conceptual complexity and self-confidence scores are only 0.02 points apart from each other and diminishes the confidence in the judgment that he is open to information. It is probably safe to argue that his openness to information would depend on the context. This also shows the rather difficult nature of interpreting a trait score when it is not easily distinguishable from compared to the mean or has questionable conclusions.

Turkish prime ministers also differ among themselves as to their motivation for seeking office. With the highest task focus score, Gül is definitely a problem-focused leader; Demirel and Erbakan are rather relationship-focused leaders according to their task focus scores in comparison to others. Yılmaz, Erdoğan, and Ecevit remain above the mean for Turkish prime ministers, but are not one standard deviation away from it; likewise, in the reverse direction, Çiller is below the mean, but has a higher task focus score the low mark. The motivations of these four leaders, then, would be context-specific. They might have a problem or relationship focus depending on contextual factors.

Regarding their motivation toward the world (distrust of others and in-group bias scores), the majority of Turkish prime ministers (Ecevit, Erdoğan, Gül, and Yılmaz) perceive the world as not a threatening place and they rather focus on taking advantage of opportunities and relationships. These leaders have low scores of distrust of others and in-group bias compared to the average Turkish prime minister profile. Çiller and Erbakan, however, have high scores in both distrust of others and in-group bias; according to the leadership traits method, their focus is on eliminating potential threats and problems. These leaders perceive the world to be centered on adversaries and they intend on spreading their power. Moreover, such leaders are expected to take risks because they think it is a moral imperative to challenge those adversaries—a profile that might very well fit to Erbakan's view of the world. Lastly, Demirel has a low (close to the mean) distrust of others score, but a high in-group bias score. Demirel, then, would perceive the world as a zero-sum game that has a set of international norms but also ongoing confrontations with adversaries. His focus would be on dealing with threats and solving problems.

Turkish prime ministers' leadership styles as a function of responsiveness to constraints, openness to information, and motivation suggest significant differences among them. One must note that case-based research of foreign policy decisions under each leader would suggest more insights into the leadership traits and styles of Turkish prime ministers.[45] The leadership styles as suggested here fit very well with broad foreign policy orientations of the Turkish prime ministers. However, due to space limitations, this discussion will feature some discussion about Erbakan, Çiller, and Erdoğan. Most notably, if Erbakan's openness to information is considered as "closed," then an evangelistic leadership style definitely explains Erbakan's foreign policy vision. As such, among Turkey's recent prime ministers, Erbakan, the leader who exploited religion most explicitly and consistently throughout his political career, stands out as a unique leader.[46] The Islamic international organizations such as a Muslim NATO or a Muslim United Nations desired by Erbakan were indeed his attempts to mobilize other Muslim nations around a mission. Erbakan's two major visits abroad to the East and then to Africa were based on similar motivations to per-suade other Muslim nations such s Pakistan, Indonesia, Libya, and Nigeria to come together and work closely with Turkey—certainly under Erbakan's guidance and vision.

Once Erbakan's coalition partner, Çiller, who is considered a secular person, shares some traits with Erbakan. Çiller has lower than average scores in all but distrust of others[47] and in-group bias traits. In the rankings of these both traits in the norming group, Tansu Çiller is second only to Erbakan. According to Çiller, Turkey was the central state in the world and its culture and status were of the utmost significance. For her, Turkey was "the only stable country in the Middle East" and its "democratic heri-tage," its historical, ethnic, religious ties to Central Asian and other Muslim nations, its geopolitical location, Turkey was an indispensable country.[48] According to the LTA, it is predicted that leaders with high scores in both distrust of others and in-group bias will focus on eliminating potential threats and problems. Çiller's militarism may very well be an outcome of her high distrust of others and in-group bias scores.[49] One can trace the impact of these two traits in the example of the Kardak crisis with Greece.[50] During the Kardak crisis in late 1995, Çiller's discourse and policy preferences reflected her desire for a strong move. In reaction to the news that there was a Greek flag on the Kardak islets and that Greek soldiers had "occupied" them, Çiller quickly declared, "that flag will come down, those soldiers will go back to Greece." Furthermore, Çiller said "This is our legacy: We do not give away territory. We do not concede even an inch of territory or a pebble. We can sacrifice lives, but not pebbles..."[51] In fact, as Turkish policy-makers formulated their response to these events, Çiller is said to have suggested even tougher policies than those of the Turkish military.[52]

The findings here also point out that Erdoğan can legitimately be considered an actively independent leader. The "zero problems policy" and "strategic depth" doctrine initiated by the Justice and Development Party governments since November 2002 are very much based on increasing Turkey's maneuverability and status in its region and in the world.[53] Erdoğan's policies and leadership mirror these principles. Prime Minister Erdoğan significantly altered Turkey's foreign policy choices in its immediate neigh-borhood and its visibility around the world. For instance, Erdoğan publicly and mul-tiple times collided with Israel over the Palestine, and in 2010, against the rest of the United Nations Security Council (siding with Brazil), voted against more sanctions on Iran. One ramification of Erdoğan's "zero problems" and "strategic depth" approach to foreign policy is that, aware of the utility of Turkey for the West as a dominantly Muslim, secular, democratic society, Erdoğan is motivated to make the most of this opportunity. Erdoğan's talk about "marketing Turkey" corresponds to his understand-ing of how Turkish foreign policy should be formulated. In response to a question about how there are accusations that the Turkish government is "selling Turkey to Western, Arab, and Israeli investors," Erdoğan says: "I am not selling, I am promoting. These people know nothing about the issue and do not know the meaning of marketing or promotion. We tell them: Learn and study management. Politics, social life, and economy are marketed and you have to do this."[54]

Finally, according to these results, especially when compared to a Turkish prime minister average as its reference, Turkish prime ministers display different leadership

Table 6. Leadership Styles of Turkey's Prime Ministers

	Norming group: 214 world leaders	Norming group: 83 Middle Eastern leaders	Norming group: 104 World leaders	Norming group: 44 Arab/Islamic leaders	Norming group: Turkish prime ministers
Demirel	Directive/evangelistic	Directive/evangelistic	Actively independent/directive	Actively independent/directive	Directive
Çiller	Directive/evangelistic	Directive/evangelistic	Expansionistic/evangelistic	Actively independent/expansionist	Collegial
Yılmaz	[a]	[a]	Opportunistic	Actively independent	Opportunistic/collegial
Erbakan	Evangelistic/directive?	Evangelistic?	Evangelistic/directive	Evangelistic/directive	Directive/evangelistic
Ecevit	Collegial/influential	Directive/evangelistic	Actively independent/directive	Actively independent	Opportunistic/collegial
Gül	Actively independent/expansionist?	Actively independent	Actively independent	Actively independent	Opportunistic
Erdoğan	[a]	Evangelistic/directive	Actively independent/directive	Actively independent	Actively independent

[a]Openness to information and motivation are context dependent; hence, based on this norming group, leadership style can be expansionistic, evangelistic, actively independent, or directive.

styles. Table 6 also illustrates that, expectedly, leadership style suggested by this method depends on the norming group. Arguably, the findings here suggest that the Turkish prime ministers norming group matches rather well with the perceptions of Turkey's prime ministers. The discussion so far used this norming group for comparison purposes. While other norming groups (world or regional) still suggest different leadership styles, the national norming group captures the leadership styles of Turkey's post-Cold War prime ministers very well. Moreover, these leadership styles challenge reducing Turkey's leadership to a dichotomy of secular and religious leaders.

Indeed, following the common portrayals of Turkish leaders, Table 7 presents leadership traits scores for secular and religious leaders. The LTA scores for individual leaders and their leadership styles already suggest that Erbakan is the only Islamist leader who would significantly differ from Turkey's other post-Cold War prime ministers. Moreover, the discussion about Erbakan, Çiller, and Erdoğan finds rather similarities between Erbakan and Çiller than Erbakan and Erdoğan. Obviously, one can claim that at times Erdoğan's discourse—for instance, on Israel—and actions are more similar to Erbakan than to Turkey's other secular leadership. However, it needs to be conceded that Erdoğan's rationale (at least, so far) is quite distinct than that of Erbakan, and Erdoğan can possibly be likened to Ecevit in matters like Turkish–Israeli relations. Finally, Table 7 also reports the results of an analysis of variance (ANOVA) test of leadership traits of secular and religious leaders. This test shows whether the categorization of leaders as "secular" and "religious" is statistically valid given the ProfilerPlus results. According to the findings in Table 7, these categories suggest absolutely no statistical significance between these two types of leaders.

Conclusion

"Who leads matters."[55] In addition to domestic and international constraints, decision-making processes are bound by leaders' cognition. Psychological

Table 7. Turkey's Secular and Religious Leaders: LTA Scores and ANOVA Results

	Secular leaders, monthly average $N = 119$	Religious leaders, monthly average $N = 98$	F	Significance
Belief can control events	0.340	0.371	2.635	0.106
Conceptual complexity	0.580	0.578	0.136	0.713
Distrust of others	0.124	0.132	0.257	0.613
In-group bias	0.140	0.123	1.669	0.198
Need for power	0.273	0.272	0.011	0.915
Self-confidence	0.390	0.404	0.135	0.714
Task focus	0.636	0.649	0.416	0.520

approaches to international relations offer scholars the tools to explain the individual (as well as group) level limitations on decision-making. The broader inquiry into the effects of cognition on international relations remains a relatively young research agenda and much is still left to do.[56] This study contributes to the broader literature by introducing the profiles of Turkish prime ministers. Moreover, it offers a solid ground for further debate about this topic in the study of Turkish politics. Finally, this essay contributes to the broader literature on the methodology that it employs: in the Turkish example, it is evident that norming groups matter. It is essential that political leaders be compared to a norming group that shares certain characteristics with the leader. While the current leadership traits literature attends to this by calculations of regional profiles (hence, creating regional norming groups), the findings here suggest that a national norming group may serve the goal of political leadership assessment better.

Building on extant research in political leadership studies, this study shows that at-a-distance assessments of political leaders provide the means to conduct research on world leaders in a systematic manner. Furthermore, their conclusions go well beyond subjective appraisals of political leaders. This piece illustrates that LTA, as a method is applicable to non-Western leadership. In fact, this approach can remedy the simplistic accounts of leaders—in the case of Turkey, the dichotomous image of secular and religious leader. This study contributes to the study of Turkish foreign policy by introducing a well-established method of assessing political leadership. Utilizing such methods (operational code analysis, image theory, etc.), scholars as well as policy-makers of Turkish foreign affairs can reach methodologically sound and theoretically informed understanding of factors influential in Turkey's foreign policy.

Accordingly, one can hope that simpleminded interpretations of Turkey's political leaders would be questioned and explored further if they apply to many leaders of Turkey. This piece shows that one prevalent conceptualization of Turkish leaders as seculars and Islamists does not necessarily get at delineating differences among the many secular and Islamist leaders. A secular leader, Çiller has leadership traits that one can compare with Erbakan, the archetypical Islamist. Likewise, the current prime minister of Turkey does not necessarily share traits with Erbakan or Gül. The clustering of Turkey's post-Cold War leadership into seculars and Islamists does not return much for a scholarly understanding of Turkish leaders' impact on policymaking.

In conclusion, as such a common reference to secular and religious leaders becomes highly questionable if not invalid based on the findings here, one must mention the value of research that puts individuals at its centerpiece. The field of political psychology and its various methodologies offer such an approach, which can be very fruitful to the understanding of Turkish politics. This paper illustrates one of the possibilities in this vein of research.

Acknowledgements

The author thanks Cengiz Erişen, Esra Çuhadar, Binnur Özkeçeci-Taner, all the participants to the workshops hosted by TOBB University of Economics and

Technology in Ankara, and anonymous reviewers, as well as Jessica Epstein and Christina Xydias. In addition, thanks are due to Juliet Kaarbo, Philip Schrodt, and Brent Steele for their support. Finally, the author is grateful to Social Science Automation for making ProfilerPlus available.

Notes

1. Yavuz and Özcan, "Crisis In Turkey: The Conflict of Political Languages."
2. Yavuz, *Secularism and Muslim democracy in Turkey*, 98.
3. Not all Turkish leaders have had the same level of interest in foreign policy. Experience and interest/ training in foreign policy were employed as measures in earlier political leadership studies but are not in current at-a-distance assessment of leadership: see, Hermann, "Explaining Foreign Policy Behavior Using the Personal Characteristics of Political Leaders."
4. Obviously, Erdoğan did not assume an office in government until he was elected to parliament after a by-election in the province of Siirt in March 2003. Here, the reference is to Erdoğan's party ascending to government in the aftermath of November 2002 elections and Erdoğan's capacity to influence foreign policy as the party chairperson.
5. Heper and Sayarı (eds.), *Political Leaders and Democracy in Turkey*. In addition to Sayarı's introduction and Heper's concluding remarks, included in this book are chapters on Atatürk, İsmet İnönü, Celal Bayar, Adnan Menderes, Süleyman Demirel, Bülent Ecevit, Necmettin Erbakan, Alparslan Türkeş, Turgut Özal, Mesut Yılmaz, and Tansu Çiller.
6. Demir (ed.), *Türk dış politikasında liderler: süreklilik ve değişim, söylem ve eylem.* This edited book contains studies of Adnan Menderes, Süleyman Demirel, Bülent Ecevit, Necmettin Erbakan, Alparslan Türkeş, and Turgut Özal.
7. Görener and Uçal, "The Personality and Leadership Style of Recep Tayyip Erdoğan: Implications for Turkish Foreign Policy." A forthcoming study of Tansu Çiller by the author would be another contribution to this research: Kesgin, "Leadership Traits and Foreign Policy of Tansu Çiller." These two, among many others, represent a new interest developed in leadership and Turkish foreign policy: Ak, "Liderlik Profili Analizi ve Dış Politika: Turgut Özal ve Recep Tayyip Erdoğan." Kesgin, "Political Leadership and Foreign Policy in Post-cold War Israel and Turkey." Kesgin, "How Do 'Secular' and 'Religious' Leaders Shape Foreign Policy Behavior Towards the United States?" Özdamar, "Dış Politika Karar Alımı Sürecinde Lider Merkezli Yaklaşım: Akılcı Tercih Kuramı ve Türkiye'nin Irak Savası'na Katılmama Kararı." In addition, on a broader scale than a specific interest in personality, some research now looks at the role of psychological factors in Turkish foreign policymaking: see, Erişen and Kesgin, "Dış Politika ve Psikolojik Unsurlar: Türk-Yunan İlişkilerinin Analizi."
8. See, for instance, a literature about the Islamization of Turkey's foreign policy: among others Bird, "The Impact of Political Islam on Turkish Foreign Policy: Myth or Reality?" Oğuzlu, "Middle Easternization of Turkey's Foreign Policy: Does Turkey Dissociate from the West?" Sasley, "Foreign Policy Variation and Islamist Governments in Turkey: From Neglect to Advocacy."
9. Cited in Byman and Pollack, "Let Us Now Praise Great Men: Bringing the Statesman Back In."
10. Snyder, Bruck, and Sapin, *Foreign Policy Decision Making* Hudson, "Foreign Policy Analysis: Actor-Specific Theory and the Ground of International Relations." In stark contrast, the assumptions of classical and structural realism run counter to this claim. Then, neo-classical realism engages with the individual level more so than its classical and structural variants; there is a great opportunity for interaction between neo-classical realism and political leadership studies. However, presently, this remains quite limited. For some short discussion, see Renfro, "Presidential Decision-Making and the Use of Force."
11. Hermann, "Explaining Foreign Policy Behavior Using the Personal Characteristics of Political Leaders," 12.
12. Hudson, "Foreign Policy Analysis: Actor-Specific Theory and the Ground of International Relations."

13. Here, "Foreign Policy Analysis" refers to the academic study of foreign policy as a subfield of International Relations. For a review, see Levy, "Political Psychology and Foreign Policy." Also, see Erişen, "An Introduction to Political Psychology for International Relations Scholars."
14. Hermann, "When Leader Personality Will Affect Foreign Policy: Some Propositions." Schafer, "Issues in Assessing Psychological Characteristics at a Distance: An Introduction to the Symposium." Winter et al. "The Personalities of Bush and Gorbachev Measured at a Distance: Procedures, Portraits, and Policy."
15. Winter, "Personality and Foreign Policy: A Historical Overview of Research." Winter, "Personality and Political Behavior."
16. Major exceptions would include: Feldman and Valenty (eds.), *Profiling Political Leaders: Cross-cultural Studies of Personality and Behavior*. Malici and Buckner, "Empathizing with Rogue Leaders: Mahmoud Ahmadinejad and Bashar al-Asad."
17. Young and Schafer, "Is There Method in Our Madness? Ways of Assessing Cognition in International Relations." Other techniques, Young and Schafer identify are operational code analysis, image theory, and cognitive mapping. For recent reviews about leaders' cognition, see Preston, "Leadership and Foreign Policy Analysis"; also, see Rosati and Miller, "Political Psychology, Cognition, and Foreign Policy Analysis."
18. Dyson, *The Blair Identity: Leadership and Foreign Policy*. Dyson, "'Stuff Happens': Donald Rumsfeld and the Iraq War." Dyson and Lorena Billordo, "Using Words as Data in the Study of the French Political Elite."
19. Hermann, "Assessing Leadership Style: Trait Analysis."
20. Ibid., 181.
21. Ibid., 182.
22. Kaarbo and Hermann, "Leadership Styles of Prime Ministers: How Differences Affect the Foreign Policymaking Process."
23. Hermann, "Assessing Leadership Style: Trait Analysis," 192.
24. Ibid., 197.
25. Ibid., 183.
26. Dyson, "Personality and Foreign Policy: Tony Blair's Iraq Decisions." Here, Dyson reports scores for all the seven personality traits in LTA; however, in his discussion he focuses exclusively on these three traits.
27. Ibid., 303.
28. These individuals are: President George W. Bush, Vice President Dick Cheney, Secretary of Defense Donald Rumsfeld, National Security Adviser Condoleezza Rice, Secretary of State Colin Powell, Deputy Secretary of State Richard Armitage, and Deputy Secretary of Defense Paul Wolfowitz.
29. Shannon and Keller, "Leadership Style and International Norm Violation: The Case of the Iraq War."
30. Rasler, Thompson, and Chester, "Foreign Policy Makers, Personality Attributes, and Interviews: A Note on Reliability Problems."
31. Hermann, "On 'Foreign Policy Makers, Personality Attributes, and Interviews: A Note on Reliability Problems'."
32. Hermann "Assessing Leadership Style: Trait Analysis," 211.
33. Mahdasian, "State, trait, or design? A critical examination of assumptions underlying remote assessment."
34. While it is possible that some content may be lost in translation, earlier studies indicate that translation was not an issue in profiling leaders. Hermann reports that there was a high degree of correlation between the profiles of a leader coded in the original and translated languages.
35. Word counts for each Turkish leader are as follows: Demirel, 19357; Çiller, 27402; Yılmaz, 18162; Erbakan, 10147; Ecevit, 34843; Gül, 6799; Erdoğan (till 2010), 100482. Notably, the Erdoğan profile is based on almost double the word count in Görener and Uçal "The Personality and Leadership Style of Recep Tayyip Erdoğan: Implications for Turkish Foreign Policy."
36. One must note that leadership traits and operational code analyses differ in their preference of the type of material used for assessing political leaders: respectively, they use spontaneous and scripted materials. For a discussion about the contradictory conclusions about the utility of scripted (prepared) and spontaneous statements in profiling leaders, see Mahdasian, "State, trait, or design?" and Renfro, "Presidential Decision-Making and the Use of Force."

37. Because opening statements in press conferences are often prepared remarks, these are omitted from the analysis. Only the "Q and A" parts of press conferences are coded.
38. An approach also adopted by Astroff, "Fear of Heights: Foreign Policy Decision-Making in the Israeli–Syrian Conflict, 1988–2001" and Crichlow, "Idealism or Pragmatism? An Operational Code Analysis of Yitzhak Rabin and Shimon Peres"; though, both collected only a sample of leaders' speeches or interviews.
39. Social Science Automation (Columbus, OH: 2008).
40. Dyson (2006) offers a summary of LTA coding procedures—see, specifically, a table on page 292. Otherwise, programming details of ProfilerPlus are beyond the focus and interest of the present study.
41. This list excludes Erdal İnönü, who served as acting Prime Minister for about a month after Süleyman Demirel was selected as president and until Tansu Çiller's accession to Demirel's seat in the True Path Party and then in the coalition. With the exception of governments under Gül and Erdoğan, all governments were coalitions.
42. Robins, *Suits and Uniforms: Turkish Foreign Policy since the Cold War*.
43. Here, primarily, the role of the military in making Turkey's foreign policy is implied.
44. Kaarbo, "Power and Influence in Foreign Policy Decision Making: The Role of Junior Coalition Partners in German and Israeli Foreign Policy." Özkeçeci-Taner, *The Role of Ideas in Coalition Government Foreign Policymaking: The Case of Turkey Between 1991 and 2002*.
45. The author wishes to thank Binnur Özkeçeci-Taner for highlighting this point.
46. It is worth noting that the average profiles of Turkish Prime Ministers were calculated from their monthly scores, likewise the average profile of a Turkish Prime Minister was calculated from all available scores for 218 months. As one would expect, when leaders speeches are aggregated to a single document and their profile is assessed from this document, there might be some differences in their leadership styles compared to the method used here. For instance, Erbakan's self-confidence score drops from 0.502 to 0.261 when all his foreign policy relevant speeches are aggregated and a single score is calculated for him.
47. Çiller's distrust of others score is not significantly higher than the average score; yet, if Erbakan (with a score more than two standard deviations higher than the mean) is an outlier in this trait, then Çiller's distrust of others becomes more significant.
48. Interview with Public Broadcasting Company (April 18, 1995).
49. Arat, "A Woman Prime Minister in Turkey: Did It Matter?" In the meantime, Arat also observes that Çiller "justified" her militarism, or more specifically her hawkish policies on the Kurdish problem, with reference to being a mother (ibid., 16).
50. On the domestic front, Çiller's approach to the fight against the PKK would be another example.
51. "Premier Says Flags and Soldiers 'Must Go' from Disputed Islet" (BBC Summary of World Broadcasts, January 30, 1996).
52. Civaoğlu, "Kardak'ta derin kulis."
53. Davutoğlu, "Turkey's Zero-Problems Foreign Policy"; Davutoğlu, "Turkey's Foreign Policy Vision: An Assessment of 2007."
54. "Without Borders," Al Jazeera network (November 16, 2005).
55. Hermann et al. "Who Leads Matters: The Effects of Powerful Individuals."
56. Schafer, "Issues in Assessing Psychological Characteristics at a Distance: An Introduction to the Symposium."

Bibliography

Ak, Ömer. "Liderlik Profili Analizi ve Dış Politika: Turgut Özal ve Recep Tayyip Erdoğan." In *Dış Politika Teorileri Bağlamında Türk Dış Politikasının Analizi*, edited by Ertan Efegil and Rıdvan Kalaycı, 501–527. Ankara: Nobel Yayınevi, 2012.

Arat, Yeşim. "A Woman Prime Minister in Turkey: Did It Matter?" *Women and Politics* 19, no. 4 (1998): 1–22.

Astroff, Robert E. "Fear of Heights: Foreign Policy Decision-Making in the Israeli-Syrian Conflict, 1988–2001." Unpublished PhD Diss., University of Toronto, 2008.

Bird, Alexandra. "The Impact of Political Islam on Turkish Foreign Policy: Myth or Reality?" Paper presented at the 47th ISA Annual Convention (San Diego, CA), 2006.

Byman, Daniel, and Kenneth M. Pollack. "Let Us Now Praise Great Men: Bringing the Statesman Back In." *International Security* 25, no. 4 (2001): 107–146.

Crichlow, Scott. "Idealism or Pragmatism? An Operational Code Analysis of Yitzhak Rabin and Shimon Peres." *Political Psychology* 19, no. 4 (1998): 683–706.

Davutoğlu, Ahmet. "Turkey's Foreign Policy Vision: An Assessment of 2007." *Insight Turkey* 10, no. 1 (2008): 77–96.

Davutoğlu, Ahmet. "Turkey's Zero-Problems Foreign Policy." *Foreign Policy*. Accessed September 27, 2010. http://www.foreignpolicy.com/articles/2010/05/20/turkeys_zero_problems_foreign_policy

Demir, Ali Faik, ed. *Türk dış politikasında liderler: süreklilik ve değişim, söylem ve eylem*. Cağaloğlu, İstanbul: Bağlam Yayıncılık, 2007.

Dyson, Stephen B. "Personality and Foreign Policy: Tony Blair's Iraq Decisions." *Foreign Policy Analysis* 2, no. 3 (2006): 289–306.

Dyson, Stephen B. *The Blair Identity: Leadership and Foreign Policy*. Manchester: Manchester University Press, 2009a.

Dyson, Stephen B. "'Stuff Happens': Donald Rumsfeld and the Iraq War." *Foreign Policy Analysis* 5, no. 4 (2009b): 327–347.

Dyson, Stephen B., and Lorena Billordo, L. "Using Words as Data in the Study of the French Political Elite." *French Politics* 2, no. 1 (2004): 111–123.

Erişen, Cengiz, and Barış Kesgin. "Dış Politika ve Psikolojik Unsurlar: Türk-Yunan İlişkilerinin Analizi." In *Dış Politika Teorileri Bağlamında Türk Dış Politikasının Analizi*, edited by Ertan Efegil and Rıdvan Kalaycı, 553–580. Ankara: Nobel Yayınevi, 2012.

Erişen, Elif. "An Introduction to Political Psychology for International Relations Scholars." *Perceptions* 17, no. 3 (2012): 9–28.

Feldman, Ofer, and Linda O. Valenty, eds. *Profiling Political Leaders: Cross-Cultural Studies of Personality and Behavior*. Westport, CT: Praeger, 2001.

Görener, Aylin, and Meltem Uçal. "The Personality and Leadership Style of Recep Tayyip Erdoğan: Implications for Turkish Foreign Policy." *Turkish Studies* 12, no. 3 (2011): 357–381.

Heper, Metin, and Sabri Sayarı, eds. *Political Leaders and Democracy in Turkey*. Lanham, MD: Lexington Books, 2002.

Margaret G Hermann. "When Leader Personality Will Affect Foreign Policy: Some Propositions." In *In Search of Global Patterns*, edited by James N. Rosenau, 326–333. New York: Free Press, 1976.

Hermann, Margaret G. "On 'Foreign Policy Makers, Personality Attributes, and Interviews: A Note on Reliability Problems'." *International Studies Quarterly* 24, no. 1 (1980a): 67–73.

Hermann, Margaret G. "Explaining Foreign Policy Behavior Using the Personal Characteristics of Political Leaders." *International Studies Quarterly* 24, no. 1 (1980b): 7–46.

Hermann, Margaret G. "Assessing Leadership Style: Trait Analysis." In *The Psychological Assessment of Political Leaders: With Profiles of Saddam Hussein and Bill Clinton*, edited by Jerrold M. Post, 178–212. Ann Arbor, MI: University of Michigan Press, 2003.

Hermann, Margaret G., Thomas Preston, Baghat Korany, and Timothy M. Shaw. "Who Leads Matters: The Effects of Powerful Individuals." *The International Studies Review* 3, no. 2 (2001): 83–131.

Hudson, Valerie M. "Foreign Policy Analysis: Actor-Specific Theory and the Ground of International Relations." *Foreign Policy Analysis* 1, no. 1 (2005): 1–30.

Kaarbo, Juliet. "Power and Influence in Foreign Policy Decision Making: The Role of Junior Coalition Partners in German and Israeli Foreign Policy." *International Studies Quarterly* 40, no. 4 (1996): 501–530.

Kaarbo, Juliet, and Margaret G. Hermann. "Leadership Styles of Prime Ministers: How Differences Affect the Foreign Policymaking Process." *Leadership Quarterly* 9, no. 3 (1998): 243–263.

Kesgin, Barış. "How Do 'Secular' and 'Religious' Leaders Shape Foreign Policy Behavior Towards the United States?" Paper presented at the annual convention of the International Studies Association-Midwest (St. Louis, Missouri), 2009.

Kesgin, Barış. "Political Leadership and Foreign Policy in Post-Cold War Israel and Turkey." Unpublished PhD Diss., University of Kansas, 2011.

Kesgin, Barış. "Leadership Traits and Foreign Policy of Tansu Çiller." *Perceptions* 17, no. 3 (2012): 29–50.

Levy, JackS. "Political Psychology and Foreign Policy." In *Oxford Handbook of Political Psychology*, edited by David O. Sears, Leonie Huddy, and Robert Jervis, 253–284. New York: Oxford University Press, 2003.

Mahdasian, Sarkis A. "State, Trait, or Design? A Critical Examination of Assumptions Underlying Remote Assessment." Unpublished PhD Diss., Washington State University, 2002.

Malici, Akan, and Allison L. Buckner. "Empathizing with Rogue Leaders: Mahmoud Ahmadinejad and Bashar al-Asad." *Journal of Peace Research* 45, no. 6 (2008): 783–800.

Oğuzlu, Tarık. "Middle Easternization of Turkey's Foreign Policy: Does Turkey Dissociate from the West?" *Turkish Studies* 9, no. 1 (2008): 3–20.

Özdamar, Özgur. "Dış Politika Karar Alımı Sürecinde Lider Merkezli Yaklaşım: Akılcı Tercih Kuramı ve Türkiye'nin Irak Savası'na Katılmama Kararı." In *Dış Politika Teorileri Bağlamında Türk Dış Politikasının Analizi*, edited by Ertan Efegil and Rıdvan Kalaycı, 479–500. Ankara: Nobel Yayınevi, 2012.

Özkeçeci-Taner, Binnur. *The Role of Ideas in Coalition Government Foreign Policymaking: The Case of Turkey Between 1991 and 2002*. Dortrecht: Republic of Letters Publishing, 2009.

Preston, Thomas. "Leadership and Foreign Policy Analysis." In *International Studies Encyclopedia Online*, edited by Robert A. Denemark. Blackwell Publishing, 2010. Blackwell Reference Online. Accessed March 9, 2010. http://www.isacompendium.com/subscriber/tocnode? id=g97814443365 97_chunk_g978144433659712_ss1-8

Rasler, Karen A., William R. Thompson, and Kathleen M. Chester. "Foreign Policy Makers, Personality Attributes, and Interviews: A Note on Reliability Problems." *International Studies Quarterly* 24, no. 1 (1980): 47–66.

Renfro, Wesley. "Presidential Decision-Making and the Use of Force." Unpublished PhD Diss., University of Connecticut, 11–17, 2009.

Robins, Philip. *Suits and Uniforms: Turkish Foreign Policy since the Cold War*. Seattle: University of Washington Press, 2003.

Rosati, Jerel A., and Colleen E. Miller. "Political Psychology, Cognition, and Foreign Policy Analysis." In *International Studies Encyclopedia Online*, edited by Robert A. Denemark. Blackwell Publishing, 2010. Blackwell Reference Online. Accessed March 9, 2010. http://www.isacompendium.com/subscriber/tocnode?id=g9781444336597_chunk_g978144433659716_ss1-10

Sasley, Brent. "Foreign Policy Variation and Islamist Governments in Turkey: From Neglect to Advocacy," Paper presented at the ISA-Midwest Annual Convention (St. Louis, MO), 2006.

Schafer, Mark. "Issues in Assessing Psychological Characteristics at a Distance: An Introduction to the Symposium." *Political Psychology* 21, no. 3 (2000): 511–527.

Shannon, Vaughn P., and Jonathan W. Keller. "Leadership Style and International Norm Violation: The Case of the Iraq War." *Foreign Policy Analysis* 3, no. 1 (2007): 79–104.

Snyder, Richard C., H. W. Bruck, and Burton Sapin. *Foreign Policy Decision Making*. New York: Free Press, 1962.

Winter, David G. "Personality and Foreign Policy: A Historical Overview of Research." In *Political Psychology and Foreign Policy*, edited by Eric Singer and Valerie M. Hudson, 79–101. Boulder: Westview Press, 1992.

Winter, David G. "Personality and Political Behavior." In *Oxford Handbook of Political Psychology*, edited by David O. Sears, Leonie Huddy, and Robert Jervis, 110–145. New York: Oxford University Press, 2003.

Winter, David G., Margaret G. Hermann, Walter Weintraub, and Stephen G. Walker. "The Personalities of Bush and Gorbachev Measured at a Distance: Procedures, Portraits, and Policy." *Political Psychology* 12, no. 2 (1991): 215–245.

Yavuz, Hakan M. *Secularism and Muslim Democracy in Turkey*. Cambridge: Cambridge University Press, 2009.

Yavuz, Hakan M., and Nihat Ali Özcan. "Crisis in Turkey: The Conflict of Political Languages." *Middle East Policy* 14, no. 3 (2007): 118–135.

Young, Michael D., and Mark Schafer. "Is There Method in Our Madness? Ways of Assessing Cognition in International Relations." *Mershon International Studies Review* 42, no. 1 (1998): 63–96.

Public Opinion toward Immigration and the EU: How are Turkish Immigrants Different than Others?

BAŞAK YAVÇAN

Department of Political Science, TOBB University of Economics and Technology, Ankara, Turkey

ABSTRACT   *Public preferences on immigration and attitudes toward the European Union (EU) have been shown to be closely related. In this article, it is argued that, to better understand this relationship, people's opposition to immigration should be differentiated based on the ethnicity of the prospective immigrant group. Specifically, in the case of Germany, Turkish immigrants constitute a special case. The results of the original survey experiment conducted in Germany suggest that, controlling for other explanations, categorizing immigration attitudes by ethnic group reveals that fear of EU enlargement and future Turkish immigration is actually a more important reason for Euroskepticism than has been shown so far. That is, people's opposition to immigrants from Turkey explains their overall Euroskepticism much better than their attitudes toward immigrants from within EU member states, suggesting that their attitudes are informed by opposition to further enlargement rather than a general dislike of multiculturalism.*

Introduction

The Eurostat report on population projections in Europe indicates that immigration will be Europe's sole source of population increase by 2015.[1] In 2005, the European Union (EU) had an overall net gain from international migration of 1.8 million people, which accounted for almost 85 percent of Europe's total population growth that year. Previously, in 2000, Der Spiegel reported that Germany needed more than 300,000 immigrants per year just to maintain its population size because of the declining birthrates of native Europeans. This means that the EU will require large-scale immigration of young workers if the functioning of the welfare state is to be maintained and labor shortages in a variety of sectors to be offset.

However, while often presented as a panacea that would allow the aging populations of Europe to maintain a functioning welfare state, immigration also provokes very strong public opposition from host societies, and engenders significant intergroup tensions. Some of these include the rise of extreme right-wing parties, violent acts of Neo-Nazis, the Danish cartoon crisis, French banlieu riots and mass deportations of immigrant Roma in France and Italy. Public opinion toward immigrants is particularly negative toward those from outside the EU, and immigrants of Turkish descent constitute a large part of this group. Such attitudes are not only important in relation to existing Turkish minorities living in Europe, but they have also been shown to be closely related to several issues: voting behavior, especially for extreme right-wing parties and in European referenda,[2] public attitudes toward globalization, and Euroskepticism[3] and opposition to integration-related policies. Not surprisingly, therefore, the immigration attitudes of Europeans are also a strong predictor of opposition to Turkey's EU membership.

In this article, the relation between immigration and EU attitudes is analyzed in great detail. Both opposition to EU integration in general, also known as Euroskepticism, and EU enlargement in particular, a process which also includes Turkish EU membership, will be the focus of this inquiry. In order to understand these two issues in relation to immigration attitudes, the special case of Turkish immigrants will be further discussed and compared to the cases of immigrants of other ethnic backgrounds. The rationale for this is twofold.

First, a recent surge of scholarship has demonstrated that attitudes toward immigration heavily depend on the immigrant group in question. This is because, contrary to conventional wisdom, immigrants are not necessarily perceived as one homogeneous group.[4] Given the critical role of immigration attitudes in explaining people's preferences regarding the EU, there is reason to believe that a heterogeneous perspective on immigration attitudes, which would also account for the special case of Turkish immigrants, may provide some useful new insights.

Second, a substantial part of the scholarly discussion on attitudes toward EU integration revolves around the relative role of cultural concerns compared to economic concerns, and the importance of the values of multiculturalism and the mass media's portrayal of them. Scholars have argued that symbolic or in other words culture or value-related concerns manifested as fear of immigration, and the possible cultural invasion resulting from this immigration, seem to be major reasons as to why people oppose the EU integration as well as enlargement, more so than their economic concerns.[5] However, little research has been done to investigate whether or not the fear of immigration applies to all prospective immigrant groups, or only to some of them. Given the close relationship between EU attitudes and immigration attitudes, as well as related symbolic concerns, a nuanced understanding of attitudes toward immigrants may also shed light on EU-related attitudes, especially in terms of an improved causal model that takes account of the ethnicity of immigrants.

Therefore, in this article, a new model that combines levels of support for EU integration and enlargement with a potential heterogeneous perception of immigrants according to their ethnic origin will be presented. First, the effect of differentiating immigrants by ethnicity in relation to addressing some gaps in the existing literature will be shown. Then, taking the conditionality of immigration attitudes toward different ethnic groups as an independent variable, it will be investigated whether immigration concerns regarding some groups matter more than others in relation to the EU in order to provide a better understanding of the underlying causal mechanisms. In order to achieve this, an original survey, with an embedded newspaper priming experiment about immigration, conducted in Germany in the summer of 2009 will be utilized.

Literature

While there was a dearth of studies on EU public opinion in the early years of EU integration, a bourgeoning literature has been developed in the last two decades due to the EU's increasing need to replace its earlier permissive consensus with a policy approach more responsive to public attitudes. One line of research, begun by scholars Gabel and Palmer,[6] theorized a self-interest model of public opinion. This approach emphasizes the role of utilitarian cost-benefit calculations in forming people's preferences.[7] Many scholars used this perspective to analyze support for the EU, focusing on both the individual level and on the national level economic variables, such as the role of intra-EU trade, possible benefits from EU structural and Common Agricultural Policy funds, and benefits from new employment opportunities.[8] These studies have found that income, education, and occupation all play important roles in forming individuals' preferences regarding the EU. This is because, for those individuals who are better off economically, the EU project appears to be a much more beneficial and desirable process than it is for poorer, less educated and lower class individuals. People's perceptions of how much their country benefits from being an EU member also have an important impact on their attitudes toward the EU.

Another line of research has focused on the more symbolic, value-based, and identity-related explanations of support for the EU. This work has emphasized the role of national perspectives,[9] ideology,[10] religion,[11] and xenophobia.[12] Some of those scholars stressing the role of symbolic concerns suggest that, when people feel their nation state or its cultural integrity is threatened, they develop reservations against the EU.[13] These scholars measure this feeling of cultural threat via variables capturing exclusionary attitudes toward out-groups, arguing, through an extension of social identity theory, that exclusionary behavior is actually a manifestation of protection of the in-group.[14] Seeing immigration attitudes as distinct from national identity,[15] they develop this argument by suggesting that Europeans holding negative attitudes toward immigrants will show a greater readiness to categorize others in general, which is likely to yield unfavorable evaluations of out-groups. Even though the exact reasoning is not elucidated, immigration attitudes appear to be the one of the most important predictors of support for or opposition to the EU.[16]

These results are consistent with studies that model support for EU enlargement in that, while economic considerations play a minor role in informing attitudes toward enlargement, immigration attitudes, and perceptions of cultural threat have major explanatory power.[17] Intuitively, it seems likely that fear of out-groups may lead to fear of EU enlargement. However, EU integration, with all the different policy areas it encompasses, is a process, which includes, but goes beyond the inclusion of new member states into the Union. Hence, the causal link between immigration attitudes and integration is less direct than it is with enlargement. One possibility is that people only think of immigration via enlargement when they are asked about EU integration. Another is that they see the EU as a proxy of globalization in a way that threatens the cultural unity of their community. A third is that their fear of immigration is a proxy for a more overarching attitude against multiculturalism. Unfortunately, because the current literature assumes that the European public has a homogeneous understanding of immigration, it does not address these alternatives adequately, as explained in more detail in the following section.

Implications of Heterogeneous Immigration Perceptions on EU Attitudes

Most research on attitudes toward immigration is based on the assumption that immigrants are perceived as a homogeneous category by the host society.[18] This is evident by their measurement of immigration attitudes based on a single item in the European Social Survey or Eurobarometer surveys. However, a recent surge of scholarship has challenged this assumption by illustrating that attitudes toward immigration heavily depend on the immigrant group in question, indicating that, contrary to conventional wisdom, immigrants are not necessarily perceived as a homogeneous group.[19]

In particular, scholars Wasmer and Koch[20] argue that, in developing attitudes toward equal civil rights for immigrants, the German population makes clear distinctions between different groups of foreigners, favoring Italian over Turkish immigrants and Turkish immigrants over asylum seekers. Similarly, Brader et al.[21] found that people in the USA are much more inclined to perceive harm and less inclined to support the immigration of Hispanics than Russians, who they perceive as being culturally similar. Finally, Ford[22] shows that British citizens form an ethnically based hierarchy of immigrants, in which they show less opposition to supposedly culturally proximate "white" groups than more distinct "non-white" groups.

The results of the cognitive interviews conducted as a pilot study for the survey experiment reported here were consistent with these results. In this pilot study,[23] German interviewees were presented with a commonly used immigration question, asking about their views about immigration into their country without specifying any ethnic group. Having answered this question, the interviewees were then asked if there were any specific groups that came to their mind, and if they could name these groups. About two-thirds of the sample named Turkish and/or Muslim immigrants as the first group that came to their mind when answering the immigration question. Also, the previous experimental research,[24] in which respondents were primed with stimuli representing Turkish, Polish, and Italian groups, showed that those primed with a Turkish immigrant had very similar immigration attitudes to those in the unprimed control group. Thus, the results of both the cognitive interviews and this experimental survey indicate that the default immigrant group for the majority of the interviewees in both studies was Turkish immigrants.

These research findings regarding categorization of immigrants by ethnicity has potential implications for the study of EU attitudes. As elaborated earlier, studies have already shown that immigration attitudes are a strong predictor of support for EU integration and enlargement, but these analyses rest on surveys using a single question for understanding immigration. On the other hand, recent studies on immigration suggest that, when the immigrant group is not specified (as is the case with many of the surveys that most scholars use), a large proportion of people probably think of immigrants from outside EU member states. It is, therefore, argued that the strong relationship between immigration attitudes and EU attitudes regarding integration and enlargement actually stems from a specific fear of Muslim or other culturally alien immigrants, possibly due to Turkey's potential EU membership.

In the light of these, it seems reasonable to predict that, when Europeans consider EU enlargement, they mostly consider the Turkish case, since Turkey is a candidate country with a large Muslim population perceived to be culturally different, whose EU membership bid is a highly politicized and contentious issue. Hence, public opposition to EU enlargement in general, as reported by earlier studies, may actually represent opposition to Turkish membership specifically, out of fear of immigration from this country. This implies that differentiating attitudes toward immigrants according to their ethnicity may help us to better understand the impact that the fear of immigration from Turkey, a candidate country that has been mostly framed as an "other", has on attitudes toward EU enlargement.

Therefore, regarding enlargement, this study first hypothesizes the following:

Hypothesis 1: For those who are exposed to a Muslim or Turkish group compared to another group (Polish or Italian), there should be a stronger positive relationship between opposition to immigration and opposition to EU enlargement.

Regarding Polish or Italian immigrants, their home countries have had been EU members for at least 5 years at the time of this study's fieldwork, with the Italians being one of the European Community's six founding members. Both groups have been entitled to freedom of movement within the EU since the early years of EU integration. This leads to the second hypothesis of this study:

Hypothesis 2: For those who are exposed to a Western European group (Polish or Italian) as opposed to other groups, there should be a weaker positive relationship between opposition to immigration and opposition to EU enlargement.

With regards to attitudes toward EU integration, on the other hand, the relationship is less straightforward, as evidenced by the lack of agreement in the literature. Some studies see immigration attitudes as a proxy for a larger concept, such as multiculturalism. Following this argument, the ethnicity of the immigrant should not matter as someone who is against multiculturalism would tend to be against immigration on principle, without much regard for the particular ethnicities of the immigrants.

However, as the aforementioned studies suggest, for most people, culturally different immigrants are the first ones that come to mind. When these findings are considered in conjunction with the literature illustrating a close link between attitudes toward immigrants (assumed to be perceived homogeneously) and EU attitudes, this suggests a possible fusion of these two concepts by many individuals.[25] Put differently, it could be that Europeans associate the EU directly and very closely with enlargement, and more specifically with being an avenue for members of culturally different out-groups to culturally invade their territories.

In this case, the ethnic background of the prospective immigrant informing their immigration attitudes may matter a lot. As a result, if EU enlargement is the factor informing attitudes toward the EU, which some recent literature suggests to be the case, there should be major differences in the way immigrant attitudes relate to attitudes toward EU integration depending on the ethnicity of immigrant groups. Figure 1 illustrates this line of causal expectation in that, as the main concern is EU enlargement, attitudes toward Muslim or Turkish immigrants should be a more important determinant of Euroskepticism than attitudes toward immigrants from existing member states. This leads to the following hypothesis:

Hypothesis 3: For those who are exposed to a Muslim group compared to another group (Polish or Italian), there should be a stronger positive relationship between opposition to immigration and Euroscepticism.[26]

Since attitudes toward EU integration are widely understood as the amalgamation of a range of converging policies affecting its members, many may disagree with the line of reasoning proposed here. This is because, both conceptually and operationally, EU integration is measured as an overarching entity involving many diverse policy areas besides freedom of movement, integration speed, direction, benefit *vis-à-vis* each member state. Enlargement, as just one of the many aspects of EU integration, may therefore not relate so closely as expected to integration.

Accordingly, the strong relationship between immigration and EU attitudes evidenced in many studies may suggest that integration is associated with certain

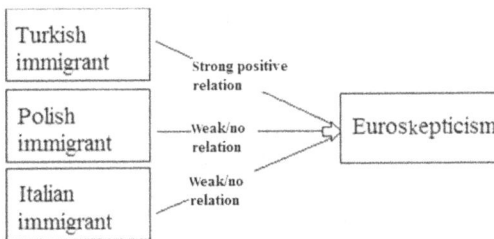

Figure 1. Hypothetical Expectation of Immigrant Ethnicity Influencing Euroskepticism

values that promote diversity and multiculturalism. Therefore, public opposition to immigrants, taken as an all-inclusive, homogenous group, may indicate that the public feels a general threat to the unity of their country. In this case, the ethnic background of the prospective immigrant should not matter much, as immigrants from every group would heighten the public's fear of multiculturalism similarly. If fear of immigration, in general, stands as a proxy for fear of multiculturalism informing attitudes toward EU integration, one immigrant group should not have much more effect than any other on the relationship between immigration attitudes and Euroskepticism. However, as indicated in the earlier discussion of previous research, this is not expected to be the case here.

Data and Methods

In order to test the above hypotheses, a novel priming experiment was conducted in Germany. The respondents for this survey experiment were recruited from the participant database of the German market research company Schmiedl gmbh. About 208 individuals (103 male, 105 female) were recruited to participate in the study, all of whom were residents of the city and suburbs of Berlin. A company employee called every participant to set up an appointment for taking the survey experiment in return for a financial incentive. All participants were required to have German-born parents to ensure that they were all ethnically German. To enable a comparison of contextual differences half of the subject pool consisted of individuals born and raised in former Eastern Germany.

In addition to the quotas on gender and East/West background, recruitment was also designed to ensure a wide variation in age, income, and education. The median respondent was 41-years-old with some college education and a household income of 24,000 Euros. Recruited respondents were welcomed and seated in the computer lab within the premises of the market research firm. The entire procedure was conducted by employees of the survey firm, all of whom had German-born parents with no immediate immigrant descent.[27]

Via the consent forms, all participants were told that they were about to participate in a survey regarding current social issues, informed about the possible risks associated with the survey experiment, and offered 15 Euros as a compensation for their participation. All of the recruited subjects agreed to complete. The median interview length was 14 min and 40 s. The study followed a 3 (ethnic group: Turkish *vs.* Italian *vs.* Polish immigrant frame) x 2 (tone: evaluation of costs *vs.* benefits of immigration) x 2 (issue: on economic *vs.* symbolic frame) randomized between-subjects design with a control group.[28]

Twelve subjects were recruited for each condition combination and presented with the manipulations in the form of fabricated newspaper articles. For the ethnic group manipulation, equal numbers of the respondents were randomly assigned to read a newspaper article about one of the three ethnic groups (Turkish, Polish, or Italian), featuring the relevant immigrant along with an appropriate stereotypical headshot. The control group did not read any article, instead immediately receiving the question about immigration that all the other groups received as a follow-up to reading the newspaper article. The rationale for setting up the control group this way was to see how the control group respondents differed from the treatment groups in relation to their immigration preferences. Respondents in the control group were informed that the study was a simple survey on social and political issues, and they were given no way of guessing the real purpose of the study. The reason for picking the three nationalities portrayed in the newspaper articles was that they were considered, due to their relative population sizes and consequent visibility in Germany, to best represent the three groups that respondents had named in the earlier cognitive interviews, namely West European, East European, and Muslim.

As given in Table 1, there are currently a variety of immigrant groups in Germany. In addition to Italian and Turkish immigrants who arrived as guest workers many decades ago, there has also been a surge of immigrants from Eastern Europe, Russia, and especially neighboring Poland. Besides their objectively large numbers, their selection is further justified by the consistent references to these groups in the media and by policy-makers in relation to their particular characteristics, unemployment rates, and levels of integration into German society. Finally, these groups also provide a variation relation to their home country's EU membership status, with Italy being a founding EC member state, Poland being a recent member following the Eastern enlargement, and Turkey being a controversial candidate.

To better identify the impact of ethnicity on immigration attitudes, it was necessary to control for the effect of other variables such as ordering effects or social desirability bias that might contaminate this relationship. For this reason, each article contained the picture mentioned above of a "recent immigrant", who appears to be Turkish, Polish, or Italian. The picture's caption read: "[Ali Yilmaz / Alexander Kowalski / Massimo Rizzo] is one of many immigrants who arrived in Germany recently".

To maximize control over the experimental treatment, the pictures were selected from the University of Essex face database,[29] containing 7900 images of 395 individuals of various ethnic backgrounds, with 20 images per individual. The sample face

Table 1. Citizenship of Foreigners Residing in Germany as of December 31, 2011

Turkey	1,607,161
Italy	520,159
Poland	468,481
Greece	283,684
Croatia	223,056
Russian Federation	195,310
Austria	175,926
Bosnia and Herzegovina	153,470

Source: Table generated using the population statistics of German Statistics Bureau https://www.destatis.de/EN/FactsFigures/SocietyState/Population/MigrationIntegration/ForeignPopulation/Tables/PlaceOfBirth.html

images are of 24-bit 180×200 pixel color JPEG, shot with an S-VHS camcorder. From 15 possible photos, 3 male faces were selected based on the ratings of their ethnicity by an independent panel of 8 naïve German judges. They rated how much each male appeared ethnically Turkish, Polish, or Italian, as well as how attractive and friendly they found them. The pictures selected at the end were the ones rated as being most characteristics of the ethnicities in question, while being similar to each other in terms of the extraneous characteristics of attractiveness and friendliness. The selected photos had a plain green background and only showed the head of the immigrant, with their outfit not being clearly shown to eliminate other possible factors than ethnicity. An English translation of a sample article for the Turkish-Positive-Economic prime, one of the 12 versions of the article, is shown in Appendix 1.

Upon reading the article, respondents were asked about their position on immigration to Germany without specifying any particular group. This was followed by a battery of survey questions, serving as distractors and then questions on prejudice, and political, economic and sociological attitudes, as well as personal traits. The participant was then invited to complete a second survey on EU-related attitudes.

The first-dependent variable "support for EU enlargement" was measured by the sum of the respondents' support for the possible membership of Albania, Ukraine, Croatia, Bosnia, Turkey, Norway, and Switzerland, measured on a seven-point scale. The ranking of the countries from most to least supported with the average score of support in parenthesis was as follows: Norway (4.96), Switzerland (4.93), Croatia (3.85), Bosnia (3.65), Turkey (3.34), Ukraine (3.25), and Albania (3.20). The second-dependent variable "Euroskepticism" is measured as the sum of five survey items: whether or not the respondent was in favor of unification; the respondent's preferred speed of EU integration; the respondent's perception of Germany's benefit from the EU; whether they thought Germany's EU membership was a good thing or not; and the overall image of the EU for the respondent.[30] Chronbach's alpha for this scale was $\alpha = 0.86$ indicating a very good-scale reliability.

Using these data, separate models predicting for support for EU enlargement and EU integration were estimated. This way it is hoped to reveal the underlying mechanisms linking immigration attitudes to EU attitudes, and the extent to which the ethnicity of the immigrant in question supported this study's hypothesis that a heterogeneous understanding of immigrant groups affects attitudes toward the EU. In other words, the models tested whether the relationship between support for immigration and support for EU enlargement and/or EU integration was conditional upon the specific immigrant groups that came to the minds of the respondents.

Analysis and Discussion

For a preliminary analysis of the relationship between attitudes toward immigration and the EU, the sample is categorized based on which ethnic group the respondents in the treatment groups were primed with. Then, simple Pearson's r coefficients were calculated to probe the plausibility of my expectations regarding the relationship between these two attitudes. Figure 2 illustrates the correlations between opposition

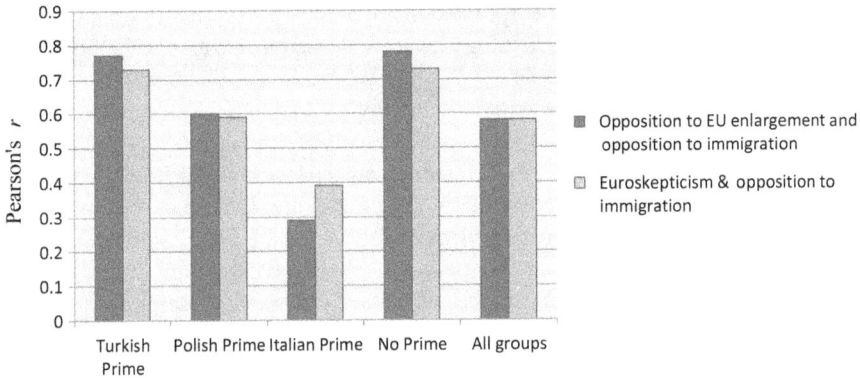

Figure 2. Relationship between Euroskepticism, Opposition to EU Enlargement and Immigration Attitudes when Primed with Different Ethnic Groups

to immigration and Euroskepticism on the one hand, and opposition to EU enlargement on the other hand, depending on the three different ethnic primes.

The preliminary results illustrated in Figure 2 confirm that there is a strong relationship between immigration attitudes and EU attitudes and that this relationship differs across the different immigrant groups. The strongest correlation coefficients for both the immigration-Euroskepticism and immigration-Enlargement relationships were obtained when the respondent was primed with the newspaper article about a Turkish immigrant, while both relationships were weaker for the respondents primed with articles about the culturally similar Polish and Italian immigrants. For the control group, which was not primed with any ethnic group and received the immigration question directly, the relationships are similar to the treatment group that read about the Turkish immigrant. This supports the prediction that, when not primed with any group, as would be in the case in a conventional survey question, respondents think of Turks as the default immigrant category. This finding casts serious doubt on the reliability of findings from studies that rely on a single immigration question and then generalize their results from this to all potential immigrant groups.

Given these preliminary results, there is good reason to further examine the relationship between immigration and EU attitudes to see if this relationship is statistically significant in a multivariate analysis. For this purpose, an OLS regression analysis with interaction effects and clustered robust standard errors is estimated. Even though alternative explanations are assumed to be randomly distributed in an experimental design, this form of analysis allowed me to test if this relationship pattern continued to hold even if this assumption was not fully justified, and once all the possible explanations of EU attitudes had been integrated into the model. As the purpose of this section is to illustrate the effect of priming respondents with different ethnic groups on the relationship between their immigration attitudes and EU attitudes, the discussion of the results will focus on these variables only.

Nonetheless, the models also incorporated many of the other variables found to have impact on EU attitudes, such as ideology, education, sociotropic and pocketbook concerns, age and income as controls.

For this analysis, ideology was represented by a variable measured with a seven-point scale, where the value (1) corresponded to the extreme left, (4) to the exact middle, and (7) to the extreme right. Income was measured in 10 levels, where (1) corresponded to a monthly income below 300 Euros and (10) to an income above 5000 Euros. Education was measured by a four-category scale, where (0) corresponded to no qualification, (1) to primary school qualification, (2) to middle school qualification, and (3) to a higher education degree. Sociotropic and pocketbook concerns were measured by an additive index of a number of Likert-scaled items, measuring prospective and retrospective evaluations of the respondents' individual and national economic well-being, where (10) indicated high concern and (1) indicated low concern.

Table 2 illustrates OLS regression models for opposition to EU enlargement.

Models 1 and 2, given in Table 2, show that, after controlling for the impact of extraneous factors, when respondents were led to think about Turkish immigrants, the relationship between immigration attitudes and attitudes about EU enlargement was strongest, closely followed by the prime for Polish immigrants. However, this relationship disappeared or weakened when their respondents' attitudes toward

Table 2. Explaining Opposition to EU Enlargement through Immigration Attitudes Interacting with Turkish, Polish, and Italian Ethnic Primes

Independent variables	Model 1	Model 2
Anti-immigration	0.154* (0.080)	0.503** (0.000)
Turkish prime	0.239 (0.131)	−0.094 (0.547)
Polish prime	0.288* (0.085)	–
Italian prime	–	−0.453** (0.006)
Anti-immigration × Turkish prime	0.429** (0.009)	0.010 (0.950)
Anti-immigration × Polish prime	0.405** (0.020)	–
Anti-immigration × Italian prime	–	−0.539** (0.001)
Prospective socio-tropic concern	0.083 (0.207)	0.090 (0.167)
Prospective pocketbook concern	0.050 (0.445)	0.033 (0.616)
Household income	−0.038 (0.519)	−0.028 (0.630)
Education	−0.086 (0.132)	−0.098* (0.086)
Age	−0.007 (0.906)	−0.012 (0.829)
Ideology (left to right)	0.317** (0.000)	0.307** (0.000)
Adjusted R^2	0.49	0.50
N	191	191

*Statistical significance with 90 percent or greater confidence.
**Statistical significance with 95 percent or greater confidence.

Italian immigrants had little relationship with their attitudes toward EU enlargement. This finding, therefore, supports the first two hypotheses, and shows how distinguishing the specific immigrant groups under consideration matters for a nuanced understanding of EU attitudes.

The conditional impact on immigration attitudes was statistically significant for all three ethnic primes, as shown by the coefficient of the interaction term in Table 2. However, a more statistically nuanced and substantially meaningful interpretation of these conditional effects requires additional analysis[31] that enables a more thorough exploration of the conditional impact of one variable at different levels of the other variable. That is, the effect of each ethnic prime on the relationship between EU and immigration attitudes may differ at different values of the latter two attitudes. On the one hand, for those who have little opposition to either immigration or EU enlargement and/or integration, no ethnic prime has much influence on their attitudes. On the other hand, for those who score high on both attitudes, particular ethnic primes may have statistically more significant effects.

To illustrate this more clearly, graphs for the predicted values of opposition to immigration and EU enlargement were generated for different levels of these variables being interacted for each of these models. In the areas where the two lines follow a very close or a similar pattern to each other, the conditional impact is weak; where they differ from each other, the conditional impact is strong. Figure 3 illustrates the effect of immigration attitudes on the predicted value of opposing EU enlargement, conditional upon the ethnicity of immigrants for all three immigrant groups separately at different levels of immigration support.

A brief glance at the three graphs confirms the predictions of this study that the three immigrant primes result in different relationships between respondents' attitudes toward immigration and EU enlargement. The first graph in Figure 3 illustrates the conditional impact of being primed with a Turkish immigrant on opposition to EU enlargement at different levels of anti-immigration attitudes, where the x-axis represents opposition to immigration, ranging from (1) to (5) and the y-axis represents opposition to EU enlargement, ranging from (-5), indicating no opposition, to (15), indicating high opposition. The solid line corresponds to cases where the Turkish immigrant prime was present, while the dashed line corresponds to cases where it was absent. The distance between the two lines indicates the magnitude of the conditional impact of immigrant ethnicity on attitudes toward immigration and EU enlargement. For those already highly opposed to immigration (represented here by a value of (5) on the x-axis), the Turkish prime shown with a solid line leads to even higher opposition to EU enlargement, whereas for those relatively unopposed to immigration (a value of (1) on the x-axis), the Turkish prime leads to even higher support for enlargement. In other words, if an individual is primed with a Turkish immigrant, the steeper solid line suggests that immigration attitudes are a stronger predictor of opposition to EU enlargement as compared to other primes.

The second graph in Figure 3 illustrates the conditional impact of being primed with a Polish immigrant on opposition to EU enlargement at different levels of immigration opposition. The conditional impact of this prime is quite distinct in that being

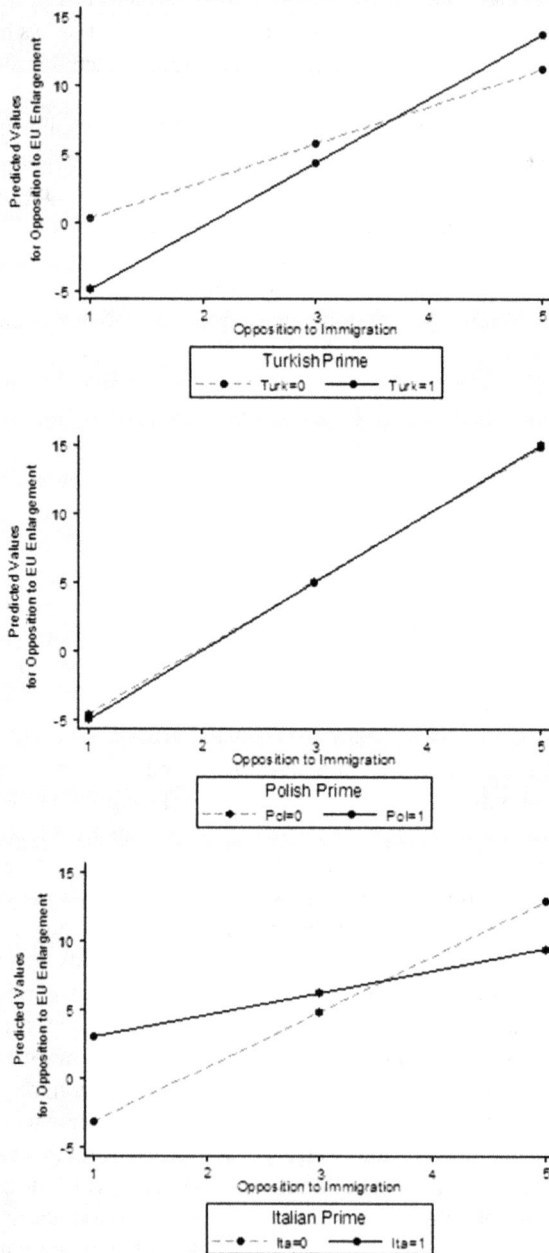

Figure 3. Conditional Effects of Ethnic Prime on opposition to EU Enlargement at different levels of Opposition to Immigration

Table 3. Explaining Euroskeptic Attitudes with Immigration Attitudes Interacting with Turkish and Polish Ethnic Primes

Independent variables	Model 1	Model 2
Anti-immigration	0.213** (0.016)	0.384** (0.000)
Turkish prime	0.041 (0.790)	−0.172 (0.271)
Polish prime	0.206 (0.213)	–
Italian prime	–	−0.276* (0.090)
Anti-immigration × Turkish prime	0.176 (0.273)	−0.042 (0.786)
Anti-immigration × Polish prime	0.226 (0.191)	–
Anti-immigration × Italian prime	–	−0.271* (0.095)
Prospective socio-tropic concern	0.112* (0.076)	0.116* (0.066)
Prospective pocketbook concern	0.083 (0.187)	0.072 (0.254)
Household income	−0.104* (0.074)	−0.102* (0.075)
Education	−0.108* (0.071)	−0.108* (0.054)
Age	0.011 (0.844)	0.010 (0.854)
Ideology	0.444** (0.000)	0.445** (0.000)
Adjusted R^2	0.58	0.58
N	170	170

*Statistical significance with 90 percent or greater confidence.
**Statistical significance with 95 percent or greater confidence.

primed with a newspaper article about a Polish immigrant does not seem to exert any conditional impact at any level of immigration attitudes. Finally, the relationship of the Italian prime to attitudes, shown in the third graph in Figure 3, is completely different from the previous two immigrant group primes in that, as illustrated by the steeper line, for those who received the Italian prime, the relationship between immigration and EU enlargement attitudes are weaker as compared to the other primes and the control group.

Confirming the first and second hypotheses, these results show that it is the thought of immigration from outside the EU, in this case from Turkey, which negatively affects the attitudes of Europeans toward EU enlargement. This result also proves that the ethnic manipulation in the experimental design of this study worked as intended. The models presented here also suggest that, for this sample at least, immigration attitudes are more predictive of attitudes toward enlargement than economic variables.

Having explained the impact of ethnic primes on the relationship between immigration attitudes and opposition to EU enlargement, their conditional impact on Euroskepticism can be analyzed. Table 3 illustrates the results of an OLS regression estimating opposition n to EU integration (or Euroskepticism).

Models 1 and 2 in Table 3 show that, controlling for the impact of extraneous variables, when respondents were led to think about Italian immigrants, the relationship between immigration attitudes and Euroskepticism was weaker compared to other ethnic primes, whereas it was stronger when they were led to think of Poles or Turks. However, the conditional impact of ethnic prime on immigration attitudes was statistically significant only for the Italian prime. As mentioned earlier, Euroskepticism was measured by a composite index of various items related to EU integration, and the presence of missing values for different items across respondents forced the sample size to be reduced for this variable, which may have prevented the coefficients from being statistically significant. Nevertheless, the previous analysis suggested that the impact of priming might vary across different levels of opposition to immigration. To explore this possibility, Figure 4 evaluates this interaction at different levels of the relevant variables.

Figure 4 shows the effect of changing immigration attitudes on the probability of opposing EU integration (or Euroskepticism), conditional on the ethnicity of the immigrant prime, for all three immigrant groups separately. Here, the x-axis represents opposition to immigration, ranging from (1) to (5), and the y-axis represents the level of Euroskepticism, ranging from (-5), indicating no opposition, to (15), indicating strong opposition. As can be seen, the conditional impact of ethnic primes on Euroskepticism follows an almost identical pattern to that seen in Figure 3 for opposition to EU enlargement, both in terms of magnitude and in the relationship of the pattern to the particular immigrant priming groups. This pattern partly supports this study's claim that it is actually people's fear of enlargement that makes immigration attitudes so important for explaining attitudes toward EU enlargement and integration.

More specifically, as the second graph in Figure 4 shows, the Polish prime did not seem to have any substantial conditional effect on the relationship between immigration attitudes and Euroskepticism. However, especially at high levels of immigration support, being primed with a Turkish immigrant increased the odds of a respondent being Euroskeptic, as represented by the steeper line for those primed by this immigrant group (see the first graph in the same figure). In contrast, being primed with the Italian immigrant led to a weaker relationship compared to the other primes, as evidenced by the flatter line for those who received the prime.

These results disprove theories that assume immigrants are perceived homogeneously by the host society. They also show that the influence of immigration attitudes on support for EU integration is probably not because these attitudes are a proxy for greater support for multiculturalism or immigration from within the EU. On the contrary, these results suggest that, while the relationship is not statistically significant for all primes and for all values of both variables, the ethnicity of the immigrant in mind does matter when explaining attitudes toward the EU *vis-à-vis* their level of opposition to immigration.

In particular, these findings partially confirm Hypothesis 3, by suggesting that the link between opposition to EU enlargement and Euroskepticism is closer than mostly assumed. In other words, the fear of Turkish immigration constitutes a different case compared to attitudes toward other immigrants in that opposition to Turkish immigration seems to increase Euroskepticism more than does opposition to immigration

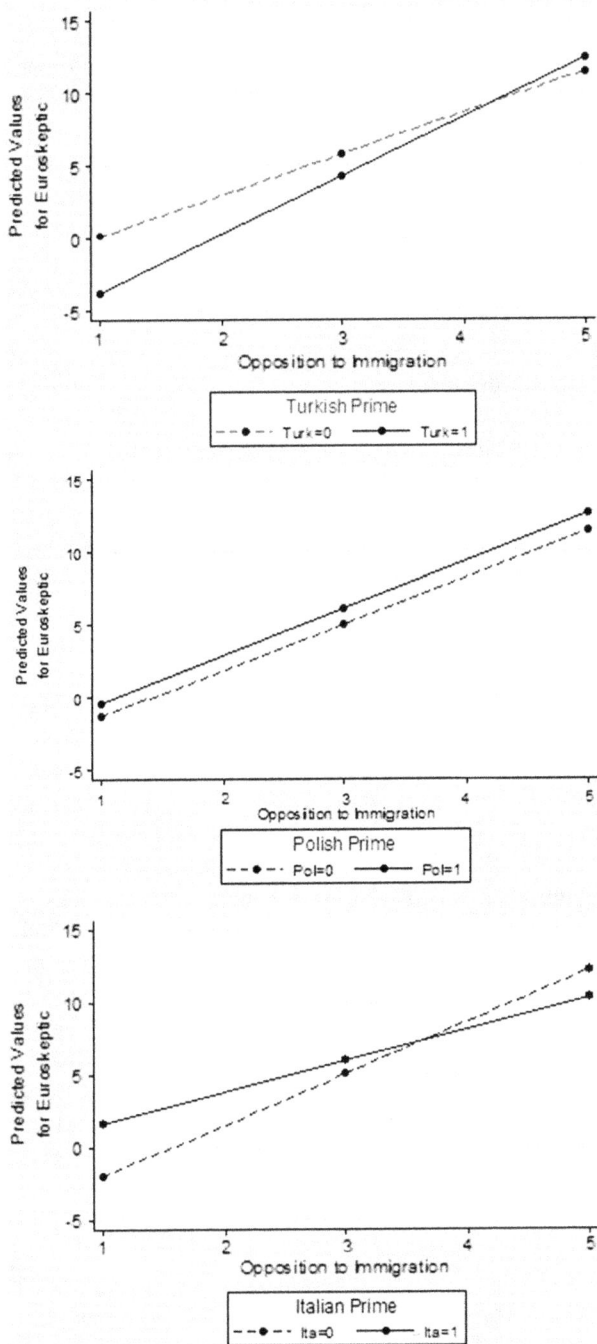

Figure 4. Conditional Effects of Ethnic Prime on Euroskepticism at different levels of Opposition to Immigration.

from other countries, so much so that alternative explanations remain limited in their predictive power. Being primed with a Turkish immigrant has a strong effect on people's expression of support for EU integration. Considering that Turkey is the only candidate country among the primes in this study, this analysis implies that EU integration attitudes are filtered through their EU enlargement attitudes. This is an important finding because it suggests that, from the European public's perspective, even a multifaceted concept such as EU integration can be reduced to a single symbolic concern if that concern is something that can trigger a strong reaction, as with the ethnicity of the immigrant in mind.

Conclusion

This study has shown that a heterogeneous understanding of immigration attitudes can illuminate areas in public opinion other than immigration itself. In particular, this study's findings demonstrate that, when understanding attitudes toward immigration-related issues such as EU integration and enlargement, the ethnicity of the immigrant interacts with immigration attitudes in important ways. In this particular instance, triggering an apparent fear of Turkish immigration led to a stronger relation between immigration attitudes and EU attitudes. Specifically, for those primed with the Turkish immigrant group in the experimental setting, the aforementioned relationship was stronger, whereas for those primed with the Italian immigrant, it was the weakest. This relationship was very similar for both EU enlargement and integration attitudes. Furthermore, while not directly tested due to the design of this experiment, this finding suggests that it is predominantly a fear of enlargement that informs Euroskepticism rather than immigration from within the EU or some other-related anti-diversity attitude. Therefore, future studies aiming at explaining immigration-related attitudes should consider possible implications of this heterogeneous perception of immigration by the public. To enable this kind of refined examination, future surveys should find some way of inquiring about people's attitudes regarding immigration and the EU with respect to different national origins or ethnicity separately.

These findings also have important policy implications because they suggest that the hierarchy people have in mind when considering potential immigrant groups extends to their attitudes toward areas that they see these anti-immigration attitudes as closely linked to. EU integration is one of these areas, and this study has shown that, regardless of all other aspects of integration, people tend to perceive the EU as a symbol of freedom of movement across boundaries, particularly from the EU's external boundaries via the most visible EU policy of enlargement. Any national or supranational policy aiming at mitigating Euroskepticism or opposition to EU enlargement should first focus on this fear of immigration, and in particular immigration by certain groups.

These findings also have important relevance to similar contexts across the industrialized world. For example, Magrebi immigrants in France, Pakistani immigrants in the UK, or Turkish, and Bosnian immigrants in Austria may not be perceived similarly to other immigrants, and as a result may exert a more powerful influence on people's political preferences, such as voting for extreme right-wing parties, opposing immigration politics, or developing Euroskeptic attitudes. The implication of this study is that, to address this issue, the ethnicity of the immigrant concerned should be taken into account in explaining relevant political phenomena.

Acknowledgements

I am grateful to Aaron Abbarno, Cengiz Erişen and Ciğdem Şirin for their valuable comments and suggestions.

Notes

1. Eurostat 2008. From 2015, Deaths Projected to Outnumber Births in the EU27. http://europa.eu/rapid/pressReleasesAction.do?reference=STAT/08/119
2. Givens and Luedtke, "European Union Immigration Policy," 145–65; Hobolt, *Europe in Question*.
3. Scheve et al., "Labor Market Competition," 133–45.
4. Brader et al., "What Triggers Public Opposition to Immigration?," 959–78; Ford, "Acceptable and Unacceptable Immigrants," 1017–37; Yavcan Ural, "Who are the Immigrants in Germany."
5. Hooghe and Marks, "Calculation, Community and Cues," 419–43; McLaren, "Public Support for the European Union," 551–66; Garry and Tilley, "The Macroeconomic Factors," 361–79.
6. Gabel and Palmer, "Understanding Variation", 3–19.
7. Gabel and Palmer, "Understanding Variation"; Dalton and Eichenberg, "Citizen Support for Policy Integration," 250–82; Tucker et al., "Transitional Winners and Losers," 557–57; Hooghe and Marks, "Calculation, Community and Cues".
8. Gabel, "Economic Integration and Mass Politics," 936–53; Eichenberg and Dalton, "Europeans and the European Community", 507–34; Gabel and Palmer"Understanding Variation"; Schoen, "Identity, Instrumental Self-Interest and Institutional Evaluations," 5–29; Van Spanje and de Vreese, "So what's wrong with the EU?" 405–29, 25p.
9. Deflem and Pampel, "The Myth of Post-National Identity," 119–43.
10. Hooghe and Marks, "Calculation, Community and Cues," 419–43.
11. Nelsen and Guth, "Religion and Attitudes toward the European Union"; Hobolt et al., "Religious intolerance and Euroscepticism," 359–79.
12. De Master and Le Roy, "Xenophobia and the European Union," 419–36; McLaren, "Public Support for the European Union."
13. Christin and Trechsel, "Joining the EU?," 415–43; McLaren, "Public Support for the European Union."
14. Henri and Turner, "An Integrative Theory," 33–47.
15. De Vreese and Boomgaarden, "Projecting EU Referendums," 59–82.
16. McLaren, "Public Support for the European Union"; Hooghe and Marks, "Calculation, Community and Cues"; De Vreese and Boomgaarden, "Projecting EU Referendums."
17. Kessler and Freeman, "Public Opinion in the EU," 825–50; McLaren, "Public Support for the European Union". Mclaren, "Explaining Mass-Level Euroskepticism," 233–51.
18. McLaren, "Public Support for the European Union"; Hooghe and Marks, "Calculation, Community and Cues"; De Vreese and Boomgaarden, "Projecting EU Referendums"; Luedtke, "European Integration, Public Opinion," 83–112; Sides and Citrin, "European Opinion about Immigration," 477–504.
19. Ford, "Acceptable and Unacceptable Immigrants," 1017–37; Brader et al., "What Triggers Public Opposition to Immigration?"; Yavcan Ural, "Public Opinion Towards Immigration in Europe."
20. Wasmer and Koch, "Foreigners as Second-Class Citizens?," 95–118.

21. Brader et al., "What Triggers Public Opposition to Immigration?"
22. Ford, "Acceptable and Unacceptable Immigrants."
23. Yavcan Ural, "Who are the Immigrants in Germany."
24. YavcanUral, "A Heterogeneous Approach."
25. Yavcan Ural, "Who are the Immigrants in Germany."
26. Hence, a weaker relationship between immigration and Euroscepticism for those who considered an Eastern or Western European immigrant group.
27. While the sample is more representative than a student sample caution should still be exercised when generalizing these results. The sample is drawn from a cosmopolitan city in Germany and consists of more urban, more educated, more well and three times more former Easterners.
28. For this study, only the ethnic group manipulation will be discussed as the rest of the manipulations were related to hypotheses of another study.
29. Dr Libor Spacek, http://cswww.essex.ac.uk/mv/allfaces/index.html
30. To avoid possible ordering effects, the EU integration questions were asked before the EU enlargement questions.
31. For this purpose, I used the lincom command in Stata, which computes confidence intervals for linear combinations of coefficients.

Bibliography

Brader, Ted, Nicholas A. Valentino, and Elizabeth Suhay. "What Triggers Public Opposition to Immigration? Anxiety, Group Cues, and Immigration Threat." *American Journal of Political Science* 52, no. 4 (2008): 959–978.

Christin, Thomas, and Alexander H. Trechsel. "Joining the EU? Explaining Public Opinion in Switzerland." *European Union Politics* 3, no. 4 (2002): 415–443.

Dalton, Russell J., and Richard Eichenberg. "Citizen Support for Policy Integration." In *Supranational Governance: The Institutionalization of the European Union*, edited by Wayne Sandholtz and Alec Stone Sweet, 250–282. New York, NY: Oxford University Press, 1998.

Deflem, Mathieu, and Fred C. Pampel. "The Myth of Post-National Identity: Popular Support for European Unification." *Social Forces* 75, no. 1 (1996): 119–143.

De Master, S., and M. K. Le Roy. "Xenophobia and the European Union." *Comparative Politics* 32, no. 4 (2000): 419–436.

Eichenberg, Richard C., and Russell J. Dalton. "Europeans and the European Community: The Dynamics of Public Support for European Integration." *International Organization* 47, no. 4 (1993): 507–534.

Ford, Robert. "Acceptable and Unacceptable Immigrants: The Ethnic Hierarchy in British Immigration Preferences." *Journal of Ethnic and Migration Studies* 37, no. 7 (2011): 1017–1037.

Gabel, Matthew. "Economic Integration and Mass Politics: Market Liberalization and Public Attitudes in the European Union." *American Journal of Political Science* 42, no. 2 (1998): 936–953.

Gabel, Matthew, and Harvey Palmer. "Understanding Variation in Public Support for European Integration." *European Journal of Political Research* 27, no. 3 (1995): 3–19.

Garry, John, and James Tilley. "The Macroeconomic Factors Conditioning the Impact of Identity on Attitudes towards the EU." *European Union Politics* 10, no. 3 (2009): 361–379.

Givens, T., and A. Luedtke. "European Union Immigration Policy: Institutions, Salience and Harmonization." *Policy Studies Journal* 32, no. 1 (2004): 145–165.

Henri, Tajfel, and John C. Turner. "An Integrative Theory of Intergroup Conflict." In *The Social Psychology of Intergroup Relations*, edited by William G. Austin and Stephen Worchel, 33–47. Monterey, CA: Brooks/Cole, 1979.

Hobolt, Sara. *Europe in Question: Referendums on European Integration*. Oxford: Oxford University Press, 2009.

Hobolt, Sara B., Wouter Van der Brug, Claes H. De Vreese, Hajo G. Boomgaarden, and Malte C. Hinrichsen. "Religious Intolerance and Euroscepticism." *European Union Politics* 12, no. 3 (2011): 359–379.

Hooghe, Liesbet, and Gary Marks. "Calculation, Community and Cues: Public Opinion on European Integration." *European Union Politics* 6, no. 4 (2005): 419–443.

Kessler, Alan. E., and Gary P. Freeman. "Public Opinion in the EU on Immigration from Outside the Community." *Journal of Common Market Studies* 43, no. 4 (2005): 825–850.

Luedtke, Adam. "European Integration, Public Opinion and Immigration Policy." *European Union Politics* 6, no. 1 (2005): 83–112.

McLaren, M. Lauren. "Public Support for the European Union: Cost Benefit Analysis of Perceived Cultural Threat?" *The Journal of Politics* 64, no. 2 (2002): 551–566.

Mclaren, M. Lauren. "Explaining Mass-Level Euroskepticism: Identity, Interests, and Institutional Distrust." *Acta Politica* 42, no. 2 (2007): 233–251.

Nelsen, Brent L., and James F. Guth. "Religion and Attitudes toward the European Union: The New Member States: A Research Note." European Union Studies Association Ninth Biennial International Conference, Austin, Texas, March 31–April 2, 2005.

Scheve, Kenneth F., and Matthew J. Slaughter. "Labor Market Competition and Individual Preferences over Immigration Policy." *Review of Economics and Statistics* 83, no. 1 (2001): 133–145.

Schoen, Herald. "Identity, Instrumental Self-Interest and Institutional Evaluations: Explaining Public Opinion on Common European Policies in Foreign Affairs and Defence." *European Union Politics* 9, no. 1 (2008): 5–29.

Sides, John, and Jack Citrin. "European Opinion about Immigration: The Role of Identities Interests and Information." *British Journal of Political Science* 37, no. 3 (2007): 477–504.

van Spanje, Joost, and Claes de Vreese. "So What's Wrong with the EU? Motivations Underlying the Eurosceptic Vote in the 2009 European Elections." *European Union Politics* 12, no. 3 (2011): 405–429, 25p.

Tucker, Joshua A., Alexander C. Pacek, and Adam J. Berinsky. "Transitional Winners and Losers: Attitudes toward EU Membership in Post-Communist Countries." *American Journal of Political Science* 46, no. 3 (2002): 557–557.

de Vreese, Claes H., and Hajo G. Boomgaarden. "Projecting EU Referendums: Fear of Immigration and Support for European Integration." *European Union Politics* 6, no. 1 (2005): 59–82.

Wasmer, Martina, and Achim Koch. "Foreigners as Second-Class Citizens? Attitudes toward Equal Civil Rights for Non-Germans." In *Germans or Foreigners: Attitudes toward Ethnic Minorities in Post-Reunification Germany*, edited by Richard Alba, Peter Schmidt, and Martina Wasmer, 95–118. New York, NY: Palgrave McMillan, 2003.

Yavcan Ural, Basak. "Who are the Immigrants in Germany." Paper presented at Midwest Political Science Association Conference, Chicago, April 3–6, 2008.

Yavcan Ural, Basak. "A Heterogeneous Approach to Public Opinion towards Immigration in Germany: Prejudice and Economics as a Function of Cultural Similarity." Paper presented at Midwest Political Science Association Conference, Chicago, April 2–5, 2009.

Yavcan Ural, Basak. "Public Opinion Towards Immigration in Europe: A Heterogeneous Approach." Dissertation, University of Pittsburgh: ProQuest/UMI, 2011. (Publication No etd-08192011-143725.)

Index

Page numbers in **bold** type refer to **figures**
Page numbers in *italic* type refer to *tables*
Page numbers followed by 'n' refer to notes

For Product Safety Concerns and Information please contact our EU
representative GPSR@taylorandfrancis.com
Taylor & Francis Verlag GmbH, Kaufingerstraße 24, 80331 München, Germany

www.ingramcontent.com/pod-product-compliance
Lightning Source LLC
Chambersburg PA
CBHW070427270326
41926CB00014B/2973